Managing IT/Community Partnerships in the 21st Century

Jonathan Lazar
Towson University, USA

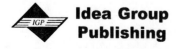 **Idea Group Publishing**

 **Information Science Publishing**

Hershey • London • Melbourne • Singapore • Beijing

Acquisition Editor: Mehdi Khosrowpour
Managing Editor: Jan Travers
Development Editor: Michele Rossi
Copy Editor: Maria Boyer
Typesetter: LeAnn Whitcomb
Cover Design: Tedi Wingard
Printed at: Integrated Book Technology

Published in the United States of America by
    Idea Group Publishing
    1331 E. Chocolate Avenue
    Hershey PA 17033-1117
    Tel: 717-533-8845
    Fax: 717-533-8661
    E-mail: cust@idea-group.com
    Web site: http://www.idea-group.com

and in the United Kingdom by
    Idea Group Publishing
    3 Henrietta Street
    Covent Garden
    London WC2E 8LU
    Tel: 44 20 7240 0856
    Fax: 44 20 7379 3313
    Web site: http://www.eurospan.co.uk

Library of Congress Cataloging-in-Publication Data

Managing IT/community partnerships in the 21st century / [edited by] Jonathan Lazar.
    p. cm.
  Includes bibliographical references and index.
   ISBN 1-930708-33-5 (cloth)
   1. Community and college. 2. Information technology--Study and teaching (Higher) 3. Industry and education. 4. Education--Computer network resources. I. Lazar, Jonathan.

  LC237 .M36 2002
  378.1'03--dc21   2001059440

  eISBN 1-59140-022-0

British Cataloguing in Publication Data
A Cataloguing in Publication record for this book is available from the British Library.

NEW from Idea Group Publishing

- **Data Mining: A Heuristic Approach**
  Hussein Aly Abbass, Ruhul Amin Sarker and Charles S. Newton/1-930708-25-4
- **Managing Information Technology in Small Business: Challenges and Solutions**
  Stephen Burgess/1-930708-35-1
- **Managing Web Usage in the Workplace: A Social, Ethical and Legal Perspective**
  Murugan Anandarajan and Claire Simmers/1-930708-18-1
- **Challenges of Information Technology Education in the 21st Century**
  Eli Cohen/1-930708-34-3
- **Social Responsibility in the Information Age: Issues and Controversies**
  Gurpreet Dhillon/1-930708-11-4
- **Database Integrity: Challenges and Solutions**
  Jorge H. Doorn and Laura Rivero/ 1-930708-38-6
- **Managing Virtual Web Organizations in the 21st Century: Issues and Challenges**
  Ulrich Franke/1-930708-24-6
- **Managing Business with Electronic Commerce: Issues and Trends**
  Aryya Gangopadhyay/ 1-930708-12-2
- **Electronic Government: Design, Applications and Management**
  Åke Grönlund/1-930708-19-X
- **Knowledge Media in Healthcare: Opportunities and Challenges**
  Rolf Grutter/ 1-930708-13-0
- **Internet Management Issues: A Global Perspective**
  John D. Haynes/1-930708-21-1
- **Enterprise Resource Planning: Global Opportunities and Challenges**
  Liaquat Hossain, Jon David Patrick and M.A. Rashid/1-930708-36-X
- **The Design and Management of Effective Distance Learning Programs**
  Richard Discenza, Caroline Howard, and Karen Schenk/1-930708-20-3
- **Multirate Systems: Design and Applications**
  Gordana Jovanovic-Dolecek/1-930708-30-0
- **Managing IT/Community Partnerships in the 21st Century**
  Jonathan Lazar/1-930708-33-5
- **Multimedia Networking: Technology, Management and Applications**
  Syed Mahbubur Rahman/ 1-930708-14-9
- **Cases on Worldwide E-Commerce: Theory in Action**
  Mahesh Raisinghani/ 1-930708-27-0
- **Designing Instruction for Technology-Enhanced Learning**
  Patricia L. Rogers/ 1-930708-28-9
- **Heuristic and Optimization for Knowledge Discovery**
  Ruhul Amin Sarker, Hussein Aly Abbass and Charles Newton/1-930708-26-2
- **Distributed Multimedia Databases: Techniques and Applications**
  Timothy K. Shih/1-930708-29-7
- **Neural Networks in Business: Techniques and Applications**
  Kate Smith and Jatinder Gupta/ 1-930708-31-9
- **Information Technology and Collective Obligations: Topics and Debate**
  Robert Skovira/ 1-930708-37-8
- **Managing the Human Side of Information Technology: Challenges and Solutions**
  Edward Szewczak and Coral Snodgrass/1-930708-32-7
- **Cases on Global IT Applications and Management: Successes and Pitfalls**
  Felix B. Tan/1-930708-16-5
- **Enterprise Networking: Multilayer Switching and Applications**
  Vasilis Theoharakis and Dimitrios Serpanos/1-930708-17-3
- **Measuring the Value of Information Technology**
  Han T.M. van der Zee/ 1-930708-08-4
- **Business to Business Electronic Commerce: Challenges and Solutions**
  Merrill Warkentin/1-930708-09-2

Excellent additions to your library!

**Receive the Idea Group Publishing catalog with descriptions of these books by
calling, toll free 1/800-345-4332
or visit the IGP Online Bookstore at: http://www.idea-group.com!**

0281595

Managing IT/Community Partnerships in the 21st Century

Table of Contents

Section II: Educational Partnerships

Section III: Business Partnerships

Section IV: Digital Divide Issues

Preface

Many people have a stereotypical view of the university as an "ivory tower" of scholars who keep to themselves and are not involved with the day-to-day activities of the communities around them. In reality, most universities have multiple partnerships through which they make an immediate impact in the local communities. Community partnerships cross all boundaries within the university – faculty, staff, and students; academic departments; administrative departments; student affairs; and athletic departments – all can make a difference in their surrounding communities. Many universities even have offices of community service, or offices of community partnerships. The relationship between universities and their communities is a living, breathing relationship.

Academic departments of information technology can play a major role in these community partnerships. While these academic departments may have a variety of titles (Information Systems, Management Information Systems, Computer Information Systems, Information Sciences, Management Science), and may fall under multiple academic units (Colleges of Business, Engineering, Mathematical and Natural Sciences, Library Sciences, etc.), these departments all have an important role to play, and important resources to share. As the importance of information technology increases, there are many technology needs in the community that go unfulfilled. Information technology must be not only for those who are economically privileged. Information technology must be used to improve the quality of everyone's life.

The chapters in this book provide a sampling of the many different types of partnerships taking place between communities and academic departments of information technology. The partnerships described take place in different universities, large and small, with different missions, in many different countries. They demonstrate the wide range of partnerships that have taken place, and they can provide a base of literature with which to build future partnerships.

I have organized the chapters along four major themes: course partnerships, educational partnerships, business partnerships, and digital divide partnerships. Although these themes, and the related partnerships, are not mutually exclusive, they provide a conceptual framework in which to present these partnerships. For instance, many of the course partnerships involved partnerships with local primary and secondary schools. Some of the business partnerships involve course curricula. Some of the business partnerships involve the educational system—local primary and secondary schools. Some of the course partnerships involve the digital divide. These different types of partnerships should not be viewed as individual solutions;

rather, combinations of all of these partnerships should be sought to best meet the needs of the university and the community.

The first chapter, "Service-Learning Partnerships in the Information Systems Curriculum," by Lazar and Lidtke, provides a background on service-learning courses within the information systems curriculum. Service-learning courses involve students taking part in community service that is structured in a way to build on the classroom curriculum. In this chapter, the advantages and disadvantages of service-learning are discussed, and the infrastructure needed to successfully operate a service-learning class is presented. The major courses in an information systems curriculum are then presented, with corresponding information on how to present the class as a service-learning class, and where possible, examples of how service-learning has been successfully utilized. From personal experience and the published literature, the lessons learned can assist those attempting to implement service-learning in their classes. Finally, important issues that impact on the information systems curriculum, such as cheating and accreditation, are presented in the context of service-learning.

"Active Learning in Higher Education: A Model and Roadmap, " by Venkatesh and Small (Chapter 2), continues the discussion on service-learning and other experiential learning processes. The chapter provides an excellent discussion of the educational theories that inspire experiential learning in universities. The authors discuss their experiences with field projects at Syracuse University, including a number of design and networking-related courses. Venkatesh and Small also provide a discussion of the infrastructure at Syracuse University that has allowed their experiential learning programs to flourish.

In Chapter 3, Ruppel and Ruppel describe in detail a service-learning class that has worked with the same community partner for five semesters. In this Systems Analysis and Design class at the University of Toledo, students have helped a small K-8 private school with their computer networking needs. In the different semesters, the student groups assisted with the planning, design, and wiring of the computer network for the school. The students also assisted with grant writing, cost-benefit analyses, and web site development. This chapter provides an interesting view of a service-learning class, because students and faculty worked with the same non-profit organization over five semesters. Ruppel and Ruppel discuss the benefits of this course to both university students and the local school, and present their lessons learned, to be applied in courses that focus on networking or systems analysis and design.

Roberts and Boyle present the partnerships at the University of Leeds, a large university in the United Kingdom, which is surrounded by economically disadvantaged neighborhoods. This chapter, entitled "University/Community Partnerships: Capstone Projects that Make a Difference," describes the final-year projects that have benefited the community. All undergraduates are required to take part in capstone projects that last a minimum of 300 hours, and students can choose to do things such as perform research or develop new informational systems. Many of these final-year projects have been structured to assist local schools in meeting their information technology needs. These students have helped local schools with tasks such as infusing information technology into the curriculum, developing summer school programs in technology, organizing student clubs for those interested in technology, and building web sites. These projects have made a positive impact in the local community, and have also generated positive press for the university. Roberts and Boyle discuss the problem of evaluating these student projects for quality, given the variation in topics and location.

New methodologies for developing informational systems are increasingly focusing on more user participation in the development lifecycle. In participatory design, the user becomes a true member of the design team, to determine the outcome of the systems development, rather than playing only a minor role in systems development. Chapter 5, "Building Educational Technology Partnerships Through Participatory Design," by Carroll et al., presents a participatory design partnership between researchers at Virginia Tech and local public school teachers in Montgomery County, Virginia. The human-computer interaction researchers at Virginia Tech were interested in learning more about how participatory design practices could apply to building educational technology to be successfully used by teachers and students. Based on their experiences over a five-year period, Carroll et al. describe the infrastructure, as well as the challenges and successes, of developing a design partnership with local schools and teachers. A model is presented that discusses the different and changing roles of the teachers over the course of the technology development. To assist in those forming similar design partnerships, Carroll et al. discuss some of the lessons learned from this type of educational partnership.

In Chapter 6, Hawley presents a university/community partnership to help meet the technology needs of schools in Ohio. State and federal funding was increasingly available for the purchase of computer equipment and service for primary and secondary schools; however, there was a lack of school staff experience in using and managing the information technology. A partnership was formed through the University of Cincinnati to help meet the technology training needs of Ohio's schools. A summer camp program was developed in which separate groups of teachers and students would come to the university campus and take part in intensive training on the effective uses of technology in education, standard software tools (such as word processing and spreadsheets), the Internet, and maintenance of technology. The partnership grew from the university and the K-12 schools to now include other community organizations and corporations.

Coakley and Tyran present the Corporate Partnership Program at Oregon State University in Chapter 7. This partnership between Oregon State University and businesses and non-profit organizations in the Pacific Northwest offered numerous benefits. The development of the partnership program over 10 years is presented within the framework of a "stages of growth" model. At a critical time in the development of the information systems program at Oregon State, the business community was instrumental in preventing the elimination of the program. From this point, the partnership between the IS program at the university and the business community grew, and has been mutually beneficial. The business community assisted with curriculum suggestions, encouraged the university administration to increase funding for the IS program, and helped to increase the visibility of the IS program. Coakley and Tyran discuss the internship program and placement activities that help both the business community and the student population. Guidelines are presented for successful development and management of industry advisory councils.

Universities may differ based on their mission, their location, and their size, and partnerships that are appropriate for a large research university may not be appropriate for a smaller teaching university. In Chapter 8, Borton and Lassila present the "Partners in Excellence" program at the University of Southern Colorado, a regional university with fewer than 5,000 students. The program started as an industry advisory board in 1977 to help develop the curriculum and increase enrollments in the Computer Information Systems program. The partnership program grew to include partnerships with local K-12 schools for student tutoring, career counseling, a web design contest, and a summer camp program. In the summer camp program, local high school students can experience college-level courses in CIS. Business partnerships include the industry advisory board for curriculum input, a guest lecture series, job placement services, and internship programs. In addition, students in the senior capstone course assist regional for-profit and non-profit organizations in the development of information systems. Borton and Lassila postulate some of the future possibilities for the "Partners in Excellence" program, such as visiting professors from industry, a new web-based program in CIS for working professionals, a student-faculty-industry research program, and a student IT consulting center.

"Adaptive structuration" is a theory relating to organizational change through the influence of technology and social processes. In Chapter 9, LeRouge and Webb extend adaptive structuration theories to the area of IT/community partnerships. This provides an interesting theoretical framework for forming community partnerships, but LeRouge and Webb also explain the theoretical framework through university/business partnerships involving enterprise systems software, also known as enterprise resource planning or ERP. ERP software consists of modules that relate to the traditional business functions (marketing, accounting, human resources, etc.), and can be easily modified and integrated to track processes within a company. Through the adaptive structuration framework, the challenges of implementing partnerships involving ERP software are discussed. LeRouge and Webb present issues such as the technology infrastructure, educational structure, and curriculum approaches necessary for successful ERP partnerships, and the resulting beneficial outcomes.

As previously stated, different types of universities will be able to offer, and will require, different types of partnerships. In Chapter 10, Navarrete and Pick describe the need for industry advisory boards at universities in developing nations, through a case study at the Universidad Iberoamericana (UIA) in Mexico City, Mexico. Through the assistance of the industry advisory board at the UIA, the number of IS faculty was increased, IS faculty salaries increased, technical training was offered to faculty, and IS students had access to superior computer equipment, as well as industry internships. However, years later when the industry advisory board was not as active, IS faculty salaries dropped, fewer IS faculty members were employed, the IS curriculum was not being updated, student enrollment in IS programs dropped, and the IS graduate program lost accreditation status. Navarrete and Pick describe some of the challenges of successfully running an IS program in a developing nation, and how the industry advisory board can assist in overcoming those challenges. From their experiences, Navarrete and Pick provide success factors for industry advisory boards.

In Chapter 11, Pinkett presents an interesting partnership between the Massachusetts Institute of Technology (MIT) and Camfield Estates, a low-to-moderate income housing development. Researchers at MIT were interested in the role of technology for assisting those who are in low-income communities with building community, empowerment, and self-sufficiency, to help bridge the growing "digital divide." A number of foundations and companies provided funding and/or computer hardware, software, and network service, and a partnership was formed with four research groups at MIT and the Camfield Tenants Association. Among other roles, the researchers at MIT have developed software specifically for community-building, administer and maintain the computer resources in the community, and provide training sessions for the community. While research and evaluation is taking place, the Camfield Estates community and the residents of the community are becoming empowered. Pinkett presents recommendations for universities that want to take part in partnerships relating to community networks.

Digital divide issues are not limited to North America. In Chapter 12, Harris discusses some of the digital divide issues in Malaysia. After providing a background on rural economic development and community informatics, Harris focuses on the rural Malaysian state of Sarawak. A partnership between the university, the business community, and the state of Sarawak is currently under development, with the hope that providing access to technology will assist in the economic development of Sarawak and improved economic conditions. The infrastructure required to create such a partnership is presented along with the many organizations involved in this effort and the role of the university in such a complicated effort. As a part of this process, research is being performed to determine success factors, and new approaches are being developed for bridging the digital divide in rural areas.

In the final chapter, Lazar and Norcio present an agenda for service-research. In service-research, academic research is structured in a way that some sort of service is immediately provided to the local community as a part of the research process. We investigate the ways in which digital divide challenges can be addressed as a part of the data collection required for serious research. Service-research can help recruit larger numbers of subjects for research studies, and can possibly help lower the expenses to researchers of recruiting subjects. Possible applications of service-research are discussed in the context of research in areas such as: user training, interface usability, user behavior, documentation, information systems management, and design processes. Two examples of service-research are briefly discussed.

Acknowledgments

Intellectual growth can only occur when one has a supportive, insightful, and challenging group of colleagues. I am fortunate to have many such close colleagues. Thanks to James Clements, Alfreda Dudley-Sponaugle, Julie Jacko, Doris Lidtke, Chao Lu, Gabriele Meiselwitz, Anthony Norcio, Jenny Preece, Andrew Sears, Cheryl Schroeder-Thomas, and countless other colleagues at Towson University and in the human-computer interaction community. In addition, my work on community partnerships has been financially supported by the Center for Applied Information Technology at Towson University and the Shriver Center at UMBC.

Special thanks go to the enthusiastic publishing team at Idea Group Publishing. Michele Rossi was always available to provide valuable suggestions in an upbeat manner. Mehdi Khosrowpour provided continuing encouragement and the benefit of his publishing experience. Thanks also to Carrie Stull for assisting with the marketing of the book.

An edited book is a group process, and it is the contributing authors who make the book into a reality. Thanks to the authors for their valuable contributions, and best wishes for continued success in their community partnerships. In addition, I also want to thank all of the people who assisted in the reviewing process. And thanks to the continuing support of my close family–Libby and Martin Lazar, Berniece and Herbert Kumin, Mollie Lazar, and Joel and Sandra Lazar.

Dr. Jonathan Lazar, Editor
Towson University
Towson, Maryland, USA
October 2001

Section I

Course Partnerships

Chapter I

Service-Learning Partnerships in the Information Systems Curriculum

Jonathan Lazar and Doris Lidtke
Towson University, USA

Service-learning partnerships involve students taking part in structured community service that relates to their academic course experience. Students who major in information systems are increasingly being provided with real-world experiences. These real-world experiences offer numerous benefits. Students can immediately apply their course knowledge to real-world situations. Students can gain the experience of grappling with political, social, and ethical issues in a workplace setting. In addition, students can develop a sense of civic responsibility, by contributing their skills to their communities. This chapter presents the issues involved in implementing the service-learning paradigm in an information systems curriculum. Examples of successful service-learning courses are presented, and new possibilities for service-learning courses are discussed.

INTRODUCTION

Courses in the information systems curriculum are increasingly incorporating hands-on experiences for students. Student evaluation is no longer limited to exams and research papers. Projects are becoming an increasingly common part of the information systems curriculum. It is one thing to describe to students how an information system is developed, modified, or maintained. It is a totally different experience for students to experience first-hand an information system being developed, modified, or maintained. If the students can work with real users in a real-world experience to develop an information system, this is a valuable experience.

The major question is how to place students in an appropriate real-world project setting. An educational paradigm called service-learning would seem to be appropriate for forming a partnership. In service-learning, students take part in structured community service experiences relating to their coursework (Jacoby, 1996). At the same time, students learn about the social and cultural dimensions of computing, and may start to question their own role in systems development, and how they can apply their skills to help the community. This chapter will discuss opportunities for implementing the service-learning paradigm in the information systems curriculum.

SERVICE-LEARNING

Service-learning is an educational paradigm in which students take part in community service (Jacoby, 1996). This community service is structured to relate to course material, with the goal of strengthening the program experience. The idea is that the service-learning projects offer an opportunity to immediately apply the material learned in the classroom. Instead of simply discussing the concepts in a classroom setting, students get a chance to use their knowledge to assist others (Jacoby, 1996). At the same time, while gaining experience working in their community, students also strengthen their sense of civic responsibility. Service-learning can provide a strong educational experience for the students involved.

Community-based non-profit organizations are in need of assistance with technology. Non-profit organizations tend to have smaller budgets for technology, and therefore cannot afford to hire many people to work on their technology needs. For instance, schools frequently cannot afford to provide Internet training for their teachers (Lazar and Norcio, 2000). In some cases, schools might be required to spend their technology budgets on capital expenses such as hardware and software, instead of developing new resources or managing existing resources or providing training (US General Accounting Office, 1998). Other non-profit organizations, such as parent groups, and support groups, usually are dependent on donations of money and time to effectively utilize technology. Groups of technology workers may come in on a Saturday to wire a school for the Internet. Professional user groups may take donations of old computer equipment, refurbish and upgrade the computers, and then donate the now-functional computers to non-profit organizations in the local community. Many community groups are dependent on the goodwill of their local citizens to effectively use technology.

Service-learning is a useful technique for incorporating real-world experiences into the curriculum. Local community groups are in need of assistance with technology. Students are in need of real-world experiences that relate to their course material, because they gain a better understanding of user issues only by working with real users (Lazar and Preece, 1999). By getting real-world experience, students can get a sampling of the ethical and political issues that can occur in a workplace (Lazar and Preece, 1999). Through their real-world projects, students may also make contacts, and develop professional networks that can help them in their careers (Shneiderman, 1998). In addition, students frequently assume that implementing an information system consists entirely of programming. By going through the complete development lifecycle, working with users to gather requirements, develop a system, and then implement that system, students can see that there is much more than coding involved in information systems development.

There are many other advantages of service-learning. Students can "learn to learn," meaning that they learn new technologies, new techniques, and new programming languages in real-time, in the workplace. In a service-learning placement, students can learn the importance of documentation. The appreciation for the importance of documentation can be hard to instill in the classroom. By working with others in a real-world setting, students can develop the skills needed for successful teamwork. By seeing the variety of information technology positions available within an organization, students may develop a better understanding of their area of interest, which can assist students in choosing elective courses to complete their degree program. These service-learning experiences are very relevant to the experiences that students will have after they complete their degrees (Kolenko, Porter, Wheatly, and Colby, 1996). Students gain valuable experience to help them prepare for their professional career. And when students have completed their degree requirements, their service-learning placements can be used as a "portfolio" of work, to show their level of competence (Lazar, 2000).

Meeting Industry Needs

Industry frequently requests that students completing information systems programs should have a better understanding of how information systems are developed and maintained in the workplace (Lidtke et al., 1999). Service-learning certainly adds this component to the curriculum. Students gain exposure to actual systems, meaning that they improve their understanding of how the components of a system interact and function together. In addition, the students see how important requirements gathering is, and they obtain experience working with the actual users of their systems. Frequently, students get exposure to issues such as cost analyses, teamwork, workplace ethics, and the importance of documentation. All of these experiences help the student to better understand just what working as an information systems professional is all about.

REQUIREMENTS FOR A SERVICE-LEARNING COURSE

An information systems course using the service-learning paradigm is generally appropriate for juniors or seniors who have a thorough understanding of the issues involved in the process of developing an information system. To develop an information system, or even to provide a consulting report, is by no means appropriate for a freshman or those new to the information systems major. Many new students tend to think that developing an information system begins with sitting down and coding. In reality, a long process of analysis and conceptual design first takes place. Because this understanding is necessary for a successful service-learning placement, a good prerequisite for a service-learning course would be either a basic *Systems Analysis and Design* and/or *Project Management* course. Both of these courses involve the process of developing an information system, as well as the issues (political, legal, user, financial) that can arise when building an information system. With this knowledge base, students are qualified to enter an organization and build an information system. Even without this knowledge base, it is possible to design a service-learning course for freshman-level courses. However, these courses will not focus on building real-world systems (see the description of the "Computer Applications" course later in this chapter).

Good community partners are a requirement for a successful service-learning experience. Ideally, these partners should be non-profit organizations, which generally have smaller technology budgets and are frequently unable to afford assistance with their technology needs. These non-profit organizations are ecstatic to have bright students to assist them, and the students are welcomed with open arms. The students feel that they are wanted, and that they can make a difference. This makes for a very positive experience for the students. In one service-learning placement, the non-profit organization was so happy to have the students there, that the contacts in the non-profit organization hugged the students every time that they came for a client meeting, and baked cookies to thank the students for all of their hard work. Good community partners are essential to the service-learning paradigm, because if the clients do not find the time to meet with the students, the service-learning project cannot be successful. At the same time, students must understand that they have made a commitment to the community partner, and students must live up to their end of the bargain. Feeling tired, or partying the weekend before, is not an excuse for late work in the workplace, and neither is it acceptable in a service-learning project. Service-learning mirrors the responsibilities that students will face when they enter the workplace after graduation.

Models of Service-Learning

There are a few different models of service-learning that can be used for a class. The service-learning projects can be anything from a two-week project, to the main focus of the semester. The service-learning projects can be required (as a stated part of the course grading), or they can be optional. For an optional service-learning project, the students can substitute a service-learning project for other course requirements, or the students can possibly earn an extra credit ("the fourth credit option") for taking part in a service-learning experience (Sanderson and Vollmar, 2000). Although service-learning is traditionally used in conjunction with classroom-based courses, service-learning could also be implemented as a co-op or internship program. Students can apply their knowledge from a number of different classes, to assist a non-profit organization with their technology needs. Of particular value are internships which allow students to be involved in the complete process of analyzing, designing, implementing, delivering, and maintaining a system. Alternatively, students can learn a great deal from in-depth immersion in one or more of these development phases.

The Infrastructure Required

Certainly, it can take more time and require additional resources for faculty to effectively manage service-learning projects. Before the semester begins, it is important to find appropriate community partners for the service-learning course. Although some students might have possible community partners in mind, many students will be looking to the professor for suggestions as to an appropriate community partner. It is possible that resources might already exist on the university campus to assist in finding appropriate community partners. In some universities where service-learning is a frequent occurrence, there is a designated service-learning coordinator who can help find appropriate community partners (Sanderson and Vollmar, 2000). At other universities, there might be community service coordinators, or an entire office of community service, or office of community partnerships, and these can be valuable resources for the faculty member looking for community partners (Lamb, Swinth, Vinton, and Lee, 1998). These offices not only assist those who are leading service-learning classes, but also positively promote the concept of service-learning within the organization (Lamb, Swinth, Vinton, and Lee, 1998). In addition, some colleges of business have the infrastructure in place for faculty to work with local organizations, both for-profit and non-profit.

In addition to the set-up time, faculty must keep in touch with the students, as well as the community partners, on a constant basis. Constant, ongoing communication is important to make sure that the projects are running smoothly. The worst-case scenario is for the faculty member to "find out" at the end of the semester that the service-learning project has not been going well for a least a month!

SERVICE-LEARNING EXAMPLES

The following section will describe some of the possibilities for implementing service-learning in the information systems curriculum:

Web Design

As part of the requirements for a Web design course, students can develop small Web sites for non-profit organizations in the community (Lazar, 2000). In such a situation, the students must learn about both the Web design process, as well as Web programming, such as HTML and JavaScript. Alternatively, students could learn more about Web design applications, such as FrontPage and Dreamweaver. For this service-learning approach to be successful, students must have both the tools to build Web sites (coding and/or Web-development applications), as well as an understanding of the development process (Lazar, 2000). The service-learning project could consist of a series of deliverables, which is similar to a real-world work setting. At the end of the semester, the final deliverable is a completed Web site.

This approach offers numerous advantages. Students go through the full lifecycle of analysis and design, by determining user requirements, developing a Web site, and then testing and installing a Web site (Lazar, 2001). Students rarely get to experience a full lifecycle for an informational system, and many students feel that design begins by writing code. This service-learning experience gives students the opportunity to see coding in the proper context, as part of the systems lifecycle. In place of building a Web site from scratch, students can also re-design currently existing Web sites. By re-designing an existing Web site, students can get experience in maintaining information systems, a topic which is frequently left out of analysis and design courses. Throughout the semester, students should be encouraged to share their insights, their experiences, and their revelations.

Database Design

Students in database classes can apply their knowledge to help community-based organizations manage their data. Jimenez describes a class where students analyzed, designed, and implemented a database for a county department of health and human services. This relational database stored resources available related to child care (Jimenez, 1995). In this service-learning class described by Jimenez, the students performed an analysis, developed entity-relationship diagrams, designed a relational database, and then implemented the database in Windows-based database software. Users were involved in the entire development process, and functionality and usability testing were performed. Not only did students get to experience the challenges of creating a functional system, but the students also had the opportunity to deal with the challenges of designing appropriate relational structures for real-world data. Students also learned the importance of project documentation (Jimenez, 1995). A service-learning project related to database design was also utilized in a software engineering course (Sanderson and Vollmar, 2000).

Computer Applications

Many universities offer courses dealing with computer applications such as word processing, spreadsheet, and database. These courses tend to be at the 100-level or 200-level. Although word processing is a popular tool, many employees in non-profit organizations are not as familiar with the powerful features of spreadsheet and database software. As part of their course requirements, students could assist non-profit organizations in developing databases of members or mailing lists, or in developing spread-sheets for tracking finances. Because students only receive very basic training in using these software tools, these projects might be relatively small, but they can give students a good introductory experience of working with users. These types of projects would also tie-in very well with business classes such as marketing and accounting. These courses typically enroll students of freshman and sophomore rank, so it is essential to make sure that the students are well-equipped to operate in a work-place, and understand the systems development lifecycle, before sending the students out for a service-learning experience. Another possible approach to service-learning in an introductory course is to have the university students mentor local residents (such as primary school students or senior citizens) on using the basic software applications. Such an approach was used at the University of San Diego. Although it may not possible for introductory-level students to go out and create informational systems, there are still possibilities for service-learning partnerships in these introductory-level courses.

Online Communities

Online communities are network-based resources where people with common interests can go online to communicate (using listservers, bulletin boards, etc.) and share resources (Lazar and Preece, 1998). Online communities exist on the Web for people with shared interests, for instance: Communities exist for sports, hobbies, parent groups and sup-port groups. An online communities course is offered at the University of Maryland-Baltimore County, where students examine and develop online communities.

In the service-learning approach to this course, students talk with non-profit organizations (both locally and regionally) and determine where there is a need for a new online community, or where an existing online community needs to be re-designed for improved usability. Students then build or re-design online communities for groups such as parent support groups, local schools, and neighborhood associations (Lazar and Preece, 1999). In developing the online communities, the students follow the development methodology of community-centered design (Preece, 2000). By doing this, the students become familiar not only with the software tools for building online communities, but also with the user considerations in building an online community (Lazar and Preece, 1999).

Business Process Redesign

A graduate course in business process redesign (BPR) included a community partnership, where students worked in a local organization to help redesign business processes. The course objective was to teach BPR concepts and techniques (Kock, 2000). The instructor decided that the most effective way for students to learn about BPR was to re-design business processes for a local company (Kock, 2000). The specific IT processes to be re-designed included help desk call response, new employee account set-up, and asset management (Kock, 2000). Although this partnership involved a for-profit company, this same course approach could be used for a non-profit organization. By the end of the course, students had created three deliverables, describing the analysis of the current processes, possible IT approaches for process re-design, and cost/benefit analyses of the different implementation plans (Kock, 2000).

Senior Capstone Course

Many information systems programs include a "capstone" course at the end of the program. These courses tend to synthesize the knowledge gained in other courses, and therefore, these courses are very appropriate for service-learning partnerships. Projects are frequently the main component of a capstone course. Students can utilize skills gained in other courses, such as programming, database design, systems analysis and design, and networking. The type of service-learning project (database, programming, Web design, etc.) may change, based on what the needs of the community-based organization are. The service-learning project could involve programming skills, software skills, networking skills, and/or database skills. Chapter 4 by Roberts and Boyle, describes service-learning in Capstone projects.

Networking

Students in networking courses could assist non-profit organizations in implementing local area networks. Frequently, non-profit organizations such as schools cannot afford many of the costs associated with implementing computer networks. As service-learning placements, students could work with local non-profit organizations, at numerous stages of network development. For instance, students could help in the network planning stages, the physical wiring, or the implementation of working networks. For more information about such a service-learning project for computer networking, please read Chapter 3 in this book, by Ruppel and Ruppel.

Human-Computer Interaction/Usability

A topic that is increasingly becoming a part of the information systems curriculum is the area of human-computer interaction and usability. Human-computer interaction is a more general area of study, dealing with all aspects of how humans interact with computers. Usability is a sub-topic within the field of HCI, related to designing products that are easy to use. Some universities offer usability as a topic within an HCI course, while other universities offer entire courses in usability. With new laws relating to usability taking effect in the United States (Lazar, Kumin, and Wolsey, 2001) and other countries such as Australia (Astbrink, 2001), it is expected that interest in the area of usability will increase.

Depending on the focus of the HCI course, there are a number of different opportunities for service learning. For instance, if ergonomics was a major topic in the course, students could go out to local non-profit organizations and examine the physical environment in which the users are working. The students could act as consultants, examining the ergonomics of the workplace, and providing a consulting report, identifying the problems in the physical setting, and offering suggestions for improvement. If usability was a major focus of the course, then students could assist local organizations in improving the usability of either internal organizational applications or the usability of their Web sites. Other possible service-learning partnerships could involve the creation of training sessions or appropriate documentation.

LESSONS LEARNED

There are a number of lessons that can be learned, from both the research literature and from personal experience, that can be helpful when designing a service-learning course.

- **It is important to clearly specify to both students and community partners what their respective roles and responsibilities are.** Sometimes, either the students or the community partners may underestimate the amount of time that is required for a successful project. There must be clear communication channels between the students and the community partners. A lack of communication is one of the most frequent problems in service-learning projects, and sometimes it may be necessary for the professor to mediate when either the students or the partners feel that their letters, phone calls, or e-mails have not been answered in an appropriate time period.

Aside from the issue of time, there are certain processes that must be followed by the community partners and the students, as required by the professor. The community partners must be sensitive to the required course timelines, as well as the specific deliverables required. When the contact person at one non-profit organization changed, the new contact person was not willing to stick to the process required by the class, wondering "why the students can't just build us a Web site in two weeks." A written contract might be helpful in clarifying these roles. This contract is not necessarily a legally binding contract, but it is a contract that makes the students and the partners both understand their respective responsibilities and feel more accountable for fulfilling them (Kolenko, Porter, Wheatly, and Colby, 1996; McCarthy and Tucker, 1999). A contract may especially be helpful if students will have access to sensitive data, where confidentiality might be an important issue (Sanderson and Vollmar, 2000).

- **Although the students may turn in all deliverables to the professor, the students do not always turn in all required materials to the community partner**. From personal experience, two client organizations contacted the professor a month after the end of the semester, wondering where the final project deliverables were. After semester grades have been turned in, the leverage that the professor has is considerably reduced. Therefore, it is important to check with the community partner to make sure that all requirements have been completed, before final grades have been turned in. It is also helpful to mention to the students that final grades are not submitted to the registrar until the community partner gives the "green light" indicating that all required materials have been turned in.

- **This is a partnership—neither the students nor the community organization can make unilateral decisions**. It is important that both the students and the community partners understand the nature of a partnership. The students sometimes assume that they can and will decide what is best for the community organization. This is not good since the service-learning experience should meet a real community need. The opposite is also true—some community groups may see students as "free labor"— i.e., they think that they can tell students exactly what to do, and expect them to go do it, without concern for the students' educational needs. It must be clear to all that decisions require mutual agreement. If this consensus cannot be reached by the students and the community organization, the professor needs to become involved.

- **It is helpful to have an infrastructure to support service-learning projects**. If there are university staff that specifically focus on community service, they will be excellent resources, as they will be familiar with the many organizations in the area that have needs. In addition, these university staff will also have an organizational memory of community service projects, meaning that they may be able to provide feedback as to which organizations welcome students with open arms and provide wonderful experiences for students, and which organizations are not able to provide good experiences for students. (Chapter 2, by Venkatesh and Small, provides information on the infrastructure existing at Syracuse University.)

- **There are some situations that occur, that simply cannot be planned for**. By sending students out into the "real world," the professor allows them the experience of what occurs in real organizations. Unfortunately, in rare occurrences, what happens in an organization isn't very positive. In one service-learning project, the community group asked the students to illegally install software (Lazar and Preece, 1999). Luckily, the students were aware that this was wrong, and after talking with the professor, the students immediately ended their involvement with the community organization. In another service-learning project, when the contact person at the client organization changed, the organization became somewhat hostile to the students. Not only did the community partner complain about the personalities of the students, but the client organization complained that the students had "wasted the valuable time" of the organization, and expected either more work after the semester ended, or some form of compensation. In another instance, a student in a service-learning internship was asked to remove all advertising from the community organization's Web site. The Web site hosting for the community organization had been provided for free, based on the understanding that advertisements would be displayed. Essentially, the community organization asked the student to perform inappropriate acts based on the hosting agreement. After pointing out this fact to the community organization, the student terminated the internship.

- **Reflection is an important aspect of service-learning**. For the experience to truly "sink in," students should be required to reflect on their experiences. What have they learned? How was it different from what they expected? Is there anything that was surprising? There are a number of different approaches for doing this: students could write weekly journals (Kolenko, Porter, Wheatly, and Colby, 1996), students could present their reflections in class, or a reflection paper could be required at the end of the semester. In one Web design class based on the service-learning model, a student commented at the end of the semester that "my biggest surprise was that everyone in the community didn't have a cable modem. I found that many of the users were still using slow dial-up connections. I couldn't believe it! I now understand the need to design Web sites that can load quickly." This student has learned a very valuable lesson—and probably is more considerate of the digital divide problem, as well. When reflecting, students often learn what parts of the IT field interest them, and this may help guide the students in choosing their advanced electives. This can better prepare the student for an area of IT that really interests them. Students may also discover that there are certain areas of IT that do not appeal to them, and this can also be an important discovery for their future studies and career development.

- **With service-learning, students gain an appreciation for the non-technical components of systems development**. This is evident in a number of different publications, as well as personal experiences with service-learning classes. When students have completed projects working with real users in a real-world environment, they have a better understanding of the entire development process, and are more able to see the importance of activities such as requirements gathering, training, documentation, and usability testing (Hoffer, George, and Valacich, 1999). At the beginning of service-learning projects, students may tend to feel that they truly understand the users, but by the end of a service-learning project, students leave with a better understanding that they do not necessarily have the same views or experiences as the user, and they need to involve users in the development process.

CHEATING

Cheating is unfortunately present in many university settings. Students may turn in work that has been written by another student, purchased from an Internet site, or the student may turn in the same assignment for multiple courses. Service-learning projects largely eliminate the cheating problem. It is very obvious in a service-learning project whether the students actually performed the work. If students do not meet with or communicate with their community partner, it is obvious. Typically, a specific deliverable that is useful for the community partner is due at the end of the semester. If students have not turned in this deliverable, it is clear. It is nearly impossible for students to turn in work from others and represent it as their own, as both the professor and the community partner have been working with the students during the entire process.

One problem that could occur with group service-learning projects is the free rider problem. In the free-rider problem, certain group members do a larger share of the work, and other group members do a smaller share, benefiting from the hard work of the group. This is not specific to service-learning projects—this is true in all group projects. One method that is frequently used to determine group workload is simply to ask each group member to rate the other group members in terms of their participation. This also introduces the concept of peer evaluation. Students have probably had little experience with this, however, it can be very valuable to them, as preparation for their profession. It is also helpful to ask the group members to specify what specific tasks they were responsible for throughout the semester. This way, a student cannot claim that they performed a large share of work, if they cannot say which tasks they performed. In case of a disagreement between group members, it might be helpful to also ask the community partner their views on which group members fulfilled their responsibilities.

THE EFFECT OF INFORMATION SYSTEMS ACCREDITATION

Accreditation has long been a strong component of computer science programs, through the Computer Science Accreditation Board (http://www.csab.org), and beginning in 2001, through the Computing Accreditation Commission of the Accreditation Board for Engineering and Technology (ABET). Accreditation efforts in information systems have increased, and it is expected that accreditation will play a major part in information systems programs in the future. Accreditation teams are focusing on the goals and objectives of information systems programs, and then determining whether the programs are meeting their stated goals. Service-learning projects can be helpful in program assessment, by showing how well students are able to perform in real-life situations. Real-world projects completed by students can demonstrate that students, upon completing a program of study, have mastered the subject material and are able to apply their knowledge in a real-world setting to solve real-world problems. Successfully completed service-learning projects can be an additional outcome measure to evaluate the effectiveness of the curriculum in an IS program.

The service-learning projects can also be very helpful for other types of program evaluations. For instance, many universities perform internal evaluations of their academic programs on a regular basis. These service-learning projects provide assessment of students' individual and group work, which provides important feedback on the effectiveness of an academic program. These projects can also be used by a community or industry advisory board (Chapter 7 by Coakley and Tyran, as well as Chapter 10 by Navarrete and Pick, both discuss industry advisory boards) for an information systems program, to provide continuing, comparative evaluation of the ability of students.

SUMMARY

Service-learning, when implemented appropriately, can be an effective paradigm for information systems courses. Students can gain experience working in real-world settings with real users. These service experiences can help students determine which career path is most appropriate for them. At the same time, local community organizations get assistance with their technology needs, which they otherwise could not afford. Service-learning has successfully been used in courses such as Web design and database design, and it could be appropriate for other courses, such as human-computer interaction and senior capstone courses.

REFERENCES

Astbrink, G. (2001). The legislative impact in Australia on universal access in telecommunications. *Proceedings of the Universal Access in Human-Computer Interaction 2001 Conference*, 1042-1046.

Hoffer, J., George, J. and Valacich, J. (1999). *Modern Systems Analysis and Design* (2nd Ed.). Reading, MA: Addison-Wesley Longman.

Jacoby, B. (1996). *Service Learning in Higher Education*. San Francisco, CA: Jossey-Bass Publishers.

Jimenez, S. (1995). A computer science service project. *Proceedings of the CHI 95: Human Factors in Computing* (interactive posters),151-152.

Kock, N., Auspitz, C. and King, B. (2000). Using the Web to enable industry-university collaboration: An action research study of a course partnership. *Informing Science*, 3(3), 157-166.

Kolenko, T., Porter, G., Wheatly, W. and Colby, M. (1996). A critique of service-learning projects in management education: Pedagogical foundations, barriers, and guidelines. *Journal of Business Ethics*, 15, 133-142.

Lamb, C., Swinth, R., Vinton, K. and Lee, J. (1998). Integrating service learning into a business school curriculum. *Journal of Management Education*, 22(5), 637-654.

Lazar, J. (2001). *User-Centered Web Development*. Sudbury, MA: Jones and Bartlett Publishers.

Lazar, J. (2000). Teaching Web design though community service projects. *Journal of Informatics Education and Research*, 2(2), 71-75.

Lazar, J., Kumin, L. and Wolsey, S. (2001). Universal usability for Web sites: Current trends in the U.S. law. *Proceedings of the Universal Access in Human-Computer Interaction 2001 Conference*, 1083-1087.

Lazar, J. and Norcio, A. (2000). Service-research: Community partnerships for research and training. *Journal of Informatics Education and Research*, 2(3), 21-25.

Lazar, J. and Preece, J. (1998). Classification schema for online communities. *Proceedings of the 1998 Association for Information Systems Americas Conference*, 84-86.

Lazar, J. and Preece, J. (1999). Implementing service learning in an online communities course. *Proceedings of the International Academy for Information Management 1999 Conference*, 22-27.

Lidtke, D., Stokes, G., Haines, J. and Mulder, M. (Eds.). (1999). *ISCC '99: Educating the Next Generation of Information Specialists in Collaboration with Industry*. Omaha, NE: University of Nebraska at Omaha. (http://www.iscc.unomaha.edu).

McCarthy, A. and Tucker, M. (1999). Student attitudes toward service-learning: Implications for implementation. *Journal of Management Education*, 23(5), 554-573.

Preece, J. (2000). *Online Communities: Designing Usability, Supporting Sociability*. New York: John Wiley & Sons.

Sanderson, P. and Vollmar, K. (2000). A primer for applying service learning to computer science. *Proceedings of the ACM SIGCSE 2000 Conference*, 222-226.

Shneiderman, B. (1998). Relate-Create-Donate: A teaching/learning philosophy for the cyber-generation. *Computers & Education*, 31, 25-39.

United States General Accounting Office. (1998). *School Technology: Five School Districts' Experiences in Funding Technology Programs (GAO/HEHS-98-35)*. Washington, DC: United States General Accounting Office.

Chapter II

Active Learning in Higher Education: A Model and Roadmap

Murali Venkatesh and Ruth V. Small
School of Information Studies, Syracuse University, USA

In this chapter, we present lessons learned from 10 years' instructional experience with active learning through our classes at Syracuse University. As reflective practitioners of active learning, we have refined our instruction over the years, in the process conceptually extending and augmenting extant theories of experiential learning and related approaches. Our model is built around four principles: client-centered work in natural settings, task design that is attentive to the motivational properties of the active learning stimulus, learning as social participation, and community service learning. Learning through prototyping, with its emphasis on design and the making of artifacts, functions as a background to the extended model and informs each of its principles. We then present a brief history of the Center for Active Learning and the Community and Information Technology Institute, both of which, in slightly different ways, implement our active learning method.

INTRODUCTION

We report research and reflection on 10 years of practice with active learning in the local community. Over the years, we have developed a model of active learning that augments experiential learning approaches with insights from client-centered practice, task design, learning-as-participation, and service learning. We have used what we term the "field consulting project" as the primary instructional vehicle. Students work in small teams (three or four members) to provide a consulting service to a real client in the local community facing a real problem or opportunity. This service is provided free of charge to public institutions, under which we include government agencies, healthcare institutions, as well as social sector non-profits and grassroots community institutions; public institutions are the only clients we serve through our classes. The subject matter of our teaching is information and communications technologies (ICTs), computer-based systems and software applications, telecommunications and networks. Our classes cover ICT planning and design as well as training users on use of ICTs.

By locating active learning in local community institutions, we wish to sensitize our students to the social context within which ICT applications are developed and used. We are just as concerned that our students get a sense of the larger social question: the inequality in access to ICTs. A sizable number of institutions we serve through our classes have little in the way of technology or technical expertise. Working with such clients gives our students a first-hand appreciation of the divide between the technology haves and have-nots. Such institutions are also often the ones that work most directly with low-income residents. Enabling institutional access to ICTs in such cases can also mean that, directly or indirectly, the neediest individuals in the community get the benefit of technology.

As a necessary step in the training of the socially aware systems professional, we need to balance the technical with the social in educating the new workforce. Computing is a social technology (see Iacono & Kling, 1988). Students must understand that technology choices have social implications for the adopting organization. Such an understanding is part of our expanded view of "relevance" in professional education. A professional-in-training must learn to consider technology not only within the context of work practices, but also within that of organizational culture and power. We differentiate such an awareness (the holistic "micro-social") from a broader, extra-organizational consciousness that embraces social and societal issues. Both the micro- and macro-social are constitutive aspects of relevance in our use of the term in this chapter.

We need to adopt a holistic view of ICT application, to go beyond what Schon (1983) called "technical rationality" in our approach to systems education. Consider the case of a class project that drove this point home to our students (and, powerfully, to us). The recently appointed office manager of a government agency approached the first author for advice on migrating from a mainframe-centric to a PC-based LAN environment in his office. His office was part of the District Attorney's office, and had about 30 staff members. The manager and the users "hated" the mainframe system that served many county agencies including his office; it had primitive functionality and was difficult to use. The MIS "priesthood" that ministered to it was, according to him, quite indifferent to user needs. It was not uncommon for the MIS staff to take several hours, sometimes even a day or two, to generate a report for a query from the DA on, say, crime statistics in a certain part of the city over a certain period of time. The manager felt strongly that with a PC-based networked system, his office staff could be more responsive to the DA and to the public at large; above all, he would control such a system, not MIS, which he characterized as an unresponsive entity that was answerable to no one. He needed help with technical design and product specifications for the LAN, as well as advice on connecting to the mainframe for access to public, non-confidential data. He had approached MIS with this request, and they had not responded.

The student consultant team that picked the project was warmly embraced by the user group from the outset but met with immediate and hostile resistance from MIS. MIS, the team was informed, had little use for the PC and could not or would not support PC connectivity to the mainframe database on account of "security" concerns. They were unwilling to consider that only a small part of the database—public, non-confidential data—would be accessed via the LAN. Despite the frustrations, the student consulting team came up with design specifications for the LAN. But MIS was unyielding on the database connectivity, refusing to meet with the students or share any information about the mainframe or the application. This even after the project's champion had complained to the DA himself about their hostile attitude. The students did not understand the situation until one of them asked to see the organization chart for the county. They quickly realized that MIS had countywide responsibilities, reported directly to the county executive, and that the DA's office, as a relatively small operation, merited very little of their attention. MIS was supported as part of the overhead of the county executive's office and had little incentive to be responsive to users in the DA's office. They had not impeded the students' LAN design exercise, rationalizing it as an isolated experiment, but had strenuously fought the mainframe connectivity issue because they feared the PC and didn't want to find out about it; besides, they were afraid they would lose control over the database. The team learned a lesson on their own and the manager's naivete about effecting organizational change, and on organizational structure and politics that no case study, however good as a simulation, could have brought home to them quite so vividly and powerfully.

THEORIES OF EXPERIENTIAL LEARNING

The fundamental tenet of experiential learning is that the learner is directly in touch with what is being studied, as differentiated from learning in the abstract

(Keeton & Tate, 1978). The learner in an experiential learning situation learns from actually, directly, and actively working with the objects of learning, usually under controlled conditions and under the instructor's supervision. The direct action component is key to such learning: the learner actually works with the subject matter at hand. Besides John Dewey (1938), well-known proponents of experiential learning include Piaget (1970) and Lewin (1951). All three theorists view learning as a continuous, adaptive process driven by experience; the learner is seen as active and engaged.

Situated learning theorists study the social context and practices in which learning takes place, taking as their focus "the relationship between learning and the social situations in which it occurs" (Hanks, 1991, p. 7).

Learning occurs in and through social situations; it is the product of participation in actual practice, of the interactions and relationships that constitute participation (see Lave & Wenger, 1991). Dewey himself was a proponent of the situated nature of experiential learning: experience occurs in and through situations (see Findeli, 1995).

Situated learning is relevant to our interest in natural work settings as well. Experiential learning can occur anywhere: in the laboratory, where the student learns by doing in a simulated, or synthetic, setting; and out in the "real world," in the natural context of actual practice. We believe natural settings are more effective in systems education because they continually remind the learner of the social context that influences ICT use, as in the example of the student consultants attempting to bring about change in the government office. Natural settings highlight the social context and character of systems development work, and of the social agreements or contracts under which such work is accomplished, in a way that synthetic settings cannot. In the example above, the team had to be sensitive to a number of concerns that are seldom encountered in conventional class assignments. They had to manage relations with the customer, which included managing the problem scope and customer expectations. They had to manage relations with MIS and with the course instructor. As part of a self-managing task force, team members also had to manage relations with one another and keep an eye on deadlines and deliverables, while watching out for slackers or control freaks. They had to work with differing skill levels and types in the team. Such extra-task social factors, some of which operate from within the team and others from outside, exert pressure on the team's work to shape task outcomes. We expand on these themes below, but outline them here to suggest the richness that natural settings can bring to the learning experience.

Constructionism (Papert, 1991) emphasizes design and the act of making: the learner is believed to *make* new ideas, not passively *get* them. A variant, called social constructionism, expands this view to the social milieu outside the classroom, and "focuses upon the construction of activities, projects, and relationships that help define an evolving community. Through this lens, the members of the community serve as active agents in the construction of outcomes and activities that produce a developmental cycle in the social setting" (Shaw & Shaw, 1999, p. 320). The model of active learning we discuss below is similar to both, and emphasizes design and the construction of prototypes, sometimes on paper, at other times, actual, working prototypes, as integral to the learning process.

Our approach, in line with social constructionism, makes the community and the client organization participants in the education of the learner. The field project assignment operationalizes the active learning model we have used since 1991 and expands the student's instructional field beyond the classroom into the local community. Students serve as ICT consultants to public institutions in the community. As consultants, they have to consider community-wide initiatives that may impinge on the client's problem or opportunity. Since late 1996, an especially relevant community ICT initiative has been the MetroNet (Appendix A), a broadband community network being implemented in economically poor zip codes in our community. The network design process (which lasted from mid-1998 to mid-2000) provided our students an unmatched opportunity to contribute to an evolving community resource. For example, one recent client, a branch public library, asked for a report on the feasibility of a wireless link to a nearby church. The client was interested in wireless for many reasons: she couldn't wait for the bureaucratic county central library (the decision-making authority) to pick a solution; she wished to be independent of the central library in this matter, and she felt she could get a state grant to implement an innovative solution. One student on the team had worked with wireless before, and all had an active interest in wireless.

After learning about the MetroNet and its social goals (briefly, community-wide connectivity for public institutions), the team revisited the client's interest in wireless. Their report contained what the client had asked for: an analysis of competing wireless propagation methods, products and prices, pros and cons of two candidate wireless solutions and a recommendation favoring one over the other, and an implementation plan. In addition, however, the report also successfully argued why the client ought to rethink wireless in light of the MetroNet, which will not support wireless. Linking to the MetroNet would link them to the local community as well as to the Internet; in contrast, the wireless link, which would be more expensive to implement and maintain, would be restricted to a single point-to-point link. No one on the team, including the expert, had had to think about wireless for a real user and against viable alternative solutions. This was the very first time they had to "externalize" their knowledge and assumptions, technical and contextual, in a design solution. In the process, they learned to consider not just the client's need but that of the larger community as well, pointing out the client's obligation to the community (as a resource) as well as the benefits that stood to accrue to the library from being linked to other resources (such as the city's zoo) for enriched multi-media services to patrons and to hitherto untapped audiences over the Internet. With the wireless solution, the library would have to bear the capital and recurring costs. The MetroNet solution was cheaper on account of the economics of bulk buying: capital and recurring costs would be shared by all the participants, and prices would be aggressively negotiated by the "buying group" (MetroNet participants) with the telephone company (hereafter carrier).

Service learning, learning through outreach in the local community, is central to our work as well. We believe strongly in the civic dimension of learning. Service learning is a key element in Dewey's (1927) conception of an engaged citizen. Knowing, Dewey believed, should be connected with social action.

The terms "active learning" and "experiential learning" are often used interchangeably in the literature to refer to the use of direct experience to instruct students in applying methods and theories learned in the classroom. Active learning is the broader term (Drueke, 1992), and subsumes experiential learning. Active learning encompasses a broader range of activities including hands-on work of making artifacts, interactive exercises, on-site internships, and fieldwork. Active learning emphasizes the learner's active involvement in what is being learned. For these reasons, we prefer the term active learning.

THE FIELD PROJECT ASSIGNMENT

The first author has used the field project assignment in his telecommunications classes continuously since 1991. The assignment has been refined over the years, and has been used with over 900 undergraduate and graduate students enrolled in the School of Information Studies and other schools and colleges in Syracuse University. The class has provided ICT consulting services to over 75 public institutions in the community, including government departments, healthcare and human service agencies, K-12 schools, and religious institutions. All services are provided free to clients. Topics have covered telecommunications network design and implementation, database applications, systems analysis and design, and user training.

The assignment covers one semester (14 to 16 weeks long), and accounts for up to 40% of the class grade. It is handed out during the third or fourth week of the semester; final project reports are due the week after the last class. The assignment covers two parts: *planning* and *design*. Planning includes user requirements analysis, gathering of client site documentation (e.g., floor plans, systems documentation), and resources and constraints analyses (such as the size of the MIS staff and the budget, respectively). This is by far the more time-consuming, complex, and less "technical" step. Students are expected to develop a good grasp of the client's needs and the organizational context through site visits and other data-gathering activities (e.g., surveys). This phase also provides the *criteria*, and importantly, the *values*, explicit or implicit, formal and informal, quantitative and qualitative, technical and social, that the team would use to assess the goodness of fit of the solution proposed through the design step.

The planning phase is critical also in that it forces students to think about the larger questions and concerns that frame design work. What sector(s) of the community does the client serve? Who are their customers, constituents, stakeholders? What broader goal(s) is the project contributing to? Such questions are relevant to what Schon (1983) called problem setting—"the process by which we decide the decision to be made, the ends to be achieved, the means which may be chosen." These are big and "messy" questions (compared to technology questions), and the domain is uncertain. Most students, left to themselves, would rather fast forward directly to the design step, which tends to be more concrete, manageable, less ambiguous. Planning is often frustrating, students have told us. Many of our clients serve the underserved in the community, and the project is the vehicle through which many of our students get their first glimpse of the social and moral challenges clients have to work with. Admittedly, the class is about technology applications, not sociology, and the project assignment does not require students to reflect on the social issues by themselves. They are sensitized to social issues and advised of their relevance to design work, but the issues themselves are not analyzed in class. But exposure to such issues during problem setting prepares learners for the integrative nature of design work, and argues against the adequacy of a purely technical rational view (Schon, 1983) of professional practice.

Once this step is complete, the team starts on the design activity (this is not to suggest that these steps are strictly sequential; they may occur in parallel, but logically, design tends to follow planning). The *product* of design is a set of technical specifications (Gronbaek, Kyng, & Mogensen, 1997), complete with product, price, and vendor information. The *process* of design involves assembling a system of interdependent elements to meet the client's needs. While the product is technical in nature, the process cannot be reduced to its technical focus. It is holistic, essentially integrative, in nature. When technology choices are made in a real organizational context, the designer is forced to admit pragmatic, non-technical considerations.

While the design step is the more technical, design work involves a careful consideration of the relation between technology and organizational work practices. Technology can change, sometimes subtly and at other times not so subtly, the work process it is applied to. A project such as MetroNet complicates design even more because it was purported to be an inter-organizational system infrastructure.

Inter-organizational application design can be complicated to the extent that the work process that links the participating organizations may be more central to one and less so to the other. If the application demands symmetry in resource allocation and workload when the underlying work process is asymmetric, problems can surface. An ongoing prototyping project uses Internet videoconferencing for Medicaid/Chronic Care benefits certification interviews. The county government division in-charge of administering Medicaid and the county's leading hospital are participating in the trial of the prototype, which allows applications for Medicaid/Chronic Care benefits to be interviewed via video directly at intake facilities such as the hospital.

The design team was struck by the contrasts between the two organizations. The county division's head was a strong champion of the project, giving it high visibility within the organization. The hospital's telemedicine department sanctioned the project as a local effort in the patient admissions function and was only tangentially involved. While the county dedicated a good-sized room to house the video equipment and accommodate the staff participating in the video interview, the hospital assigned a corner in a noisy, busy office. The space was barely enough for one participant to be seated comfortably, yet the original project plan had envisaged a hospital staff person sitting with and assisting the applicant during the video interview.

The county division "owns" the Medicaid benefits process; the hospital is a service provider. At present, organizational resource allocation reflects this asymmetry; the county expends more to work the process, and the county's process specialists assume the bulk of the workload. Whereas the process has the county at the center and the hospital in a service role, the videoconferencing solution insists on symmetry: end-points have to have similar technical features and support infrastructure for the application to work as intended. The hospital has appeared unwilling to commit more than the minimum technologically (spare capacity on a PC being used by a staff member was assigned to the project), and the physical space allocated was barely adequate.

The prototype has constrained work practices at the end-points and has reallocated workload. The Medicaid/Chronic Care benefits certification process requires the applicant to turn in extensive original documents, or authorized facsimiles, to process specialists during the interview. The design team explored ways to transfer documents back and forth using a courier service (to protect confidentiality, faxing or electronic sharing of documents has been ruled out for the present) prior to the interview, but the hospital is opposed to using a courier to transfer documents for fear it would disrupt existing procedures. Previously, it was the applicant's responsibility to turn in documents to the county specialists; now the hospital was being asked to handle it, and the staff have complained about the increased workload. At this writing, the hospital has assigned a dedicated room to the project, but the asymmetric workload problem (wherein the hospital staff are doing more compared to before) persists. The video installation, intended originally to support real-time conferencing as well as document sharing, only supports the former.

The project is an object lesson on the need to view design work broadly and holistically—as involving, among other things, non-technical factors such as organizational motivations. Design work is essentially integrative in that it is forced to relate technology to the work processes that embed and constrain it and to the organizational realities it is a part of. The county was motivated to free up resources and experiment with novel work practices (e.g., using a courier for document transfer) because the process, benefits certification, was central to its business function; it was less so to the hospital, and these motivations were critical constraints on the design. Design is also essentially interpretive in nature. The project highlights a key function of design, design as *interpretation*. Designers gained a deeper understanding of the design task in the process of actively working through it. The project brought into relief a work process that had hitherto been transparent, taken-for-granted. The designers had to respond to facets of the process that emerged in that particular situation, and these facets emerged as a result of and during the course of the design effort, prompting the designers to *improvise*—an important element in learning by designing. Improvisation refers to responding creatively and resourcefully to unexpected design demands. Design reflects the designer's *intent* (Deforge, 1995) as informed by the context of use, calling for improvisation.

Design work can be seductive, so much so that students want to start on it before they have gathered adequate planning data (professionals are not immune to this, either). They want to act before they adequately understand the action context, which is delineated through the planning process. They want to solve the problem before they have formulated it. This should be discouraged; without adequate planning, the team has only indeterminate criteria for evaluating the goodness of fit of design recommendations. Furthermore, without adequate planning, the role of the context in shaping design is curtailed, and the resulting design is usually inadequate.

The question (which the instructor emphasizes in class) the team must address in their final report is: what solution or assemblage of solutions available in the market would best satisfy the client's needs? Each team is required to document at least two comparable candidate solutions. Both options must be described adequately in the report, and a detailed justification of why the recommended solution was picked must be provided so that an independent reader (the client or instructor) can follow the reasoning behind the choice. We believe that the responsible consultant and designer should present the client with more than one option and justify the one picked in a comprehensible manner to facilitate independent assessment of its goodness of fit. Buchanan (1995) explains:

"Making (and the practice of design) involves two components. The first is the actual work of conception and planning...the second is the ability to explain the results of designing based on reasons and principles. ...the ability to explain is an integral part of practice: it enables the designer to judge the progress of work at each stage and persuade colleagues and clients that a particular design is effective for a given situation. Designers who possess only the skills of work are technicians; they practice a trade, not a profession" (p. 83).

LEARNING THROUGH PROTOTYPING

Design work using prototyping forces on the learner a holistic view of system development. More fundamentally, it illuminates the link between knowledge and action, between stored procedures and the contingencies that shape and inform them when they are mobilized and applied in actual situations. From this viewpoint, prototyping work, which involves the making of artifacts, is fundamentally epistemic in nature; it is instrumental to learning and to emergent knowledge (see Keller & Keller, 1993).

Project-based learning can be seen as prototyping. Students externalize an idea through, say, a sketch. The sketch is shared with other team members and with the client, and is refined as a result of their participation in the process. This is akin to using "talk-back" (Schon, 1983) from the situation to refine design, and to using a prototype to elicit user participation. Sometimes the artifact used may be a system prototype, which would allow users to actually try the system out and contribute to its refinement. Project-based learning in natural settings allows, indeed forces, learning to be holistic: the learner is sensitized to the use setting just as she is to the technology itself. The design process brings together the social and technical aspects of design work; design, in the sense of *making, improvising,* and *integrating,* is the fundamental activity in prototyping-for-learning. The prototype artifact can, in turn, help reaffirm the integrative enterprise of design by helping the designer to learn the user's needs and preferences.

What happens when prototypes are not used or used ineffectually in design work? The MetroNet design process was complicated by the poor use of prototypes. System prototypes would have been effective given the novelty to the users of the ICT technologies and applications, but were not used. Stylized network diagrams and written descriptions were used at design meetings, which included community participants and carrier staff from engineering, marketing, and sales. Most of these artifacts were produced by carrier staff and showed, via computer-generated diagrams, what the community network would look like when implemented. The artifacts generated by the users (community participants representing public institutions) were reactions to these prototypes, written and spoken questions and requests for information and clarification. These were non-technical in nature and concerned the project's legal ("Are we required to set up a fiduciary authority to make payments and collect dues if we go with a limited service offering?") and contractual aspects ("Can DSL users receive financial support for customer premise equipment?"). The carrier staff did not feel competent to respond to these concerns because they were beyond their purview.

The carrier staff encouraged user participation in the design process, but users felt that their concerns were not registering with them. There was "talk-back" and participation in a sense, but users were frustrated when they did not see their concerns addressed in the next iteration of the artifacts. Feedback was solicited and provided but was not used to inform the design process or products. When this persisted over many design meetings, users (the few that stayed with the effort) began to question the process: they felt their concerns were not being addressed. Will this network happen in a way that truly served community-wide goals? This was a common concern among users. Users questioned whether the activity was indeed the integrative, collaborative process they had expected. Carrier staff's (unintentionally) evasive answers to non-technical queries contributed more to users' frustration than any technical matter. Prototyping could have been used more effectively to assure participants of the responsiveness of the *process* as well as that of the *product* (network design).

Much has been written on the multi-faceted nature of system design work. It is recursive, non-linear, unstructured, opportunistic (Bansler & Bodker, 1993; Ball & Ormerod, 1985). The MetroNet design process was non-linear, chaotic, and often frustrating. But perhaps its most striking feature was that users' non-technical concerns persisted well into the later stages of design and were aired conspicuously at design meetings. Users' spoken comments at meetings tended to elaborate on the comments they inscribed on the margins of the artifacts developed by the carrier staff.

One would have expected that, as the design process accelerated, the proportion of non-technical concerns, on fundamental aspects of the grant guidelines and interpretations thereof, would decrease. After all, if the product of design is a technical specification, one would expect the proportion of technical issues aired at design meetings to increase. But this was not so. Users' non-technical concerns persisted over several months. The users did not understand the technology very well but aired non-technical concerns seemingly much more readily than they did technical concerns. But because they did not get satisfactory answers from the carrier staff, they began to question the validity and *personal relevance* of the design process: how real or relevant is any of this for me? The carrier staff tended to view design work as a technical, instrumental activity, and they attempted (unintentionally) to decontextualize technology. From the users' viewpoint, the carrier staff's design proposals were "cookie-cutter," that is, context-insensitive. The carrier staff appeared unwilling or unable to depart from the design methods they typically used, not recognizing that the problem situation (community networking) was novel to them and quite different (per their own admission) from what they typically engaged as part of their job.

Right from the outset of the project, community participants had had questions about the grant guidelines, what was permitted and what was not; questions on contracting and on how the grant funds would be disbursed, used, and managed, and such concerns, which reflected user *needs* in the most basic sense of the term, were an integral part of the design context. Such concerns defined the psychological frame within which the MetroNet was more or less relevant to users, e.g., if DSL service was ineligible for subsidized service charges under the program, then design decisions would be of little relevance to those who could only participate via subsidized DSL. Such concerns obviously complicate design work but are integral to it. These concerns increased in number and became sharper and more specific as the process wore on, and the carrier staff appeared to retreat further into what they were best equipped to deal with: the technology.

The target output from the design process is a solution specification. The *product* of design cannot address the kind of non-technical macro-level concerns raised by MetroNet users. Such concerns affected design activity without necessarily impinging on the design product. The *process* of design, however, has to work through such concerns, and the carrier staff's failure to take them into account prompted users to question the relevance of the *product*.

Learning suffered. Community network design as a collaborative process with user participation was new to the carrier staff; they had personally never done it this way before. They were not provided any training by the carrier before undertaking this work. Community participants, had they been assured of the responsiveness of the design process, may have been more open to learning about the technical issues the design staff were wrestling with within the grant's constraints and may have been more effective in their role as participant designers. This did not occur either. We impress upon our students and clients the need for accommodation on both sides.

The first author uses this experience to highlight the importance of the holistic view of design and the role of prototyping in learning by designing. Several related ideas can be summarized from the viewpoint of learning:

Design as interpretation: Design may be understood as situated action stemming from particular interpretations of the design space. Students learn through design work in a particular situation; the design effort surfaces issues that were hitherto transparent in the situation, and allows both learners and clients to question what is assumed and taken-for-granted. Prototypes, paper or system prototypes that the learner fashions, are indispensable design communication tools, as they allow learners and clients to externalize the solution and refine it iteratively and cooperatively with the user. Prototypes help make design activity a participative, social process. Paper prototypes are perfectly feasible in semester-long projects; system prototyping is best under-taken with projects that last beyond a semester. Learners should see prototyping for design as an integral part of articulated, reflective design activity. They should understand prototypes as interpretive aids, best used to loosen and "open up" the design, not close it prematurely. The instructor has to be vigilant that premature closure does not occur.

Design as improvisation: As part of the interpretive process, learners generate and test "hypotheses" about aspects of the design space: user needs and wants, technology and design options, social and cultural realities of the use context (e.g., computer acceptance or resistance). These hypotheses may be more or less formal or explicit, but proponents of lay epistemics (see Kruglanski, 1989) argue that learning about the world entails such a process wherein hypotheses are generated and tested until the learner is ready to act on the knowledge obtained through the process. We see the situated learner as an *active* and *adaptive* inquirer who continuously tests her understanding of the world and adapts the inquiry (and the prototype) as needed. The notions of improvisation and prototyping are fully consistent with the idea of the learner as an active, adaptive operator. The notion of design as *conjecture*, wherein the designer proposes "one particular solution concept (the conjecture) which is then tested against the requirements and constraints of the problem, thus contributing to a fuller understanding, or analysis, of the problem" (Cross, 1984, p. 168), is similar.

Design as "making relevant": The "design space" represents the constellation of possible solutions given a client's needs, resources, and constraints. The *product* of design is the resolution of the issues, challenges, opportunities, concerns, raised or presented by options within that space. The *process* of design connects options within that space with what is relevant to the client. It represents the intersection of generalized potential inherent in a solution and its personal relevance for the user. It is the tailoring of the design space to the client's specific needs. In a recent project on implementing a free Internet fax server for a faith-based social action group, the design space included several comparable hardware and software options. The options represented abstract feature-sets until the student team proposed a link between the client's needs and specific features of a sub-set of these options (this sub-set was their "hypothesis" or conjecture). When they presented this mapping to the client, the client was much more engaged than hitherto and helped the team by pointing out additional benefits he could realize by going with the options that were eventually picked for implementation in a systems prototype. Design as making relevant worked for the team as well, by helping to concretize abstractions they had only known on paper until they presented their hypothesis to the client. What had been "dry" to the client and the team, became "wet" (i.e., personally relevant) to both during design.

A pragmatic view of learning, encompassing learning by doing and social engagement by the learner, informs our practice as teachers and frames our understanding of design activity. A technical rational view of design has little to say about the context of action or the social aspects of human activity. We understand these social aspects as comprising a Web of *relations,* actors acting and interacting (Lave, 1993), with other actors through the medium of the task or work process and through the medium of technology. Such a conception of the social is consistent with approaches to learning, conceived as social participation, and design work as we have discussed above. Prototyping is, in this sense, a learning through design approach to the extent that prototypes are used to articulate (draw out, surface) the *relational* potentialities inherent in the context. When a technology is made concrete in a prototype, its social dimension is highlighted; it becomes an artifact located in a social space and derives its function(s) from the contexts it may be used in. Implementors have to work with clients, users, fellow team members, and, depending on the prototype, with vendors and service providers in a complex Web of formal and informal contracts and dependencies. Prototyping can facilitate interaction by learners with their fellows, by users with other users, and promote participation by users in the design process. Everyone learns. Used well, prototypes can help interpenetrate designers' *normative* world (normative in that it stems from their understanding of design *constraints*) and the situated world of users, allowing the one to inform the other in fruitful and innovative ways.

ACTIVE LEARNING: AN EXTENDED MODEL

We have developed and refined an extended model of active learning using the field project assignment as the stimulus. Learning through prototyping functions as a background to the extended model and informs its principles. The extended model is based on four basic principles, and draws on research and practice in teamwork, learning, motivation, and community service learning. We have found that these principles help improve the practice of active learning at the collegiate level. The statement of each principle is followed by a description of steps we have taken (and the challenges we have faced) in operationalizing the principle in our teaching.

Principle #1. Client-centered work in natural settings: An active learning experience that requires the learner to deliver a product or service to an identifiable, real client has significant motivational benefits for the learner. The idea of professionalism itself is defined with reference to the customer: "Since the essence of professionalism is the delivery of a service in response to a client need, it becomes critical, if the professional is to retain his sense of professional identity, to identify clearly on whose behalf services are being rendered" (Schein & Kommers, 1972).

In a chapter entitled "New Clients, New Client Needs" in their book *Professional Education*: *Some New Directions*, Schein and Kommers (1972) provide an extensive analysis of the changing role of the client in the professions:

- The term "client" increasingly refers to an organization and not an individual.
- There may be more than one client for professional services in an organization.
- The authors differentiate between immediate or contact client, intermediate, and ultimate clients (user). The ultimate client's needs may conflict with that of the immediate or intermediate client.
- Practitioners have to learn how to involve the ultimate client in decisions.
- Practitioners have to learn how to "reconcile or integrate the needs of the individual with those of the community or society as a whole" (p.29).

Learners in natural environments learn to pay close attention to their client or clients. In the example of the government department, the team had to be sensitive to the needs of multiple clients. The administrative officer was the contact or immediate client, his staff who would use the LAN-based database were the intermediate client, and the users of the database information (members of the public, the District Attorney) were the ultimate clients. The team worked directly with the contact and intermediate clients; the contact client communicated the ultimate clients' (assumed) needs to the team. Fortunately, there were no conflicts here. But behind the contact client was the county MIS department, which was powerful and influential but declined to play any kind of role in the project despite repeated efforts on the part of the team and the contact client to bring them to the table. There was an unstated conflict between the MIS department's systems objectives and the user department's performance goals, and the project threatened to surface these differences. The team's project activities were circumscribed and controlled by the MIS department; the contact client understood the problem but was helpless, and could get only one-half of his systems goals (implementing a LAN in his office) accomplished through the project. A focus on the customer quickly sensitizes learners to the importance of managing client relations, a skill that professional programs do not adequately cover.

In cases with multiple clients, teams sometimes get different directives reflective of different priorities. This is exacerbated by staff attrition during a project, resulting in loss of continuity (non-profit agencies tend to have high rates of technical staff turnover) and momentum. A related problem occurs when, on account of staff shortage, any available worker is assigned as the project liaison. This person, who is the "client" for all practical purposes, may not have the background or know-how to be effective. Secretarial staff tend to be seen as suitable for this role simply because they are heavy users of office systems. A second challenge stems from a consulting dilemma: should the team confirm a choice that the client has already made or is leaning toward, or recommend what they believe is the better alternative? Sometimes the client's instincts are correct (as in the case of the administrative officer, who wanted a LAN); at other times they are not (the library head, who had mistakenly assumed that a wireless solution would be ideal). The assignment advises students to research and present what they believe to be the best-fitting solution; however, they are encouraged to find out what the client's preferred solution is and research it before accepting or rejecting it. Faced with such dilemmas, students are doing much more than weigh the pros and cons of comparable ICT alternatives; they are confronting basic issues of professional identity, conduct, and integrity.

Principle #2. Project task design: Students' motivation to learn is critical in learning. In project work such as the one described here, students should have a substantial degree of interest in the project task for them to want to stay with it through the semester and complete it satisfactorily. Task motivation is but one input factor in task performance (for example, workers can be motivated through a reward system), but one that can be designed and controlled relatively easily. Task design parameters influence behavior: the extent to and depth at which relevant information is processed, the level of performance, and the willingness to "go the extra mile" for the client may all be influenced through task design.

We have found Hackman and Oldham's (1980) task design principles to be useful in the way we have approached the design of the field consulting project assignment to enhance its motivational appeal. Tasks high in skill variety, significance, and autonomy (where control is invested in the team itself for managing relations within and outside the team) promote task motivation (see Hackman & Oldham, 1980). Hackman (1983) defines these task conditions as follows:

- The group task requires members to use a variety of relatively high-level skills.
- The group task is a whole and meaningful piece of work, with a visible outcome.
- The outcomes of the group's work on the task have significant consequences for other people (e.g., other organization members or external clients).
- The task provides group members with substantial autonomy for deciding about how they do the work; in effect, the group "owns" the task and is responsible for the work outcomes.
- Work on the task generates regular, trustworthy feedback about how well the group is performing.

These principles have influenced the way we define the initial problem boundary for the teams (the initial bound is often modified by the team through negotiation with the client). First, the project has to be feasible (given the skills mix available that semester) and completable in a semester. The latter is a challenge, in that what can be completed by a team has to be meaningful to the client. This is a particular challenge when there are multiple teams working on projects for the same client in the same semester. For example, the branch library had two needs: connectivity to neighborhood facilities (via wireless), and connectivity to the Internet. The first topic involved comparing wireless solutions to high-bandwidth wireline solutions for multi-media applications sharing via MetroNet, while the second required research on local Internet service providers' (ISPs') offerings and cable-based Internet access service. Admittedly, there are overlaps here: MetroNet will provide Internet access through the telephone company or its ISP partner; similarly, the Internet can support cross-agency connectivity within the community, albeit at lower speeds relative to MetroNet. Teams working on these projects were asked to keep each other informed of their progress but were instructed to focus on their project, and not on the overlaps, in order to reduce coordination overhead (in such cases, the instructor needs to function as the link between team and client). Given the relatively short one-semester timeframe, and in the interest of completability, the team should focus on the task at hand, not on coordination with other teams. Fortunately, both MetroNet and the newer Internet access solutions (wireless, cable, and digital subscriber line) can work off of standard LAN technology, which helped cut extra-team coordination by allowing the teams to base their design decisions on a flexible infrastructure that offered alternative options to the client. Nevertheless, meaningful problem bounding is a challenge to the instructor; pragmatic concerns should be weighed carefully against the problem's integrity when "chunking up" project topics.

Skill variety. The field project assignment comprises two logical processes: planning and design. Planning covers user requirements, constraints and resource analysis, and analysis of relevant environmental factors or developments (for example, MetroNet). The product of the design process is a set of implementable technical specifications. The planning process calls for a higher proportion of relatively softer skills: survey instrument development and data analysis, interviewing, listening and writing skills, client relations, and project management skills. This is not to suggest that technology know-how is not needed; it is needed, but the need for humanistic and social skills is more prominent as the clientele, non-profit and public sector institutions, often lacks technical sophistication. Talking down and technical jargon are definite turn-offs for the client.

The design process calls for a higher proportion of technology know-how. But this is not all backroom activity. Student teams may consult with professionals at the university and in the community on design questions, talk to remote experts over the phone or the Internet, and to vendors and service providers. As argued above, the use of prototypes highlights the social nature of design work. The design sub-team interacts with the planning sub-team, and with the client and the instructor. Communication and negotiation are important activities in design. We have noticed that students with technical skills gravitate toward design activity, while those with humanistic, non-technical backgrounds favor planning activity. Note that students are not assigned to be planners or designers. In fact, they are advised the opposite — to use the opportunity to acquire skills they are deficient in, but, generally speaking, students tend to play to their strengths. The mechanism of "legitimate peripheral participation" (Lave & Wenger, 1991) allows learners to learn complementary skills by working in mixed skills teams.

Work of significance to the client, with visible outcomes: The field project effort is important to the client. Many have implemented solutions recommended by our teams; others have used the reports to complete grant proposals for funding. Yet others have used the project as a goad to get their internal staff to do things. Symbolically or substantively, project outcomes (the final report, contacts facilitated by the project) usually are significant to the client.

The project effort produces one of two possible visible outcomes for the client. A client who needs a network design recommendation gets a project report from the student team. The following semester, a team from the class may actually implement the solution at the client site. The project report is delivered to the client at semester-end, and constitutes the final deliverable. If a team undertakes implementation work for its project, it writes a report on the implementation process and outcomes for the benefit of the client and future teams who may work with the same client.

Autonomy: The student team selects the project topic. This is a key principle in our teaching. We believe students have to be interested in what they undertake to do. The implication is that there is no guarantee that a client's project will be picked up by a student team. Clients understand this. They are advised by the instructor to put a sales spin on their presentation in-class on their projects for the semester to help improve their chances of being picked. A second implication is that more than one team may pick the same project topic. Very occasionally, we have persuaded teams to take on unsubscribed topics, but this is only done when interest is starkly lopsided.

Student teams enjoy considerable autonomy. They are essentially self-managing task teams. Project tasks are assigned by the team to its members. Progress monitoring and regulation of member behavior is also the responsibility of the team. The team is free to "fire" members as a last resort, but in consultation with the instructor. The team is responsible for managing client relations and the timely completion of all project deliverables. This is not to say that teams are on their own. The class serves as a supportive and nurturing environment, and class time is set aside to discuss project progress.

Feedback: Student teams get two types of feedback during the project: one from class, and the other from the client. Project discussions are a part of class meeting. Discussing a project in class allows students from unrelated projects to offer suggestions and criticism to the project team. The instructor plays coach during these discussions, orienting the team as needed, acting as a sounding board for suggestions from the team and the class, identifying design weaknesses, and suggesting follow-up steps. In-class project discussions can get quite lively mid-semester, as project work picks up pace and deadlines loom.

Clients provide both formative and summative feedback to teams. Formative feedback occurs at many points during the project; as teams work closely with the client, every meeting offers potential for feedback. As the projects are important to them, clients do not begrudge setting aside the time to meet with the team. Formal sign-offs are not required of the client; such a practice might intimidate them. Informal sign-offs are encouraged, however, before the team starts on the next activity. Clients offer summative feedback at the end of the semester, when they attend the final presentation by student teams. Teams present on both planning and design components of their project; the final class presentation is a formal occasion, and students put on quite a show. Clients are given first opportunity to question their team(s) on the project.

Principle #3. Learning as participation: Learning comes from social participation in activities that are personally meaningful to the learner. Lave and Wenger (1991) have advanced a model of "legitimate peripheral participation" (LPP) to analyze skill development in the apprentice. The learner starts out as a peripheral (i.e., not full) participant in the activity, within a learning context that allows her to actually engage in actions leading to professional skill acquisition. She takes part in actual practice, but initially in a limited sense and with limited responsibility for the final product. As an apprentice working under a master, her participation is initially peripheral, but by engaging in the actual practice of professionals, she is taking active steps toward eventual full participation in the activity, as a master in her own right. As a full participant, she has not only acquired the skills but also the identity of a competent professional, and is thereby connected, through her practice and the shared norms that govern it, to other professionals in a community of practice (see Wenger, 1998).

We have found the LPP model useful to describe the dynamics of peer learning in a project team. Students enrolled in our classes come from diverse backgrounds. Some are trained in library and information science, business, humanities, and communication, while others have a background in engineering and computer science. Undergraduates as well as graduate students enroll in the class. Team composition, usually done by the instructor, attempts to balance skills and skill levels in the team, so that technically adept students get to work with students with other skills. This is a way to spread technical skills around, as well as to simulate cross-functional teams in actual organizations. This approach to team composition has worked well. In our experience, students with technical skills tend to lead the design effort, while playing a support role in the planning. Students with backgrounds in the humanities feel more comfortable leading the planning effort, which entails interpersonal communication and listening skills, note-taking and documentation, team work coordination, and qualitative inquiry skills (e.g., interviewing). This division of labor happens naturally. In terms of the LPP model, non-technical team members can be seen as peripheral participants in design, while technical members are peripheral participants in planning. Fostering peer learning across member competencies can be a challenge; instructors cannot assume this would occur naturally.

Knowledge and information handoffs between peripheral and "central" members in a sub-team may not be, and usually are not, seamless or automatic.

Probably the biggest challenge for the instructor is this: how to get the peripheral participant to see "the big picture." Students heavily involved in the planning may not have the background to understand, or may be unwilling to make the effort to understand, the technical design and vice versa. In highly motivating task situations, members usually are enthusiastic and proactive about learning from peers to fill in the gaps in their own training and background, but such an outcome cannot be assumed. It needs to be guided and channelized by the instructor.

Peer learning across member competencies is a necessity in project teams with differential skills and skill levels. The LPP model offers a provocative perspective on peer learning in such teams without specifying how such learning occurs in practice. Recall that the field project assignment requires that the student team justify their choice from the two comparable candidate solutions considered under the project. Justifying the choice is critical. It forces the team to consider their recommendation critically. More importantly, it forces the team to revisit the client's needs, resources, and constraints in assessing the goodness of fit of the recommended solution. The planning effort, when done well, yields *the* criteria for such an assessment; these criteria might be technical and non-technical, and are of fundamental importance and relevance in a client-driven learning exercise. The importance of the written justification of the choice is emphasized in the assignment and orally in class many times. We believe that this piece, the justification of the choice, is a powerful way of bringing to bear on design the concerns of planning, and to encourage (force) the "center" and the "periphery" to educate each other through the project.

A community of peers engaged in active learning in the field helps "decenter" learning, which refers to shifting the source of learning from the instructor to the totality of resources available to the learner in that environment. The instructor's pedagogical role shifts from being a source of wisdom to a knowledgeable guide who helps identify, qualify, and structure knowledge resources in the learning environment. On our teams, resources include other team members, as well as the consultants (on and off-campus), vendors, and former students that the team may consult via the Internet, phone, or face to face, formally or informally, during the course of the project. For example, a team needing help on a critical issue relating to data sharing between an AS-400 and a LAN contacted a former student, who was then on the IS staff of a major firm in the area, and obtained detailed information on a similar solution he had successfully implemented in his firm. Project work allows learners to tap into a supportive Web of expertise in the local community and beyond, and helps link learning and socialization in professional practice. For the majority of our students, the project provides their first opportunity to do hands-on consulting work; interacting with practitioners through the project contributes to their emergent self-image as "professionals," and this self-image, and the competencies it subsumes, is an important reason why many find the experience "fun" and "rewarding."

The client (or representative) herself may start out as a peripheral participant on the project team. The interested technician or MIS staffer at the client site may start out as project contact, begins to learn by participating in the work of the team, and acquires enough knowledge at semester end to want to play a bigger role on the project the following semester. Participation by the client in the team's work is valuable for a number of reasons. First, participation allows the client to be a better client. To view the project from the participant's viewpoint is to better appreciate the challenges faced by the team in their work. Second, participation allows the client to improve their understanding of technology and can, over time, contribute to an improved ability to make informed decisions about technology. Promoting self-sufficiency among non-profits and public sector institutions in technology know-how is an important objective of our outreach effort; the client's peripheral participation is a start. Third, participation shifts the client from a reactive "user" to an active player in the developmental context. An active client can represent the "user" in a very different light to the team, and can help change the way they think about technology. For example, the MIS head in a community agency sensitized the team to the need for creative new assistive devices to empower his office staff, all of whom had disabilities. While this was outside the project's scope and was therefore not pursued that semester, he prompted the team to think of the infrastructure they were designing in new ways.

Principle #4. Community service learning: The field project assignment is usually the student's first hands-on foray into the public sector and the practice of community. Service learning is a type of experiential learning and refers to "a method...

- under which students learn and develop through active participation in...thoughtfully organized service experiences that meet actual community needs;
- that is integrated into the students' academic curriculum or provides structured time for a student to think, talk, or write about what the student did and saw during the service activity;
- that provides students with opportunities to use newly acquired skills and knowledge in real-life situations in their own communities; and
- that enhances what is taught in school by extending student learning beyond the classroom and into the community, and helps foster the

development of a sense of caring for others" (National and Community Service Act of 1990).

Active learning in the service of the community acquires its special resonance from linking learning to the broader life of the community. As we noted earlier, for most of our students, the project provides their first real introduction to the local community, not just to the client institution but to the larger socioeconomic concerns that often form the backdrop for that institution's work. Our community has one of the highest child mortality rates nationally, and a high adolescent pregnancy rate. These statistics seldom intrude into campus life. Yet they are central to the work of human service institutions in the community, and project work at these locations exposes students to a dimension of community life they rarely suspect exists.

This dimension may not directly impact their design. A distinction needs to be drawn between micro-level and macro-level impacts of social sensitivity on the designer's work. For example, micro-level impacts occur when the designer designs an artifact, a computer interface or physical access to a building, taking into account the needs of users with disabilities. Macro-level impacts occur when the designer becomes aware of the larger issues, such as inequity in access to computers and networked resources that has been labeled the digital divide. Macro-level awareness may not instrumentally inform the design of particular artifacts, but it can provide a perspective on *logically prior* concerns, raising questions such as: why is it that whole sections of a community are out of the loop in terms of computing? How can technology advance the work of relief agencies? Such questions lie in the *moral* domain. They are fundamental to the function of design in contemporary society, we believe, and provide a values-based perspective on design activity. Micro-level sensitivity is *topical* and local; macro-level sensitivity needs to be *pervasive* and fundamental to design.

Through the project experience, students get a good feel for the constraints under which non-profit and public sector institutions often function. Constraints define the problem or problems that design work attempts to solve: there are no problems without constraints. Constraints can be of different kinds: physical (e.g., site location), financial, technology-related. Constraints can be hidden and may only surface during the design process. The computing culture, the degree of receptivity to the innovation, is one such. Although one can get a sense of this during planning, its true extent often only becomes apparent during design, when the solution is concretized and specified. The LAN design project at the county department is a case in point. MIS' distrust of LAN technology was quite well known within the user organization, but it hardened and deepened during the course of the project, and expressed itself in open hostility towards the team by the end of it. Non-profits and public institutions abound in constraints, and the smaller institutions are especially hard hit. Constraints force the designer to be creative and resourceful. Combining service learning and client-centered work yokes together a service orientation with critical thinking, because the team is accountable to the client.

We have refined our active learning approach based on what our students and clients have told us. We started out with a notion of what active learning should encompass, and refined it after several years of experimentation in the field. We have made many mistakes en route. Our ideas are still evolving; we make no claims about the completeness or generalizability of the model presented above. This works for us, for now, but it is also a work in progress. (For more information on service learning, see the Lazar and Lidtke chapter in this book.)

ESTABLISHING AN ACTIVE LEARNING PROGRAM IN HIGHER EDUCATION

The first author established the Center for Active Learning (CAL) in 1996, after several years of experimentation with active learning through our classes. The field project assignment served as the active learning vehicle.

In the summer of 1991, the first author was contacted by a faculty colleague at the school with a request by a K-12 school in the local community. The school needed help with the design and implementation of a LAN for its administrative and instructional use. Would the "Information Networking" class that fall (the class has since been replaced by a more-aptly named course called "Telecommunications Project," which was developed to serve as a vehicle for CAL projects) be interested in serving as a consultant to the school? The project was taken on as a class project that semester, with 35% of the course grade assigned to it on the syllabus. Students would work in teams to provide the consulting service to the client. The class had an even balance of graduate and undergraduate students. Five teams of six students each were formed and assigned different topics carved out of the original project idea. The teams would function as self-managing teams, under the guidance of the instructor, who would serve as guide or coach.

We learned a lot that first semester. First, it became clear that what had at first seemed a straightforward project was far from being the case. We learned that no project, if one drilled down deep enough, is small. We had started out with the idea that two of the five teams would work on the LAN design problem, while the others developed an overall telecommunications plan for the school. At semester-end, five reports were produced by these teams: one on LAN design, the second on midrange integration and data migration, the third on Internet access, the fourth on the wiring plant, while the fifth addressed the telecommunications plan. Mid-course corrections and project reassignments were done in light of the emerging picture.

Second, the school's systems ran off a multi-user machine (a mid-range computer) which could not be integrated into the LAN because of its vintage. The school's wiring plant was in disrepair and poorly documented. Midway through the project, the school wanted Internet connectivity to be included in the plan. The school's leadership, the principal and vice-principal, the librarian, and the technology person, was in support of the project, but the rest of the school's faculty and staff had no knowledge of it. The LAN planning effort suggested that the implementation would be more disruptive than originally envisaged due to the nature of the infrastructure, and it wasn't at all clear that the rest of the school had been prepared for the intervention. The school's technical support staff comprised one full-time and one "technically savvy" teacher, who helped out part time. A service contract with a vendor (the contract was shared with other schools) supported the software applications. It was clear that LAN connectivity, when implemented, would place additional new burdens on the support staff, and no one at the school quite knew how the new technologies would be supported. The importance of the need for ongoing staff and user training surfaced in a powerful way.

Third, it was clear that we had to conceptualize the project as going beyond one semester. In other words, it would have to be addressed in a phased manner, starting with a self-contained departmental LAN with Internet access; access to the applications on the mid-range would have to wait because the school had neither the technology to support access nor the procedures and policies governing such access in place. In fact, they had not thought about such issues until prompted by the student teams that worked on the project that first semester. The school leadership, and the students, learned a lesson about the practical aspects of technology work, specifically the importance of planning, the need to phase in innovations, and the need to think carefully about the impacts of new technology on existing access procedures and polices. Access to the Internet re-posed these questions afresh to the school and to the team.

Fourth, the experience changed the design of the field project assignment itself. The importance of planning was emphasized in the modified description that was used in subsequent semesters. Problem setting and bounding, and analyses of user requirements, constraints, and resources, critical project management and values-based decisions, were emphasized under planning. As argued earlier, the planning effort provides the project team among others with *the operative criteria* for assessing the solution's goodness of fit. The school's grand plan called for computers for administrative reporting and update functions, as well as a computer in every classroom for Internet access and access to instructional software served out of a server. Even though the immediate project called for little more than localized connectivity, designers had to keep in view the big picture so that the solution would scale and be manageable. In the assignment description, we encouraged teams to adopt a five-year planning horizon to emphasize the need for scalability, evolution, and growth in the solution(s) recommended.

Fifth, we decided to restrict team size to three or four. End-of-semester evaluations and project debriefing sessions indicated that six members to a team made scheduling of meetings difficult. We also decided to set aside class time and use asynchronous means to deal with inter-team coordination. For example, the LAN team and the Internet access team had to work with a shared set of assumptions because their technologies were so closely related. In the same way, the wiring plant team and the LAN team had to work off the same page. However, coordinating with other teams working on related projects would increase the burden on the teams. We decided that class time would be used to highlight dependencies both *across* teams as well as between the planning and design sub-teams *within* a team, as an efficient way of dealing with information hand-offs. Listserv technology was also identified as a resource.

This initial project resulted in follow-on projects at the school the following semester, when LAN and Internet connectivity were installed. The rest of the telcommunications plan, the wiring upgrade, and integration of the mid-range, could not be implemented due to a change in leadership at the school. In the semesters since, many more projects with a broad range of public sector clients have followed.

The initial successes led to expansion of the idea. There were other clients that wished to participate, and more projects resulted. As the number of participants continued to grow, the idea for a formal entity—CAL—emerged as a way to manage the growing number of projects as well as facilitate the inclusion of a field consulting component in more courses within the school. As teams implemented telecommunications technology at client sites, clients asked for more services, such as database applications, systems analysis, and training. Formal organization was needed. With more activity all around, more management was needed. It wasn't practical to have each instructor run their own show. An umbrella organization was needed that could work with clients, students, and faculty. Such an organization would provide the administrative support needed to provide participating faculty with a pool of clients and topics, and help ensure that the experience was productive and satisfying to all constituents. Also, importantly, we needed to ensure continuity in the coordination of project work across multiple semesters, and through the summer. This was the birth of CAL. CAL arose from a need, the need to have a central function to manage all the projects.

In the years leading up to the establishment of the Community and Information Technology Institute (CITI) in 1997, four classes at the School of Information Studies used CAL to provide project work opportunities to students: systems analysis and design, database, user training, and telecommunications project. Lessons learned from the CAL experience include the following.

Legitimacy and visibility: Make sure you have buy-in from the academic unit for students to sign on for the project experience as part of a class for course credit. In the absence of this, student motivation tends to suffer. Undertaking a project for course credit promotes a higher degree of commitment on the part of the learner. It also positions the course, and the field project experience, as an acknowledged element in the curriculum and the academic program.

Learning philosophy: We presented an extended model of active learning above, with four focal elements to it: client-centered work in natural settings, project task design, learning through participation, and the social context of professional action. This model guides our practice.

Liability issues: Clients need to fully understand that they are helping further the education of students. It is important that they understand this: it relates the work they are sponsoring to larger pro-social issues, as well as protects us from potential liability. We have not had to get formal sign-offs from the client on this, nor have any liability issues come up so far. It is a social contract: the team will deliver to the client what was promised in the project scope statement (which is agreed to during the initial presentation by the client and the instructor in class), and the client will work with the team and facilitate access to organizational information and knowledge resources.

What happens when a student team report is inadequate? About 10% of the over 250 projects we have directed fall under this category. A project report may be inadequate for any number of reasons: lack of needed skills or team dysfunction, client distraction or non-availability, project scope change of a significant nature during the project. When this happens, the instructor has to identify the cause and take appropriate steps. If it is due to the client (say due to personal non-availability during the project), the instructor has to consult the client to decide if the project should be terminated. If it is due to the team, the instructor has to decide whether to apply more resources or personally complete the project. If a fall project is inadequate, a team from the following spring semester can work on the problem. If a spring project is inadequate, the instructor has two options: see if the client can wait until the following fall, or assemble a team for coverage over the summer under an independent study or internship arrangement. Occasionally, we have had to complete a project or part of a project ourselves. Quality control is critical and onerous, and falls to the instructor to enforce.

We have had our share of slip-ups with delinquent clients as well. A small number of clients have pulled out of the project mid-semester for a variety of reasons, leaving the team or teams with no project. This can be problematic. The instructor has had to step in and find a closely related problem for the team to work on, perhaps with another client or on a simulated basis.

Project management is key: The CAL Project Manager is the primary interface between the center, clients, students, and participating faculty. In this key role, she is responsible for recruiting clients, managing the request for proposals (RFP) process, working with faculty to identify appropriate classes and projects, scheduling class presentations by clients early in the semester to kick projects off, ongoing liaison with clients, faculty and student teams through the semester, scheduling client attendance at team presentations at the end of the semester, and ensuring that clients get a copy of the team report.

Working with clients: The project manager is tasked with recruiting acceptable clients into the program. The RFP process is one vehicle for recruiting clients, but not the only one. For example, the head of a local carrier's community affairs program called to see if a nursing home would qualify as a client. Referrals like this, and from current or past clients, are a steady source of project ideas. Proposals must be assessed for suitability (feasibility and completability in the timeframe of one semester). The project manager helps prepare the client for the project experience and assists them in their project sponsor role. Such assistance, which is provided on an as-needed basis, could include helping with needs assessment, preparation of the one-page needs description for the class, identifying an appropriate representative to work directly with the team, and helping with project definition.

The RFP process starts late in the previous semester or very early in the semester that project work is undertaken. The mass mailing (targeting public institutions) introduces CAL and its mission, describes the courses on offer in the coming semester and the types of projects desired for each course— information designed to help the client develop their proposals. Resources that clients must be prepared to provide are outlined. An alternative to the broadbased RFP approach is the adoption model, whereby we identify one or two clients per semester and "adopt" them — student teams work on different problems for the same client. This approach has its merits. It may be an efficient way to tackle closely related problems. A client may want to host their own World Wide Web server and Web applications. An adoption model would allow the server team and the application team to work together in the same semester. Our typical client often lacks basic infrastructure and financial resources for technology. As our clients start to look beyond the basics, we may use the adoption approach.

The project manager reviews RFP responses and collates them for faculty review. The selection of projects and clients is a collaborative effort involving the project manager and participating faculty. Decisions are based on course requirements and assessment of the client's ability to provide the appropriate level of support for students. Past projects conducted with that client (if any) are evaluated, including feedback from students. We have turned very few clients away; more often, if a client's request appears to fit another class better, it is considered for that class if the instructor is a participant that semester. If not, the client is advised to reapply in a future semester. The client is then informed of their status that semester, and their presentation in class is scheduled. Participating clients are required to present their needs in class. Failure to appear for the initial presentation will normally remove those projects from consideration unless other arrangements have been made in advance.

Some clients feel that what they get for free is worthless. They may participate as clients for one reason or another, but shirk their responsibilities. This is a tremendous disservice to the students, and to the class. Clients have to understand that they have responsibilities too. Before coming on board, the project manager (and the instructor) has to make sure that the client understands their responsibilities. By signing on as a client, the organization agrees to work with the student team and support student learning via the project, and to provide the team access to relevant information, people, and other resources in the organization. The organization also needs to designate one of their staff as project contact; this person helps coordinate on-site data-collection activities and meeting scheduling. This person also agrees to attend the team's project presentation in class at the end of the semester; this is a key responsibility. The team's final presentation is in the nature of a briefing, and is incomplete without the client's physical presence in class.

Examples of the types of problems that have arisen have been: clients missing meetings with teams, clients losing critical resources, clients failing to meet their commitments, equipment shortages or delivery delays that delay the project. The project manager has to let the client understand, as tactfully but as firmly as possible, that the project – every CAL project that is initiated – subsumes a social contract between the parties concerned and that the client has a set of responsibilities just as the student team does. Recall that the client is advised of responsibilities through the RFP process and through subsequent interaction before the project is set up. Nonetheless, such problems have occurred after the start of the project.

The project manager's goal is to finish up with a set of projects that meet the goals of the courses to be offered in the next semester or two. Because of the amount of preparation involved and because the university is on a semester schedule, it is wise to plan for the full academic year and not just one semester. Clients should be oriented to this schedule for work completion so that they can plan effectively as well. Following the release of each semester's schedule of classes, a client presentation schedule is established for early in the semester. The practice is to have clients present their needs to participating classes during the first week or two of classes.

Working with participating faculty: Many faculty want to include an active learning component in their courses, but hesitate when they estimate the coordination effort that would be required to do so. The project manager absorbs this substantial burden. She sits down with interested faculty to explain how the active learning experience works and what it entails for participating faculty. She may follow up with faculty to determine what classes will offer the active learning component and works with them to define the types of projects that will be used for each class. This is usually done well in advance of the semester start. Once they sign on, she extends to participating faculty a full range of services.

For faculty, CAL began by simply providing potential clients and projects. As multiple-semester and multiple-discipline projects evolved, a mechanism to provide continuity became necessary. CAL now assists faculty with management of proposed and ongoing client projects including progress-to-date, background information about clients and projects, project tracking across semesters and classes, and planning and coordination. CAL also handles the administrative aspects of coordinating and scheduling client presentations, screening proposals, and providing coaching and support to not-for-profit management and representatives.

Working with students: Students work on projects in self-managing teams. The team is responsible for managing its task-oriented activity as well as its interpersonal climate, and can discipline its members. As such, the team has substantial authority over its own conduct and work. The project manager has to step in to resolve disputes in the team or between the team and the client.

The team's initial contact with the client tends to color and shape the client's response to the team. Students have to understand the importance of professionalism, punctuality, courtesy, reliability, sensitivity to the client's circumstances, and professional demeanor, in dealing with the client. The instructor highlights these values in class, and the project manager reinforces them. A professional-looking team will elicit a "like" response from the client; a dysfunctional team should not expect much from the client. The project manager may use the code of conduct developed for use with the school's internship and coop program to advise and counsel students during the project.

Over 250 CAL projects have been completed in the last decade, benefiting several dozen public institutions, large and small, in the community. Some recent projects:

- Internet fax server implemented for the Urban Ministry Project, a faith-based initiative to combat inner-city social problems. The fax server is the first in the 315 area code, and will enhance UMP's ability to communicate quickly with community leaders.
- Wireless connectivity between community center and community arts center. Student team planned and designed a comprehensive networking plan for the client and demonstrated wireless solution.
- LAN and Internet access implementation for a county branch library.
- Design and implementation of AS400/LAN integration for the United Way of Central New York.
- Design for integrating AS 400 with NT/IIS Web server technology for the Rescue Mission.

THE COMMUNITY AND INFORMATION TECHNOLOGY INSTITUTE (CITI)

As outlined above, CAL played a leading role in the planning and design of MetroNet. The planning effort had revealed a strong interest in advanced multi-media applications such as videoconferencing, spawning project ideas involving advanced ICTs (e.g., Internet videoconferencing over digital subscriber line or DSL). Many of these projects were estimated to take far longer than a semester to complete, called for a higher level of research and development effort than typical CAL projects, and required significantly more coordination in that they were undertaken in concert with vendors and service providers, who donated resources, equipment, services, funding, expertise, to the projects.

Back in 1996, potential participants in MetroNet knew little about DSL or multi-media applications over the Internet. DSL was relatively new. Community institutions had questions about DSL performance. Applications like Internet video were new also. The carrier suggested that CAL mount a demo of Internet videoconferencing over DSL to test its capabilities. In 1998, CAL staff designed and set up two live demos, both linking CAL and a local Internet service provider with a public university in the midwest over the public Internet. The demos were extremely successful and launched CITI's current program in advanced technology prototyping projects.

The demos involved a great deal of work. The staff at this time comprised the director (the first author), the project manager, and two graduate students recruited to develop the demos working part time at CAL. The two graduate students assembled a team of students, graduate and undergraduate, from the school to help with the demos. The demos were developed using donated equipment and services. The carrier donated the DSL connectivity; Internet service was donated by a prominent local Internet service provider; the software and hardware endpoints and backend equipment for videoconferencing were donated by video vendors. The design, installation, testing, and trouble-shooting of the demos were done by the CAL team. The successful demos triggered other project ideas involving advanced ICTs.

Such projects were central to the evolving technology environment in the community and were welcomed by students at the school. However, these projects were also outside the original mission of CAL, which was focused on assisting public institutions with basic ICTs while providing students a forum for hands-on consulting work as part of regular classes. Under the emerging paradigm suggested by the demos, there was a need, both at community institutions as well as among our more advanced students, for projects involving advanced ICTs. We decided to expand the scope of our mission under the umbrella of a new organization, to be called CITI, the Community and Information Technology Institute. CITI was established in 1997 in the school; CAL became a component under CITI focused on active learning through class projects.

CITI was established with three staff members, the new position of associate director was created to supplement CAL's two positions. CITI's project manager oversees CAL projects (offered through regular classes) and also serves as a liaison with CITI project partners, funding agencies, and consortium affiliates. The associate director works with the director in grant-writing and developing strategic partnerships, and runs the Center for Excellence in Broadband Applications (CEBA). CEBA was established in 2000 with significant support and funding from Alcatel. CEBA's advanced ICT lab within CITI forms the foundation of CITI's research and development, technology transfer, and prototyping work.

CITI projects are offered through regular classes on a selective basis for two reasons: because of their technical and coordination complexity, they tend to span several semesters, and, as such, personnel continuity, particularly continuity of leadership, is critical. CITI projects are led by funded graduate assistants or by staff paid on an hourly basis. Project participants could be interns or students doing an independent study under the director. Project teams are self-managing, autonomous entities reporting to the associate director.

CITI's mission spans community action and research. CITI is dedicated to promoting advanced ICT use and application broadly in communities through:

- technology transfer and prototyping
- Web-enabled application development
- education, activism, and partnerships
- social science research and consulting

Through our hands-on community action initiatives, CITI promotes and facilitates access to advanced ICT applications and services in public institutions and low-income communities; through our research, we document process and effects of the introduction of advanced ICTs into communities and into institutions in the public sector.

REFERENCES

Ball, L. J. and Ormerod, T. C. (1985). Structured and opportunistic processes in design: A critical discussion. *International Journal of Human-Computer Interaction*, 43, 131-151.

Bansler, J. P. and Bodker, K. (1993). A reappraisal of structured analysis: Design in an organizational context. *ACM Transactions on Information Systems*, 11 (2), 165-193.

Buchanan, R. (1995). Wicked problems in design thinking. In Margolin, V. & Buchanan, R. (Eds.), *The Idea of Design: A Design Issues Reader*. Cambridge, MA: The MIT Press.

Cross, N. (1984). Introduction. In Cross, N. (Ed.), *Developments in Design Methodology*. Chichester, UK: John Wiley.

Deforge, Y. (1995). Avatars of design: Design before design. In Margolin, V. and Buchanan, R. (Eds.), *The Idea of Design: A Design Issues Reader*. Cambridge, MA: The MIT Press.

Dewey, J. (1938). *Experience and Education*. Kappa Delta Pi.

Dewey, J. (1927). *The Public and its Problems*. Chicago, IL: Swallow Press.

Drueke, J. (1992). Active learning in the university library instruction classroom. *Research Strategies*, 10(2), 77-83.

Findeli, A. (1995). Moholy-Nagy's design pedagogy in Chicago (1937-46). In Margolin, V. and Buchanan, R. (Eds.), *The Idea of Design: A Design Issues Reader*. Cambridge, MA: The MIT Press.

Gronbaek, K., Kyng, M. and Mogensen, P. (1997). Toward a cooperative experimental system development approach. In Kyng, M. and Mathiassen, L. (Eds.), *Computers and Design in Context*, 201-238. Cambridge, MA: The MIT Press.

Hackman, J. R. and Oldham, G. R. (1980). *Work Redesign*. Reading, MA: Addison-Wesley.

Hackman, J. R. (1983). *A Normative Model of Work Team Effectiveness*. Technical Report #2, Group Effectiveness Research Project. School of Organization and Management, Yale University.

Hanks, W. (1991). Foreword. In Lave, J. and Wenger, E. (Eds.), *Situated Learning: Legitimate Peripheral Participation*. New York, NY: Cambridge University Press.

Iacono, S. and Kling, R. (1988). Computer systems as institutions: Social dimensions of computing in organizations. In DeGross, J. I. and Olson, M. H. (Eds.), *Proceedings of the Ninth International Conference on Information Systems (ICIS)*, Minneapolis, MN.

Keeton, M. and Tate, P. (1978). *Learning by Experience—What, Why, How*. San Francisco, CA: Jossey-Bass.

Keller, C. and Keller, J. D. (1993). Thinking and acting with iron. In Chaiklin, S. and Lave, J. (Eds.), *Understanding Practice: Perspectives on Activity and Context*. New York, NY: Cambridge University Press.

Kruglanski, A. W. (1989). *Lay Epistemics and Human Knowledge: Cognitive and Motivational Bases*. New York, NY: Plenum.

Lave, J. (1993). Introduction. In Chaiklin, S. and Lave, J. (Eds.), *Understanding Practice: Perspectives on Activity and Context*. New York, NY: Cambridge University Press.

Lave, J. and Wenger, E. (1991). *Situated Learning: Legitimate Peripheral Participation*. New York, NY: Cambridge University Press.

Lewin, K. (1951). *Field Theory in Social Sciences*. New York, NY: Harper & Row.

Margolin, V. and Buchanan, R. (1995). Introduction. In Margolin, V. and Buchanan, R. (Eds.), *The Idea of Design: A Design Issues Reader*. Cambridge, MA: The MIT Press.

National and Community Service Act. (1990). See Small, R.V. and Venkatesh, M. (1998). Linking technology training and community service: An active learning approach. In Khosrowpour, M. (Ed.). *Effective Utilization and Management of Emerging Information Technologies, Proceedings of the 1998 Information Resources Management Association International Conference*, Boston, MA, May 17-20, 1998, Hershey, PA: Idea Group Publishing.

Papert, S. (1991). Situating constructionism. In Harel, I. and Papert, S. (Ed.), *Constructionism*. Norwood, NJ: Ablex.

Piaget, J. (1970). *Genetic Epistemology*. New York, NY: Columbia University Press.

Schein, E. H. and Kommers, D. W. (1972). *Professional Education: Some New Directions*. New York, NY: McGraw-Hill.

Schon, D. A. (1983). *The Reflective Practitioner: How Professionals Think in Action*. New York, NY: Basic Books.

Shaw, A. and Shaw, M. (1999). Social empowerment through community networks. In Schon, D. A., Sanyal, B. and Mitchell, W. J. (Eds.), *High Technology in Low-Income Communities: Prospects for the Positive Use of Advanced Information Technology*. Cambridge, MA: The MIT Press.

Wenger, E. (1998). *Communities of Practice: Learning, Meaning, and Identity*. New York, NY: Cambridge University Press.

APPENDIX A

New York State's Diffusion Program: An Advanced Technology Initiative Aimed At Economically Depressed Zip Codes in NY State Communities

MetroNet was funded under New York State's $50 million Diffusion Fund. In 1995, a performance-based incentive regulatory plan drafted by the state of New York, the Public Service Commission, and the state's incumbent local exchange carrier required the carrier to commit $50 million to establish a program whose stated purpose was to bring advanced telecommunications to economically disadvantaged areas of New York State. The fund was set up to develop broadband infrastructure in selected zip codes in urban-suburban and rural areas. Participation in Diffusion Program-funded community networks was limited to public, non-profit, and small business *institutions*: city/county government, social sector institutions, K-12, and higher education, healthcare agencies, and small business units located in or providing services in these zip codes.

MetroNet was proposed by community leaders and representatives of public institutions in 1996. Subsequently, the proposal was awarded $3.7 million under the Diffusion Program. MetroNet is being implemented at this writing.

Chapter III

A University/Community Partnership to Build a K-8 School Network Infrastructure

David Ruppel
University of Toledo, USA

Cynthia Ruppel
Rollins College, USA

This chapter chronologically follows a multi-phased service-learning project. The project involved graduate and undergraduate students enrolled in Information Technology (IT) courses. A network infrastructure, including the physical wiring, was planned, designed, and built for a K-8 elementary school primarily to provide Internet access. A later group also assessed the future of the network.

The self-selected students were members of their chosen team for the relevant semester and may be viewed as part of the larger team for the multi-phased project. The pros, cons, and caveats of this particular service-learning project are assessed and suggestions for similar projects are included.

INTRODUCTION

Companies today are looking for workers, particularly IS workers, who have character or core values and ascribe to corporate values. In fact, EQ, or emotional intelligence, is a testable construct being used by companies in recruitment (Anonymous, 2001; Foote, 2001; Huy, 1999; Morris, 1999). EQ techniques can guide managers in helping workers deal with problems hindering team performance. Similarly, leadership requires refocusing on core values and principles; over time, this builds character (Badaracco, 1998). Some suggest that all educational institutions need to devote considerable attention to character building (Anonymous, 2001; Foote, 2001). As we prepare our students to be effective, productive business people, how should we as educators instill values and build character in our students? This is a difficult task not simply accomplished by providing a lecture about emotional and ethical topics.

One pedagogy designed to meet this need that is receiving attention in business schools is service-learning. Jacoby (1996a, p. 5) has defined service learning as "…a form of experiential education in which students engage in activities that address human and community needs together with structured opportunities intentionally designed to promote student learning and development." She further suggests that service-learning courses integrate community service with the appropriate academic knowledge relevant to the course. The hyphen used in the term symbolizes this integration (Jacoby, 1996a).

Service-learning is particularly important in Information Technology (IT) where the students not only need technical skills and experience, but also a strong ethical foundation due to their potential ability to misuse technology. The legal aspects of technology have not been able to keep pace with rapidly advancing technology; so often IT people are confronted with complex ethical decisions. It has been argued that service-learning represents a "unique pedagogy…that enhances the ability of private-sector managers to be effective stewards of society's moral authority" (Godfred, p. 364).

Some suggest that the future of service-learning in colleges is tightly linked with K-12 education (Jacoby, 1996b). This linkage is natural due to the growing number of at-risk children, a natural vested interest for college and universities to improve the future student body, and because students will view service-learning as an appropriate college activity if they benefited from it prior to college (Jacoby, 1996b).

Also, one of the major policy concerns in the information age is the emergence of what has been termed the "digital divide." This "digital divide" is formed by a gap between those who have easy access to technology, particularly the Internet, and those who do not. References are frequently made to the information "haves" and "have nots" in an age where information is equivalent to wealth (Holloway, 2000). The "have nots" are in danger of being left out of the new economy and being marginalized into low-wage jobs (Dunham, 1999). At Comdex, in Spring 2000, then-President Clinton asked the IT community to help close this digital divide or gap for moral reasons and to ensure that the digital economy flourishes with the availability of skilled workers (Shewmake, 2000). For the reasons listed above, K-12 schools now appear to be an ideal place to conduct service-learning projects in IT classes, particularly in non-public schools which receive less funding for these projects.

This chapter describes a five-phase service-learning project that was accomplished by forming a partnership between instructors and IT students at the University of Toledo and a local K-8 parochial/non-profit school. The students were primarily enrolled in a Systems Analysis, Design, and Implementation course (SAD), although others participated. This project was undertaken to plan, design, and wire a network for the school building, and to assess and implement continuing and future computer needs. The descriptions below include the existing situation at each phase rather than representing the final state of the network. These experiences should provide insights to those who wish to implement service-learning projects in Information Technology classes.

K-8 SCHOOL BACKGROUND

The school partner is a local parochial school that has existed for over 125 years. Recent total enrollment is approximately 200-250 students per school year. The school consists of a preschool class, grades K-8, and an after-school program. All grades have a dedicated classroom, and a computer lab and a library are also provided.

Existing computer equipment consisted of a classroom set of stand-alone, older Macintosh computers in the 8th grade room. Also each classroom had a stand-alone, older Macintosh computer for the teacher's use. Each of these Macintoshes had LAN capability through Apple Attachment Unit Interface (AAUI-15) ports. The computer lab consisted of a mix of older Apple computers (including some Apple IIes) that were used in the primary grades for computer literacy and keyboarding skills. The school secretary had a relatively "newer" Macintosh computer that had been donated by a parent; the principal also had a relatively "newer" Macintosh computer in her office. All of the hardware was based on dated technology. The primary issue in deciding to upgrade software was determining whether the hardware would support the software rather than the increased educational and productivity benefits that the upgrade would provide.

PHASE 1 – SPRING 1998 – A NETWORK PLAN

Background

The school had accumulated funds earmarked for educational computing and had, in anticipation of a major computer initiative, hired a teacher for the 8th grade who was near completion of a Master's degree in Educational Technology. The school was not sure whether the money saved was sufficient or how to best spend these funds while planning for future growth. A parent of one of the students worked for an organization that commercially provides networking services. The school received a quotation from this firm that was at least 66% more than the amount the school had accumulated.

At the same time one author was contacting organizations to find "real-life" (ideally service-learning related) projects for a graduate SAD class to complete as group projects. The teacher and principal were very receptive to using students to undertake this project, particularly since the estimate from the local company well exceeded the amount of money earmarked for the project. While the teacher had knowledge of computers from an educational use standpoint, he did not possess the technical expertise to assess the quotation received or to determine the relevant technical aspects of the network. At the same time, the teacher and principal indicated that they hoped to apply for a grant but needed technical background information to complete the grant application.

Project Definition

The students self-selected into the project that was defined as: *The goal of the school was to educate themselves as to alternatives, costs and provide background information concerning networking to prepare a grant application*. It was designed to be a traditional SAD project and was one among a list of several projects proposed.

The students had the opportunity to visit the school, examine existing computer equipment and classroom layouts, and interview both the teachers and principal. The student group apparently selected the project because at least one member of the group was employed in the capacity of writing network plans/quotations for a local company. As the project proceeded through the semester, it became apparent that the group lacked a member with the appropriate technical knowledge. The student who was employed in the area had technical experts within his firm to provide him the relevant information to write and price the plan. At the same time, there was an undergraduate student who requested an independent study. Since this undergraduate student was employed in a technical capacity for a local networking/ISP firm, he became the technical consultant to the group.

Although a blueprint of the building was obtained, the undergraduate student and a group member walked through the building with a trundle wheel and measured the areas to be networked. Since this was a crucial part of the project, an instructor also "walked" the building, including climbing into attic areas. It was informative and necessary since the teacher pointed out locations where asbestos existed that could not be disturbed without requiring expensive abatement procedures. Thus, any wiring plan had to avoid disturbing these areas. The teacher and principal were interviewed to determine the number of "drops" (where the cable terminates and the connection is established) required in each classroom based on intended use, both immediately and in the future. Two drops were deemed necessary in each classroom – one for the teacher's computer connection and one that would eventually accommodate a classroom network. Initially, however, the second drop was planned for the classroom computer used in the Accelerated Reader program. Previously, the machines with the students' reading records had been physically moved from classroom to classroom as the students advanced grade levels. It was determined this was an ideal application to illustrate the value of storing the records on a server and making student records available from any classroom.

The group's class project was a plan submitted to the school that included alternatives, costs, and technical information as to the design of the campus network; and the plan further included a design for the 8th grade classroom that positioned the computers around the perimeter of the room to facilitate the wiring process. While this configuration was easier from a network design standpoint, the teacher also cited its importance from an educational standpoint since it allowed the teacher to monitor student activity more easily. The existing classroom design used tables to form rows with the backs of the computers and monitors facing the front of the classroom. The redesign of the classroom was accomplished over the summer (shelving was placed along the wall for the computers and conduit was run along the wall), because it was deemed important from an educational standpoint, regardless of the implementation of the entire network plan.

PHASE 2 – FALL 1998 – GRANT PREPARATION AND PHYSICAL NETWORKING

Phase 2 involved submission of a grant proposal and the physical networking of the building by a different group of students. These students were taking an undergraduate SAD class. This project proved to be very popular and resulted in more students wanting to participate in the project than were needed. Therefore, there was some instructor selection of the students participating. One of the students chosen worked for a local networking firm in a hands-on position. Another was a student who had been a student worker in the college phone service department and had experience running retrofit wiring in buildings. Thus at least two students had previous experience that would prove useful. The others were chosen based on enthusiasm and a desire to learn the "hands-on" aspects of networking. One stated he was considering obtaining certification and before he paid for the courses, he wanted to see if he liked the networking area.

Grant Proposal Preparation

Within the first few weeks of the semester, the grant proposal was due. Using the commercial quotation and the project the students from the previous class had submitted, the authors, the student employed in the networking firm, the principal, and the teacher all met to work on the proposal to be submitted to Ohio SchoolNet Telecommunity. The Public Utilities Commission of Ohio, the State of Ohio Department of Education, and local telephone companies covering 97% of the state established Ohio SchoolNet Telecommunity in 1995 (http://www.osn.state.oh.us/about/frameset.asp). Its purpose was to support distance learning in public and state-chartered non-public schools within the State of Ohio. The stated purpose of the grant funding was to network schools to provide student Internet access. The proposal requested the maximum amount that could be awarded to a parochial school: $8,000.

In the grant-writing meeting, we discussed with the student employed in the networking firm the current costs of wiring and connectors to update the previous student project (the project had been completed in the previous semester and the summer had passed). Also, the principal was asked to select one of the alternatives the students had suggested so the technical aspects could be determined. The principal further provided cost figures for the physical remodeling of the classroom since these costs represented a part of the school's financial commitment to the project. The grant proposal provided evidence of the school's commitment to the project and provided a clear plan of the necessity and educational use of the networking project. The involvement of the university students was documented in the grant proposal, and the authors were listed as consultants to the school to provide additional credibility and expertise.

The grant proposal writing was divided among the authors, the teacher, and the principal. The grant guidelines required the submission of both a technology plan for the school and a specific grant request. The authors agreed to undertake the writing of the more technical aspects of the proposal, including costs figures and the technical aspects of the technology plan, while the principal and the teacher undertook the sections that described the educational plans for the use of the Internet access via the network. The proposal was submitted in September 1998. However, it is important to note that the school's accumulated funds were sufficient to undertake the physical wiring of the building (the purchase of the tools, wiring, and other supplies such as network hardware) regardless of the outcome of the grant proposal. Therefore, the students' wiring project could proceed regardless of the outcome of the grant award. Near the end of the semester, we were informed that the grant proposal had been approved and the school was awarded the maximum allowable amount.

Physical Networking

The wiring plan to be completed by the students and chosen by the school was an Ethernet LAN using Category 5 unshielded twisted pair (UTP) for the student computers located in the 8th grade room. In addition, a campus LAN was to be wired with two drops in all classrooms and some larger, multi-use offices, and with one drop in some private offices. The authors selected and ordered the wiring and the school purchased it. The students began by wiring the LAN in the 8th grade classroom. This portion of the wiring project used non-plenum UTP, which was run through surface-mounted wall conduits placed there during the remodeling of the 8th grade classroom. The outer sheathing of plenum UTP is fire-resistant and is typically used for wiring above ceilings, while non-plenum UTP is used in situations where the increased fire-resistance of plenum wiring is not as important. Plenum wiring is significantly more expensive and less physically flexible than non-plenum wiring, making it more difficult to use. The wiring closet consisted of two hubs in a corner of the classroom. The students also learned to crimp the connectors (wires were left purposely long in case it took several tries). This involved placing the eight individual wires in the cable into the correct order, inserting them into the plastic RJ-45 connector, and then closing the connector with a crimping tool. This is similar to telephone wires except that there are four pairs rather than the two or three pairs typically found in telephone wire. Since crimping connectors went faster than running wires to other places, it provided both practice in the technique of proper connections for the students and a more immediate sense of gratification. The physical LAN wiring of the 8th grade classroom was completed on a Friday evening and Saturday afternoon.

The software portion of the LAN installation involved adding an RJ-45 Ethernet transceiver and 32 MB of memory to each of the Macintoshes followed by an upgrade of the Macintosh Operating System (7.5.3 to 7.5.5) and installation of Open Transport to enable TCP/IP networking capabilities. Microsoft Windows NT Server 4.0 with the Services for Macintosh (SFM) component installed was chosen as the network operating system (NOS). This NOS was chosen because the school needed to use networked administrative software that would only run in a Windows environment. In addition, the Accelerated Reader program ran under DOS and, as previously stated, a project goal was to migrate this to a networked environment using DOS clients. Using SFM makes the server running Windows NT Server appear as an Apple Server to the networked Macintoshes. It was determined that Windows NT Server would best support this heterogeneous network.

The NOS was installed on a high-performance (at that time) Pentium II desktop machine. Two network interface cards were installed, as the ultimate function of this server was to be a gateway to the rest of the network. This machine was connected to the Internet through a dial-up connection in the classroom. Installing Microsoft Proxy Server 2.0 and Cyber Patrol on the server provided Internet proxy and content-filtering services. This provided low-bandwidth Internet access to all of the machines in the 8th grade classroom. This was a temporary setup until a high-speed connection could be installed after the entire network installation was completed. The server also provided secure home directory (folder) storage for each network user.

Concurrently, running the wiring throughout the building (the campus network) was begun. Part of a storage room was used as a wiring closet where hubs were installed and all wiring runs in the building terminated. Since the computers were used in the classroom on a regular basis, we could not proceed with software-related issues until we were relatively certain they could be done over a weekend so the computers would be usable on Monday. This work was also done on Friday evenings and Saturdays. This posed some problems with students who went home on the weekends. Thus some students were consistently present while the attendance of others varied based on their personal situations.

Due to building codes, the wiring in the ceiling was plenum Category 5 UTP. Wiring was run into each room to the location where the teacher indicated they wanted the drop. This involved climbing up and removing ceiling tiles and running the wire in the halls and classrooms. We also ran into unanticipated problems that caused delays once we had begun. For example, we found that the building had been constructed in stages; therefore, we ran into what had been exterior walls that had to be drilled through to run the wire.

After the completion of the wiring, a server was installed in the wiring closet. This server was used as a file server for administrative applications and as an intranet e-mail server (Microsoft Exchange Server 5.5). In addition, a DAT drive was installed on this machine to provide backup services for the network. It should be noted that both servers were purchased with funds from the Ohio SchoolNet Telecommunity grant award. This completed the students' project for that semester (Fall 1998).

PHASE 3 – SPRING 1999 – INTERNET ACCESS FOR THE BUILDING

The next step of the project was to install high-speed Internet access through the server in the wiring closet. The school receives continuing funding from the State of Ohio to partially defray the cost of Internet access. This funding had been used for several years to provide a dialup connection. With the installation of the network, dialup access did not provide sufficient bandwidth. This funding is channeled through the North West Ohio Computer Association (NWOCA), one of 24 data acquisition sites in the Ohio Education Computer Network (OECN) (http://www.oecn.k12.oh.us/Overview/ overview.htm). The authors remained as consultants for this portion of the project, and, in Spring 1999, they recommended the installation of a T-1 line (1.554 Mbps) for Internet access. Fortunately, the local cable company was just beginning to offer these services, so a very competitive price was obtained for installation and continuing service. One of the students from the Fall 1998 project team assisted in the hardware configuration and software installation as an independent study project. Once the T-1 access was installed and operational in Fall 1999, the dialup access from the 8th grade room was disabled, and Proxy Server was removed from that server. This completed the network installation project.

The current network consists of three servers, each running Microsoft NT Server 4.0. Combined storage capacity is over 40 GB. One server is connected to the Internet, which provides proxy and content-filtering services using Proxy Server and Cyber Patrol. It is also contains the DAT drive for network backup and acts as the Web server. Finally, the external Domain Name Service (DNS), which converts Internet addresses such as www.microsoft.com to numeric Internet Protocol (IP) addresses, is housed on this server. The second server provides home directory storage for network users, internal DNS service, and Dynamic Host Control Protocol (DHCP) services that automatically assign IP addresses to the computers on the local network. This server also acts as a gateway to the 8th grade LAN. The third server (located in the wiring closet) is an Internet e-mail server and administrative file server. A high-speed network laser printer is available to all network clients. Over 50 clients run various operating systems including Mac OS (7.5.5, 8 and 9), DOS 6.22, Windows 95, and Windows 98.

PHASE 4 – FALL 1999 – UPDATING AND REFINING THE PLAN

Once the physical wiring was completed, it was time to decide how the outdated equipment would be replaced while again providing information necessary to apply for equipment grants to upgrade the teachers and classroom computers. During this semester (Fall 1999), one of the authors was teaching both graduate and undergraduate SAD classes, so the resulting group membership included both graduate and undergraduate students.

Again students self-selected into this project, and met with the 8th grade/technology teacher and the principal. One of the main issues they addressed was whether the replacement equipment should be Apple or Windows-based machines. Pertinent factors were the educational needs, the existing equipment, and the availability of expertise in the school. Their analysis included existing factors within the school as well as a survey of surrounding schools (both elementary and high schools) to determine the norms in the geographical area. Since it is a parochial school, once the students graduate from 8th grade, they attend a variety of local high schools.

This was a very traditional SAD project, and the students were able to look at the alternative types of equipment, assess them, and write a report based on their research into costs and local computer norms. The report included a recommendation for the replacement equipment. This report and recommendation was designed to serve as the groundwork for additional equipment grant applications.

With the wiring completed and access provided, it was obvious that the teacher and student computers, while useful, were slow and needed to be replaced. A goal of the initial networking project was to minimize expenses by maximizing the usefulness of outdated equipment. For example, as noted previously, the computers required memory upgrades to run a Web browser. An earlier version of the Web browser had to be used since the machines' capabilities, even with the memory upgrade, prohibited the use of current versions. While the clients are slow, the network provides Internet access where none existed before. However, in today's world, fast access is a necessity. Revenaugh (2000) suggests that access is not the same as equity; just putting a wire to a school does not mean it will be used well. Integration of the Internet into the curriculum was an objective of the grant proposal and is currently an ongoing project within the faculty. In addition, the browser security certificates have expired, so these browsers cannot access secure (https) websites. This limits Internet access particularly for the teachers, who would generally have the need to access services such as e-business and knowledge bases provided through secure websites.

PHASE 5 – FALL 2000 – WEBSITE DEVELOPMENT AND ANOTHER GRANT PROPOSAL

The Second Grant Proposal

In Fall 2000, when the school was notified of its eligibility for another round of grant monies, the students' work was put to use and a second Ohio SchoolNet grant proposal was prepared. In this second proposal, the school again requested the maximum award to augment local funds and to purchase new computers for the teachers. To make efficient use of the Internet and the school's new high-speed network infrastructure, new computers were necessary. These new computers are also necessary for the teachers to develop and maintain individual classroom websites. In keeping with the philosophy of leveraging all available equipment whenever possible, the replaced computers will be placed in the classrooms in small networks for student use in accessing the Internet. While the inferior capabilities of these machines will somewhat limit their use, they should be acceptable for student use for the near future. In addition, access is again provided where none previously existed. This also gives the school time to find other funding for their eventual replacement.

The school was notified that a second maximum award ($8,000) to replace the teacher's computers was granted. Recently (Spring 2001) the teacher's computers were replaced with Apple PowerMac G4s.

Website Development

Concurrently, during Fall 2000, another group of university students worked on a project to design a website for the school. The use of e-mail had become prevalent among the faculty and staff, and it was desired to provide the teachers with Web access through Microsoft Outlook Web Access (OWA) to their e-mail so they could work at home. While a preliminary school website had been created about two years earlier, it was out-of-date (the expertise to update it was scarce) and the use of OWA requires a website (although the default provided by Internet Information Server was used temporarily). This system improvement provided the impetus for the website project to proceed. The students were asked to produce a factually up-to-date and easily maintained (given current expertise) website that would give teachers default webpages they could maintain independently.

It should be noted that the out-dated computer lab no longer exists. Any usable equipment was offered to the teachers for use in their classrooms. Also, the school and church is currently involved in a major new building initiative. The plan at this time is to have the contractors lay conduit for the wiring in the ceilings. However, based on the perceived success of the projects to-date by the school, volunteers were designed into the plan to complete the wiring, and currently have completed running the cabling in the new addition. This group of volunteers included students, and even one of the students from the original wiring project group that wanted to return and see the progress and contribute to its updating.

The school has hired a full-time technology coordinator. The eventual need for this position had been anticipated at the outset of the project and will be funded by the school and church. Once the building expansion is completed, the network will be rather large. This person will be expected to care for all the hardware and software in the school, apply for grants, provide training and support for the teachers and administrators, upgrade the network, and deal with outside services providers. There has been enough success in grants, and the network has grown and proved useful to a point where the school is willing to invest in its growth and maintenance.

LESSONS LEARNED

- *There must be a very close working relationship between the community organization and the university faculty involved in a service-learning project.*

For example, we needed keys to the building. Since the students could not complete the project while the elementary school was in session, all work needed to be completed in the evenings and on weekends. It turned out that the students preferred the weekends since some of them had night classes, including the SAD class. Also, trust was necessary between the school and the instructors because we needed the authority to order materials and to be able to obtain quotations on behalf of the school. The instructors then relied on the school to order them. Since the project was completed during one semester, the materials needed to be there on the weekend or a week of the semester was lost.

- *Since a project of this nature is being undertaken for a functioning organization, it cannot be left partially finished.*

This is a new experience for students accustomed to an academic environment where, at times, the "partial credit" mentality prevails. The project must be carefully analyzed and divided so that the project tasks can be completed within the available time. Student self-selection should be combined with faculty approval since the faculty member(s) have the ultimate responsibility for completion of the agreed-upon project.

- *Students appreciate being part of a project that benefits others and being treated with respect.*

The school parent/teacher organization had a fund-raising spaghetti supper that took place the first day the students began to physically wire the classroom. The principal gave the students tickets to attend the dinner (which was in part to raise money for the project), which motivated them. Subsequently, snacks were provided to the students on Saturdays when they were working on the project since it often ran over lunchtime. It served both to motivate the students and to keep them from leaving and taking the chance they would not return. This also gave the student social time to relax and discuss the project among themselves and with the instructors in an unstructured setting as recommended by the service-learning literature (Godfrey, 1999; Kenworthy-U'ren, 1999).

- *It was interesting to hear the students make comments about the animals and activities in the classrooms.*

A student even noted that he watered a guinea pig in the room he was wiring. Once, one of the students arrived at the school prior to the designated time and prior to the instructors' arrival to begin working on his own. By that time, he knew where the ladders were stored and had begun wiring in the ceiling since he had to leave early. The students clearly took ownership of the project.

- *A project such as this must be a true partnership.*

The school gave full support to the project by purchasing materials in a timely fashion and by giving the students and instructors significant access to the building. The instructors received needed supplies or tools without question. The school appreciated and valued the work the students did, particularly since they had received a commercial bid and had a dollar amount to attach to these services. We recommend this procedure for all student projects to eliminate the perception that free means valueless. Once the value of the work was clear, future projects completed for the school were easier to obtain and less justification was required to facilitate cooperation.

- *It is important to choose the students associated with the project carefully both to ensure its completion as well as to make it a learning experience for a variety of students.*

The chosen students who volunteered were chosen to ensure the skills necessary existed in at least some students and then included students who really wanted to learn "hands-on" networking. This facilitated a sharing of knowledge and maximized learning, giving those already possessing the required skills leadership experience.

- *There will be unanticipated problems even in a well-planned project.*

The building apparently had been built in many stages, so without warning (we had a set of blueprints) we often found that we needed to wire through what had previously been an exterior wall. At one point the students had to purchase (with the instructor's funds) a stronger/larger drill bit. We also ran to the store to purchase twine for pulling wire through places with difficult access. In one classroom, we found a Christmas tree and decorations left by a former teacher above the ceiling; in other places, we were showered with blown-in insulation. There was no lack of surprises we had not anticipated.

- *One thing we wish we had explored more fully was the insurance coverage for the students while working on the project since it involved physical labor with the potential for injury, and the labor was more complicated than we anticipated.*

This could be incorporated as another element of the students' project design. The students did work in the individual classrooms in pairs at all times. We had breathing masks available for working in the ceiling, but their use was not popular among the students.

- *It is important to seek knowledge from a variety of sources in such a complex project.*

Knowledge and experience with Apple computers was in short supply among both the students and the instructors. None of the volunteers seemed to have Apple experience. A student, who was not part of this project, was familiar with the school from an independent study in which he worked on designing their initial website. Since he was aware of the project and had some familiarity with Apples from working in the University Computer Center, he made relevant suggestions. It was his recommendation to check for built-in AppleTalk capabilities on the student computers in lieu of installing expensive network cards. This resulted in a reduction in complexity (the capabilities were there) and a reduced cost. Following up on this suggestion led to the exploration of Farralon's (a commercial network equipment supplier) website, which was very useful in that it contained an extensive document (with diagrams) of a plan for networking a school. While visiting the site, an instructor registered and won a $500 product certificate that was used to obtain an intelligent switch for the school. Also, a former student was contacted who works with Apple computers in his employment at a local hospital. He also supplied information, agreed to troubleshoot a few Apple computers, and, once involved, even made a CD containing the software set-up of the computers for the classrooms and teachers and included a custom-designed screen saver for the school. He also showed the students how to install the set-up. As an aside, he was so impressed with one of the group members that he arranged for the student to interview at the hospital, and it resulted in a job offer.

- *In the service-learning literature, one of the frequently cited caveats is the amount of time required of the instructor(s), particularly relative to the current reward systems such as tenure (Godfrey, 1999; Kenworthy-U'ren, 1999; Kolenko, Porter, Wheatley, & Colby, 1996).*

The amount of instructor time varied with the student projects undertaken. For those in which the students completed traditional SAD analysis and reporting, the instructor time was the same as for any other project. In some ways, it required less time, for when the inevitable questions arose, the students went directly to the appropriate source rather than the instructor being required to "fill-in" the gaps in written cases. Alternately, the instructor was responsible for contacting the organization, writing the project proposal, and dividing the project into appropriate size phases. This is consistent with the findings of Bush-Bacelis (1998), who suggests that when modifying an existing project, it does not require more work, but rather a different type of work both for the students and the instructor. The wiring project, on the other hand, required a significant amount of dedicated instructor time, as did the grant writing. Nonetheless, the students indicated they found the wiring project particularly fulfilling, especially since the feedback was a working network and a tangible skill set was learned. When the network was constructed and working, confidence levels increased that something "real" had been learned.

STUDENT ASSESSMENT

The students participating in these projects are enrolled mainly in Systems Analysis, Design, and Implementation, either at the graduate or the undergraduate level. The undergraduate course was redesigned as part of a recent conversion to semesters. Previously, the undergraduate Information Systems (IS) students were required to take both a quarter-long traditional Systems Analysis and Design course and a quarter-long capstone course, which was an Implementation course in which they completed a project. The curriculum revision that accompanied the semester conversion combined these two quarter-long courses into one semester course. The graduate course contains students from a number of degree programs, including those pursuing a Master's in Manufacturing Management and those who are taking an area of "concentration" in their MBA in Information Systems. Currently, the IS/MBA students are only required to complete two IS courses to have a "concentration."

In all group projects in the SAD courses, students are asked to assess each member's contribution to the group, and the individual project grade received reflects their contribution to the grade the group receives on the project.

Therefore, those who did not participate did not receive a passing group grade in their weighted average for the SAD course grade. To assess the project grade for those completing the physical wiring, the instructors were present in the building. For the more traditional SAD projects, the instructor assessed quality and adherence to SAD principles after obtaining feedback from school representatives with respect to perceived usefulness.

BENEFITS TO THE SCHOOL

The age of the existing computers had limited their usability, and the school did not have the funds to replace the equipment. By placing them on a network (after adding memory), their useful life was greatly extended, and the cost of replacing them was postponed, thus allowing the school the time to both plan and raise funds.

The school could not have completed all phases of the project without student help. Two groups were instrumental in preparing information used to produce two successful grant proposals by providing technical information the school did not possess. Similarly, the school did not have the funds to hire a commercial company to complete the physical wiring of the building, nor did they possess the technical expertise to assess the quotation. Therefore, for lack of knowledge and lack of enough funds, the school would not have been able to complete this project without the assistance of the students and instructors.

BENEFITS TO THE STUDENTS

Kenworthy-U'ren (1999) suggests that service-learning projects should be grounded in experiential learning and not merely be a service-related activity. These projects were designed to do what is proposed—allow the students to be involved in projects closely related to their career objectives and skills. The students gained "hands-on" experience on the projects. One student noted in the SAD class evaluation that the project was the "best part of the course." The students were able to combine their experience with a feeling of accomplishment. They could see what they were providing to the school, and the partnership allowed the projects to be completed in increments designed to allow the students to see the completion of their portion of the larger project. For those students in the group who physically wired the building, and for those who had some networking skills, they were able to receive leadership experience; those with no experience gained valuable networking experience.

The students who participated in more traditional SAD projects were able to go to the school and interview the "client" in a traditional way. We found the students to be determined to provide a high-quality product because it was being given to a "real" organization and because it would actually be used in decision-making. These projects, if carefully planned, can be win-win situations for both the students and the community partner.

REFERENCES

Anonymous. (2001). The feelgood factor series: Britain. *The Economist*, February, 59.

Badaracco, J. L. (1998). The discipline of building character. *Harvard Business Review*, 76(2), 114-124.

Dunham, R. S. (1999). Across America, a troubling 'digital divide.' *Business Week*, 3640 (August), 40.

Foote, D. (2001). What's your 'emotional intelligence'? *Computerworld*, February.

Godfrey, P. C. (1999). Service-learning and management education: A call to action. *Journal of Management Inquiry*, 8(4), 363-378.

Holloway, J. H. (2000). The digital divide. *Educational Leadership*, 58(2), 90-91.

Huy, Q. N. (1999). Emotional capability, emotional intelligence, and radical change. *Academy of Management Review*, 24(2), 325-345.

Jacoby, B. (1996a). Service-learning in today's higher education. In Jacoby, B. (Ed.), *Service Learning in Higher Education: Concepts and Practices*, 3-25. San Francisco, CA: Jossey-Bass Publishers.

Jacoby, B (1996b). Securing the future of service-learning in higher education: A mandate for action. In Jacoby, B. (Ed.), *Service Learning in Higher Education: Concepts and Practices*, 317-335. San Francisco, CA:Jossey-Bass Publishers.

Kenworthy-U'ren, A. L. (1999). Management students as consultants: An alternative perspective on the service-learning "call to action." *Journal of Management Inquiry*, 8(4), 379-387.

Kolenko, T. A., Porter, G., Wheatley, W., and Colby, M. (1996). A critique of service-learning projects in management education: Pedagogical foundations, barriers, and guidelines. *Journal of Business Ethics*, 15, 133-142.

Morris, L. (1999). Are you emotionally intelligent? *The British Journal of Administrative Management*, November-December, 8-10.

Shewmake, B. (2000). Clinton to IT execs: Help close digital divide. *InfoWorld*, 22(7) 12.

Chapter IV

University/Community Partnerships: Capstone Projects that Make a Difference

Ann Roberts and Roger Boyle
University of Leeds, UK

The University of Leeds is the largest campus-based university in the United Kingdom in terms of student numbers. The School of Computing has, in recent years, sought to share its academic and technical advantages with schools in economically deprived inner-city areas. This chapter describes some of the projects which have been initiated and managed by the School of Computing. We discuss how these have benefited both the schools and our participating undergraduate students. The chapter concludes with a discussion on some of the difficulties encountered and those factors that, from our experience, help to achieve success.

INTRODUCTION

As cited above, the University of Leeds is the largest campus-based university in the United Kingdom in terms of student numbers. It is based in the economically deprived inner city, and many of our near-neighbor schools demonstrate the problems often associated with inner-city schools. The School of Computing has, in recent years, sought to share its academic and technical advantages with these schools to their benefit, and that of our graduating students. It is the aim of this chapter to explain how we have worked with these schools and at the same time benefited a section of our own students.

BACKGROUND

The Town

Leeds is among the largest industrial urbanized areas (population one million) in the UK. It came to prominence during the nineteenth century as a northern industrial city, and its original university, the current University of Leeds, was founded approximately 100 years ago. During the twentieth century, it suffered the economic readjustments seen in many other places, and the current economy is "post-industrial," with a heavy reliance on the finance industry. The population has, naturally, been slower to adjust than industrial management, and there are major pockets of deprivation and under-privilege amidst the resurgence.

A second university, Leeds Metropolitan University, was founded in the '70s originally as Leeds Polytechnic. The two universities have a combined student population of over 50,000, which is very large indeed for the UK. There is thus a large undergraduate population in an environment of economic disadvantage; additionally, both universities have very central sites juxtaposed with areas of significant deprivation (as measured by government metrics). Areas in the immediate neighborhood of the University of Leeds are in the bottom 0.5 % of the UK deprivation indices (Department of the Environment, 1999). These include the number of single parents, lack of car ownership, unemployment, etc.

The city thus exhibits instabilities, with economic health for some, mixed with a vicious circle of unemployment and under-achievement for others. This is a familiar urban picture in the western world, but it is exacerbated by the presence of very large institutions of privilege and ambition in the precise areas that are suffering most.

The University

The University of Leeds, which lies in the centre of this area, is the largest single-site university in the United Kingdom, with over 25,000 students. It is research based, graduating Bachelor's, Master's and PhD students in a full range of disciplines. Traditionally, these students are recruited from among the more affluent middle classes who will travel to study; there is as a result an image of the university that it is not "for" the people who live next to it – this can be the cause of understandable tension. In recognition of this, there are several university-wide schemes underway to foster among the students the idea of giving something back to the community among which they have lived for the duration of their studies; most of these schemes represent voluntary, extra-curricula work for the students and are connected to local schools.

Schools

The British school system is usually based around primary schools (ages 5-11) and high schools (ages 11-18). High schools examine at many ages, with landmark examinations at ages 16 (GCSE, standing for the General Certificate of Education) and 18 (A-level, Examinations in Advanced Level studies). The A-level is the customary way for students to enter universities.

Schools conform to a government-imposed National Curriculum, which delivers the traditional subjects. Part of this is an element of ICT (Information and Communication Technology), although this is often a problem since many staff, particularly those in disadvantaged areas where recruitment is a special problem, lack experience in ICT.

This is especially problematic since ICT is an area in which the whole population will need experience and education, and experiencing a shortfall in underprivileged areas exacerbates the problems of imbalance. Schools in areas of deprivation suffer serious motivational problems, particularly through the two years spent studying the syllabus for the A-level examinations, when student aspiration to succeed and go on to university is often very low or absent. A major government problem is pupils leaving inner-city schools both under-qualified (in the formal sense) and under-experienced in the key skills such as ICT on which future success would depend.

Links

There is a significant history of voluntary work in the community by university personnel. Some of this is organized solely by the student body, but recently the institution has taken a greater role and responsibility with the establishment of a City and Regional Office. Part of the motivation for this is opportunistic, with a desire to boost recruitment, but at the same time a lot of the office's work addresses the social problems of the university's neighborhood.

Building on the many links into the community that had been developed over years, the School of Computing recognized that it could influence the solution to problems local schools were experiencing using the considerable pool of expertise represented by its students. We were anxious that this should go beyond the (very valuable) voluntary work which was already established, and make some curricular impact in an area that school staff were finding it difficult to approach. Many universities and colleges encourage this sort of voluntary work, but the School of Computing has taken the further step of incorporating IT support for inner-city schools in the neighborhood into part of its curriculum via final-year Undergraduate projects.

ACTION

Projects

The syllabus in the School of Computing of the University of Leeds would be recognized in most universities, and corresponds well to ACM guidelines (ACM/IEEE, 2001). In addition to standard topics, students are able to study the research specialities of the school, in particular AI, Informatics, and Visualization.

The culmination of undergraduate studies within the school's programs is a final-year project of 300 hours duration. These are intended as capstones to study, usually involving technical design, production, and evaluation, usually of significant computer codes. An explicit guideline is that such projects should exploit material from two or more advanced modules, which illustrates well their potential; it is common for the better quality projects to be published in research literature. Nevertheless, the student population in recent years has grown significantly, showing a 20% increase over five years, and there is now a small but identifiable proportion of finalists who are keen to pursue projects of a less traditional nature. In particular, some students are anxious to embark on, or continue, ICT work in connection with local schools. In some cases, this is simply philanthropic, but in others it is because the student has a stated ambition to become a schoolteacher, and seeks practical experience. In yet others the students are engaged in a Joint Honors program of which Computing is only half, while the other half offers other skills worthy of exercise (for example, Management Studies).

Potentially, we saw that project work in local schools, while clearly not exposing students to cutting-edge research, may be ideal for those who are not in the scientific mainstream. They are given the opportunity to gain hard experience of taking their very technical education and interpreting it for one of the most demanding audiences they might meet; this can represent academic activity of a different but equally valid kind.

Issues

Projects of this sort present course designers and curriculum quality control with an issue. Since normally we might expect a project to exercise the work of advanced modules, but IT activity (however defined) in a local school is unlikely to be at this sort of level, it might become hard to satisfy external examiners with respect to academic merit. It is thus necessary throughout such a project to have a keen eye on the skills the students are exercising, and how they will be assessed. Examples include skills of organization and presentation (at which Computing students are often notoriously weak), although there is always scope for raw technical skills to be exercised in the generation of software to assist in teaching. Indeed, software for teaching schoolchildren is among the most demanding to create, in terms of robustness and Human-Computer Interaction.

Since 1997 we have managed several projects of this type, with a constant stream of demand for future years. They represent various categories of work which will be discussed in detail below, and originate in a wide range of schools, all of which are within two miles of the university.

The UK government produces annual league tables for every school dealing with children from the age of 11. Some of the information for the year 2000 (*The Guardian Newspaper*, 2000) is produced below for the schools, all of which are in inner-city Leeds, with which we have worked (Table 1).

The following is the key for Table 1.

- % A*-C grade: % of students achieving 5 or more GCSE passes at A*-C grade. C is the lowest grade that would permit a student to take that subject forward to 16-18 study.
- % A*-G grade: % of students achieving 5 or more GCSE passes at A*-G grade. A G grade is a bare pass.
- Average GCSE point score: The average point score per 16-year old.
- Number of A-level pupils: Number of pupils entered for 2 or more Advanced level subjects.

Table 1: Annual league table for 2000

School	% A*-C grade	% A*-G grade	Average GCSE score	Number of A-level pupils	Average A-level score	% SEN	Total number of pupils
1	21	68	20.7	23	6.2	25.5	483
2	20	78	26.5			28.5	467
3	20	76	26.9			31.4	500
Local Mean	40.4	85.7	34.0		18.6		
National Mean	49.2	88.9	38.9		18.5		

- Average A-level point score: Average point score per student, computed as A=10, B=8, C=6, D=4, E=2; E is a bare pass.
- % SEN: % of pupils with Special Educational Needs. This is a Department for Education and Employment (DFEE) measure of need where physical, mental, educational, social, or behavioral factors prevent normal access to the curriculum.
- Total number of pupils: All pupils in the school. (The point score is a measure of attainment. The higher the point score, the better the results.)

Schools 2 and 3 have students for the first five years of secondary education (the years when education is compulsory up to the age of 16), while School 1 also has a "sixth form" (ages 17-18). As can be seen from the table, the results for the national examinations are very low by national standards, and low even by the Leeds standards to which they contribute. They are relatively small schools by secondary standard, but can be seen to have high percentages of students with Special Educational Needs. On the plus side the staff, despite working in this difficult environment, are usually very committed to the students' development, and encourage any help available.

When the student projects took place, none of the schools had up-to-date computing equipment available for the students, but in the last two years School 1 has become a one of Leeds' City Technology Centres. (These CTCs are a UK government initiative to make modern technology available in the local neighborhood.)

We also work with two primary schools (A and B). These schools deal with children between the ages of 5 and 11 with a nursery for those between 3 and 5.

School B has a very high proportion of children from ethnic minorities, and had an enthusiastic, but very busy ICT (Information and Computer Technology) coordinator, who by the time of the second project was working full time in a temporary capacity for the local education authority to provide ICT support for the area, leaving the school with little experienced support in the area. Thirty percent of the pupils at School A arrive at the school unable to speak English. Much of the equipment available in the school at this time was old and based on Acorn technology, and many of the class teachers lacked ITC skills. Neither school is large by Leeds standards, each having around 190 pupils.

A departure this year from our work being with our close neighbors are two projects to support the teaching staff of a high school around 10 miles away. This is one of the largest schools in Britain with more than 2,000 pupils.

One project is to build an intranet for the school and special tools to allow teachers from all specialties to put their course notes and coursework on line and to receive submissions on line. The second is to produce a secure database on which teachers can store students' marks, student information, reports for university applications, etc.

These projects are underway at present and it is not possible to provide any evaluation of the outcome for either the project students or the school staff.

Procedures

The university has a unit called the City and Regional Office whose responsibility is to build links between the university and other groups in the local area: schools, businesses, local council, charities, etc. Many of our original links with these schools come from the fact that the City and Regional was already working with them. Sometimes the school will ring us to ask if we are willing to do another project for them. New schools, if approached, sometimes refuse to be involved fearing the extra workload of "supervising a student," but those who have worked with us before are always pleased to have us back, seeing the benefits to the school, in particular the children, as greatly outweighing any time spent on talking with the students.

Sometimes the projects are suggested by the school as meeting a particular need at the time, as was the case with the new school this year; at other times a project, thought by a supervisor to be appropriate for a student, requires us to "find a home" and one of the schools is contacted.

The characteristics of a project suitable for a final-year student are:

- *Size*–The project must have sufficient content to merit an award of credits towards an honours degree.
- *Intellectual Level*–The intellectual level of the project should be sufficient to stretch the student at Senior Honours level.
- *Computing content*–There should be sufficient computing content to qualify for an award in a computing discipline.

These school-oriented projects certainly meet the size requirement, being intensive and time consuming. The intellectual level is also sufficient. The issue of sufficient computing content is also satisfied by the need to assess and respond to user requirements and then produce robust software, in a way in which more research-driven projects do not.

To a degree the students doing these projects are a self-selected group. Only a certain type of student wishes to do the kind of project which requires good interpersonal skills and the outcome of which is in part dependent on the people they are working with. The student has to be "service" or "support" minded in contrast to the kind of student who wants to do a project directly linked to research or one demonstrating immediately employable skills. The kind of student who would be encouraged to do a project of this kind if interested is an outgoing student who has to have some interest or experience in interacting with people of the appropriate age group for the school with which they will be working.

Because we would have to supervise these students doing some sort of project in their final year, these projects are in a sense resource free, but do depend on suitable staff to supervise them. It is also the case that the local school facilities are invariably inferior to those available in the university, so all the required technology is already in place. There is a small group of staff committed to supervising these projects, sympathetic and understanding of the problems of the schools and willing to design and support a project to help alleviate some of these problems. The projects obviously have to meet the project criteria defined above for the sake of the student, while making a contribution to the school.

THE PROJECTS IN SCHOOLS

The projects require a restricted range of technical skills, but develop the student's transferable skills such as prioritizing, delegating, assessing, and analyzing along with problem-solving, decision-making, and inter-personal skills. On the technical side the students do, however, have to learn how to assess and respond to user requirements, and have to consider pedagogical issues such as how children learn.

A common feature of all the projects was the requirement for help from other students to work with the children at some part of the project. This required organizational and recruitment skills on the part of the students doing the project and also allowed the volunteers an insight into the world of education.

Project 1 – IT Skills Learning in a Primary School

The aims of this project were to help School B improve their teaching of ITC (Information Technology and Communication) and to develop a Web site for the school (http://www.comp.leeds.ac.uk/little_london).

The Web site was produced to give the school a presence on the Web and to demonstrate the ways in which the World Wide Web can be used as a teaching aid. Simply producing Web pages has insufficient academic rigor to be a project, but is often, as in this case, a part of the whole project.

The project also involved the student writing five IT Skills sessions aimed at children of around 10 years of age. The sessions broadly covered the areas of word processing, spreadsheets, and the Internet. These areas were in line with the national curriculum requirements for IT education for children of this age. The student produced student worksheets, a teacher's guide, a quick help, and a resource guide for both teachers and students. To trial the material, to introduce the children to the university on their doorsteps, and to compensate for the lack of machines at school making it impossible for all the children to work on computers at the same time, the project student recruited a group of student 'buddies' and brought the children into the university where a lab of PCs were put at their disposal for a day.

Project 2 – IT Teaching Development for School A

The aims of this project were to aid the school to improve their teaching of ICT. Based on the Government Department for Education and Employment's (DFEE) guidelines and the Qualifications and Curriculum Authority Guidelines (http://www.qca.org.uk) as to a model scheme of work for Key Stages 1 and 2, the school had produced its own Information Technology booklet detailing the stages each group should be at, exactly what skills they should have been taught, and the topic areas to be covered each year. Given the capabilities of the children, and the teachers' lack of time, resources, and computing familiarity, this book appeared unrealistic in its expectations.

The skills the children were supposed to be routinely using by the end of the year were under three main headings:
- Control, Modelling, and Measurement
- Communicating Information
- Handling Information

The IT coordinator asked the student to focus the work on "Handling Information" as this had the highest priority and was the area most lacking in the school.

The student produced a series of worksheets to use with a database program available in the school, using questions to which the children could relate, for example.

What color of eyes do the children have? What color of hair do they have? Are there connections between hair and eye color? Do people with black hair all have dark eyes?

Table 2: The English Education System Divides a Pupil's School Life into Four Key Stages

Key Stage	Age (years)	School years
1	5 to 7	1 and 2
2	7 to 11	3 to 6
3	11 to 14	7 to 9
4	14 to 16	10 to 11

This involved the student in consideration of the sort of data which could be used, compatible with asking the pupils to collect their own data, again an issue of user requirements.

After at least two years of being used, these worksheets will probably be phased out when the school finally gets its PCs and they are networked, assuming they get enough to make the old machines redundant, and further projects of a similar nature will no doubt be undertaken at some stage.

The following year the headteacher again approached the university and asked that a second project be undertaken. This is described below as Project 3.

Project 3 – Using IT to Help Teach Numeracy at School A

To begin with this followed the same route as the previous project with a study of the requirements of the National Curriculum, the DFEE, and QCA. There was also research into the school's own practices and resources.

The objective of the project was:

*   to evaluate different software/multimedia packages and then create a simple course incorporating IT to help teach numeracy in the school.
*   To help the children enhance their comprehension of numeracy by using computer interaction.

Within a final-year project, evaluation and interaction are key software engineering experiences.

Two worksheets and a teaching manual were written. These were trailed in the school. As in Project 1, to introduce the children to the university on their doorsteps and to compensate for the lack of machines at school, a half-day session in the university was run. This necessitated enlisting a group of student helpers. This has the effect of cascading out the experience of working with the school to other students, which is a further benefit of this type of project.

Summer Schools

Since 1996 the School of Computing has been running regular short summer schools, involving about eight inner-city Leeds schools, aimed at introducing 15 year-olds to the Internet. The Internet was not then available in the majority of inner-city schools, and even now it is possible to find secondary schools where the use of the Internet is very limited, and the opportunity to visit the university and spend two full days, each student with a dedicated machine, is greatly appreciated. This course is therefore still being run but will become outdated as all schools are connected to the Internet, hopefully in the not-too-distant future. It was therefore decided to implement further courses for different age groups, and these are described below as Projects 4 and 5.

Project 4 – Development of a Two-Day Course in Computer-Based Design and Presentation Skills for the School of Computing Summer School 1998

This course was aimed at 16-17 year olds. During the day the young people produced a poster on a topic of their interest. The posters were produced using materials found searching the Web. During the morning of day two, they all produced Powerpoint slides and in the afternoon gave a "poster session" with their poster and slides. This was the pupils' first experience of presenting work to a group, and for some was an immense personal achievement.

This was piloted with a small group of nine students from School 3 and was found to be highly successful, with all the students responding enthusiastically. This course is available for other schools as and when funding allows.

Project 5 – A Summer School in Computing for Key Stage Two

The aims of the project were:
- To develop a summer school program relevant to children aged 10-11.
- To encourage these children in computing, before they go on to high school, and to think about university as a possible aim beyond school.
- To develop material to aid computer awareness.

The children the summer schools are aimed at come from the sort of background where no-one in the family has ever gone to university, and one of the aims was to overcome this cultural idea that "University is not for the likes of us." Simply bringing the children into university and letting them enjoy the experience of learning in that environment is a step towards promoting wider access. While this is desirable in itself, not all children will or should aim at university, so the contents of the summer school should always have some value in themselves, hence the third aim above.

The work again took place with School B. Once again a Web site was produced as a starting point for any Internet-based activities. This not only meant that it gave the pupils an environment in which to work, which gives links to other sites which are suitable for young children, but it acted as a home site to which the young people can return if they get into difficulties. It also means that the resource is available to any other school which may wish to make (unsupported) use of it.

The work itself included designing a poster and creating a food chain (based on current work as prescribed by the National Curriculum for this age group). The children were also introduced to video conferencing and e-mail. All the content was discussed with the headteacher and the year group teacher as the development progressed.

The project student shared the Bit'94 prize for 2000, which is "awarded to the student who does most to foster good interaction of either an academic or social nature between staff in the School of Computing, students in the School of Computing, and other disparate members of the university or wider community."

Project 6 – IT's for You

The student organized and coordinated after-school clubs for Schools 1 and 2. The primary objectives of the project were:
1.   To provide a course for the two schools that will encourage the pupils to take an active and prolonged interest in IT.
2.   To give pupils a realization that they have opportunities for choice in their education, and to think about these choices.
3.   To provide an environment where pupils can learn "hands-on" skills that will be interesting and fun.
4.   To get the pupils to enjoy IT.
     The underlying principle of these was to allow them to learn while having fun.

All of these objectives were met as far as was possible given the limited facilities available in the schools (see below) which affected point 3, and accepting that the "proof" of 1 having been met relies on the comments of one of the heads of school.

As the project progressed other objectives developed:
1.   *Improving Relationships between the Local Community and Students*: It was an opportunity for students to put something back into the community they temporarily inhabit.
2.   *Benefits to the two Schools*: Included extra IT teaching and arguments to support the heads' and governors' push for improved facilities.
3.   *Benefits to the Student Tutors*: These included experience of working in a team and an improvement in their communication skills.
4.   *Benefits to the City and Regional Office*: Publicity surrounding the clubs helped raise the profile of the City and Regional Office.
5.   *Benefits to the Pupils*: Among other things the pupils experienced acceptance, individual attention allowing them to progress at their own pace, and were provided with role models in the form of the student tutors.

The clubs lasted 10 weeks and the average age of the children attending was 12. Overall 32 children participated in the clubs with 11 pupils participating in every session at their school.

School 1 had the better facilities: 16 networked 486 PCs, a black-and-white laser printer, a flatbed scanner, and a zip drive. There was also access to an adjacent room with one reasonable PC, modem, and ISDN connection. The pupils created their own Web pages.

School 2 had very limited computing facilities: 20 stand-alone Acorn Archimedes and a black-and-white inkjet printer for the first five sessions, and 20 non-networked 486 PCs for the later sessions. Occasionally one Internet connection was available. The pupils at this school used the first five sessions to create a newspaper about their favorite topics. In the second five weeks an HTML editor (Dido) was installed on the PCs and they created their own Web pages, which were later held on the server at the School of Computing.

The student won outright the University of Leeds BIT prize (as mentioned earlier) for 1999.

EVALUATION

Evaluation of this form of work is not trivial. Comparing the learning experience of the students is far from easy, and the impact on the children involved is very hard to measure indeed (from the university perspective). Nevertheless, we can observe as follows:

Student Performance

The grading of this sort of work received particularly careful attention. These were Honours students so it was important not to award grades simply because an individual was well-meaning in what they were trying to do. The criteria (e.g., design, implementation, evaluation, etc.) used for project assessment at Leeds are, by design, able to be applied to a wide range of project types, being phrased as an exercise in problem solving into which this less traditional form of work fits well (School of Computing, 2000).

The students are well motivated and it is customary for projects of this type to receive grades above the average for the cohort. Thus, from the point of view of academic advancement, the idea has been a success.

External examiners (representatives of other universities) pay close attention to these unusual projects, since in the UK university system, they have the responsibility of maintaining the school's academic integrity. The arguments for work of this type need rehearsing to them, but we have had support from them hitherto, with agreement on the quality of the work done.

Student Reaction

The students who engage in this kind of work are by their nature self-selecting; they would not do it if they did not already have some sympathy and aptitude for what they were doing. Nevertheless, we have a good index into their experience since a novel aspect (Clark & Boyle, 2000: 2001) of the project assessment in Leeds is the requirement to write an assessed summary of personal experience. Among good students this is the valued reflective phase that can be the difference between success and failure in education (Schön, 1983).

Some of the project students wrote:

- *The challenges of this project have required me to learn the skills of prioritizing, delegating, assessing, and analyzing. The demands of accommodating the needs and wishes of a wide variety of customers and clients, always mindful of the dynamics of the team, has led to improvement in my problem-solving, decision-making, and inter-personal skills.*

- *[This project] has led to a huge increase in my proficiency as an innovator.*

- *During this project I have gained valuable experience of time management skills, working to a deadline and setting milestones.*

All of the projects require support from other students, whether in the classroom or for the children to visit the university, and there is an additional benefit in the experience of these students.

One student wrote:

- *The need to create and communicate information to a variety of audiences and to make presentations to students, pupils, and teachers, sometimes in great numbers, has resulted in an increase in my self confidence.*

Another said:

- *I gained an appreciation of how challenging teaching can be.*

School Reaction

Of course, there is a peculiar relationship operating when valued volunteers enter hard-pressed environments such as the schools we describe. This means that honest opinion, especially if critical, can be very difficult to extract, since the staff in these schools will be anxious to perpetuate the relationship even if it has some flaws. Nevertheless, comments from staff at the schools involved indicate the impact the students were able to have on the children:

- *The children thoroughly enjoyed every part and are now desperate to develop their new-found skills.*

- *You managed to find a range (and) breadth of activities that kept the children interested and on task (no mean feat!).*

- *[The project student] has certainly provided a role model for enthusiasm, yet provided them with new skills and assisted in facilitating more independent learning.*

- *I watched with delight as every child succeeded and became filled with enthusiasm.*
- *I have gained enormously during the time that I have worked with [the student] in terms of my professional development (ICT coordinator).*
- *It opened up their horizons, makes university education seem both desirable and attainable.*

Furthermore, the fact that there *is* enthusiasm for further work is evidence in itself that from the staff point of view, the exercise is predominantly successful.

Articulate comments from children, particularly those with the background of the sort of schools we are serving, can be even harder to obtain. From time to time, however, we can see a genuine deep involvement in the work:

- *I learn something new every week.*
- *I wish I was there [at the university] now.*
- *I learnt about Nelson Mandella and why he was famous. Thank you for letting us use your Internet computers (sic).*

Other Issues

Unsurprisingly, these activities are popular with the local press, representing a good example of activity that the general public can easily understand and approve of, originating from an institution often regarded as an "ivory tower." Such publicity is, of course, very welcome and often of benefit in the pursuit of further funding, but is rarely academic or in any sense "deep" in its content.

It is important to remember that the drivers of this work are computer scientists and not educationalists versed in school curricular affairs, and that therefore they may not be best placed to take curricular decisions at the school level.

An authority in IT education within the university observed that the projects lacked intensive teacher involvement. Pragmatically this is not possible, as all classroom teachers are already heavily burdened, but as can be seen from the staff comments above, even without the amount of involvement that would undoubtedly be helpful, we still manage to make a worthwhile contribution to the children's learning.

CONCLUSIONS

We have described an approach to assisting with ICT requirements in hard-pressed inner-city schools that augments the university curriculum for computing students. The evidence for success is in the projects that have been completed and the students that have graduated, but it remains problematic to manage this kind of work:

- There is a financial cost involved, and even though we seek to minimize it as described earlier, we still have to seek external 'goodwill' funding to allow us to undertake some of this work.
- There remains an issue of matching students to schools and though, so far, we have not had to refuse a student who has wanted to do one of these projects, the possibility remains that someday a student with an unsuitable personality might wish to take part and have to be discouraged.
- The quality of the projects was discussed earlier and it is sometimes the case that a project proposed by a school does not meet the quality criteria and has to be either increased in scope, or declined.
- The problem of the teachers being too busy to become fully involved can lead to a failure to interlace fully with school curriculum. Nevertheless, within limits, we succeed in widening the pupils' experience of ICT and aiding teachers, limited in IT skills, to meet the demands of the curriculum.

The success of this approach depends on a number of things:
- The goodwill of suitable supervisors within the school.
- The preparedness of formal academic mechanisms to admit this sort of work as valid study.
- The willingness of schools to allow the students to be involved, although it has become clear that the advantages to the schools outweigh any extra demands placed on the staff by the presence of a student.
- The university's location in the centre of a large, predominantly urban region with surrounding areas of urban deprivation.
- Support mechanisms for liaison provided by the university City and Regional Office who provided a link with the schools.

We conjecture that these ingredients are present at many city universities; what we have contributed is the successful absorption of the activity into the computing curriculum.

We feel we can persist in maintaining the quality of our students' education while providing a high quality support service in an important discipline, in an underprivileged area. Our evidence to date suggests that, at the very least, we are building new bridges of cooperation between higher education and the community in which it operates.

REFERENCES

Clark, M. A. C. and Boyle, R. D. (2000). The characteristics of successful innovation. *Proceedings of Improving University Learning and Teaching. 25th International Conference*, Frankfurt, Germany, July, 294-299.

Clark, M. A. C. and Boyle, R. D. (2002). Successful curriculum innovation: Who is proposing what to whom? *Active Learning in HE*. Under review.

Department of the Environment. (1999). *Index of Local Conditions*. DFEE.

ACM/IEEE. (2001). *Computing Curricula*. Retrieved March 6, 2001, from the World Wide Web: http://www.computer.org/education/cc2001/.

The Guardian Newspaper. (2000). *Guardian Education*. November 16, 12.

Schön, D. (1983). *The Reflective Practitioner*. New York: Basic Books.

School of Computing. (2000). *Project Assessment Criteria*. Retrieved February 18, 2001, from the World Wide Web: http://www.comp.leeds.ac.uk/uginfo/projects/assessment-criteria.html.

Section II

Educational Partnerships

Chapter V

Building Educational Technology Partnerships Through Participatory Design

John M. Carroll
Virginia Tech, USA

George Chin, Jr.
Battelle Pacific Northwest Laboratory, USA

Mary Beth Rosson, Dennis C. Neale, Daniel R. Dunlap
and Philip L. Isenhour
Virginia Tech, USA

Over more than five years, we worked with a group of public school teachers to define, develop, and assess network-based support for collaborative learning in middle school physical science and high school physics. From the outset, we committed to a participatory design approach, in part to explore what issues and possibilities arise when participatory design is pursued more extensively. The nature of our interactions, and in particular the nature of the roles played by the teachers, did change significantly through the course of the project. We suggest that there may be a long-term developmental unfolding of roles and relationships in participatory design.

Technology development is often seen as a waterfall process, a cascade of activities each feeding the next: new technologies are invented, then elaborated and refined in demonstration applications, then transferred to real developers and deployed in real applications, and finally adopted by users. This conception derives from the belief that technology innovation is inherently good for people and organizations, and that the key engineering challenge for technology development is efficiency. However, linear waterfall processes maximize the risk that inappropriate technology will be deployed, that the technology will solve the wrong problem or conflict with commitments and practices of the people who are to use the technology.

Educational technology provides many examples of how "efficient" development and deployment is not enough. Teachers work in a complex and dynamic context in which measurable objectives and underlying values collide on a daily basis. Traditionally, teachers work in isolation from their peers; individual teachers have well-established personal practices and philosophies of education. Teachers have enormous discretion with respect to what goes on in their classrooms, yet are also routinely interrogated by supervisors, by parents and other community members, and by educational bureaucracies. This has led to an abiding tension in the culture of schools: teachers' innovative practices are often not adequately acknowledged or valued, and at the same time, teachers often passively resist school reforms that are imposed top-down.

Technology is a particularly problematic element in the culture of schools. The isolation and discretion of the teacher's work environment requires that technology for classroom use be highly appropriate and reliable. Yet it is generally assumed that teachers are to be *trained* on new technologies, not asked to *define* what those technologies should be. From the teacher's standpoint classroom technology often is itself the problem, not the solution. This culture of technology development in the schools has been singularly ineffective; film and radio in the 1920s, television in the 1950s, computer-assisted instruction in the 1980s, among others, have been notable failures (Cuban, 1986; Hodas, 1993; Tyack & Cuban, 1995).

An alternative to merely efficient technology development is *participatory design*, the inclusion of users within a development team, such that they actively help in setting design goals and planning prototypes. This approach was pioneered, and has been widely employed, in Europe since the 1970s, and now consists of a well-articulated and differentiated set of engineering methods in use worldwide (Greenbaum & Kyng, 1991; Muller, Haslwanter & Dayton, 1997; Schuler & Namioka, 1993).

In 1994, our research group began a design collaboration with two public school teachers. We wanted to investigate whether and how the teachers could contribute to a design collaboration; we were specifically interested in exploring the utility of a scenario-based design approach in this context (Carroll, 1995, 2000). We were guided by beliefs that the teachers could participate effectively in the design of educational applications, that their expertise in education could be especially critical, and moreover, that the teachers had a right to such participation. Our hypothesis was that the principal obstacles to achieving such an interaction were the culture and professional jargon of software design. Our initial investigation addressed these barriers by creating a cooperative relationship, spanning more than a year, between the teachers and a software developer who worked with them to create several novel educational applications (Laughton, 1996).

In 1995, with the support of the U.S. National Science Foundation (NSF), we formed the LiNC project (for "Learning in Networked Communities"), a partnership between Virginia Tech and the public schools of Montgomery County, Virginia, USA. The objective was to develop and investigate a high-quality communications infrastructure to support collaborative science learning. Montgomery County is located in the rural Appalachian region of southwestern Virginia. In March 2000, one of its high schools was listed among the top 100 in the U.S. by *Newsweek* magazine. However, in others, physics is only offered every other year, and to classes of only three to five students. Our initial vision was to give students in this diverse and dispersed school district access to peers through networked collaboration.

We wanted to create and study a broad framework for participatory design interactions. The NSF program that sponsored our work was directed at producing models for how new computer networking infrastructures could facilitate systemic change in public education (as opposed to producing specific curricular innovations). Thus, an important orienting goal was enhancing the autonomy of teachers with respect to our technology infrastructure. In other words, we assumed from the start that in order to succeed, we must someday fade from the project, and leave the teachers to maintain and develop its achievements. This meant that the teachers' involvement could not be limited to requirements interviews, or even to relatively active roles in conceptual design. We needed to think of them as collaborators in implementation, deployment, testing, and refinement, and as leaders in the development of courseware and classroom activities that would exploit the software.

STAGES OF COOPERATIVE ENGAGEMENT

Looking back at the past five years, we can distinguish four stages in our collaboration with the teachers: at first, the teachers were *practitioner-informants*; we observed their classroom practices and we interviewed them. Subsequently, the teachers became directly and actively involved in the requirements development process as *analysts*. Some two-and-a-half years into the project, the teachers assumed responsibility as *designers* for key aspects of the project. Through the past year particularly, the teachers have become *coaches* to their own colleagues within the public school system.

We use the term "developmental" in the sense of Piaget and Inhelder (1969) and Vygotsky (1978). We believe that the teachers have developed qualitatively different roles through the course of our collaboration. In some cases, these roles were suggested to them; in other cases, they defined and claimed new roles. But in all cases, these transitions exemplified the defining characteristics of *developmental change*: active resolution of manifest conflicts in one's activity, taking more responsibility, and assuming greater scope of action. Each successive stage can be seen as a relatively stable organization of knowledge, skills, and attitudes that resolves the instigating conflict.

In a classic Piagetian example, a child in the pre-operational stage perceives single dimensions of quantity. This produces conflicts: a given quantity of liquid poured from a short, wide container into a tall, thin container appears suddenly to be more, but of course cannot be more. These conflicts eventually precipitate a cognitive reorganization called the concrete operational stage, in which constant quantities are perceived as constant regardless of varying shapes and arrangements.

Developmental change in adults is of course more complex. The stages we describe are not singular competencies, but relatively complex ensembles of collaboration, social norms, tool manipulation, domain-specific goals and heuristics, problem-solving, and reflection-in-action. They are social constructions achieved through enculturation, constituted by the appropriation of the artifacts and practices of a community (Vygotsky, 1978).

In the Piagetian notion of stages in child development, successive stages build upon the cognitive structures and enabled activity of prior stages, but ultimately replace those structures. A child who enters the concrete operational stage can no longer function at the pre-operational stage. Adult growth, however, is not static achievement, but continual elaboration. The teachers are still practitioners whose classroom practices we regularly observe and whose classroom expertise we still interrogate; they seem to us and to themselves to be representative practitioner-informants. However, they are now *also* analysts and designers, and often coaches. Indeed, effective design coaches probably must be experienced designers, successful designers must be skilled analysts, and analysts must have attained significant domain knowledge.

A third modulation of the developmental perspective in our analysis is our relativistic viewpoint with respect to the nature of expertise. In classic developmental work, it is the child who is developing, and indeed doing so by becoming more like the adult. In contrast our situation is one of mutual learning. Through the past five years, the faculty and graduate student researchers in our group have learned a vast amount about the practices, the exigencies, the values, and the politics of public schools. The teachers could present a complementary analysis of the development of *our* capacities to collaborate in the design of educational activities and technologies. Such reflexivity is inherent in any participatory design project. We acknowledge this, and thus offer a partial analysis of the long-term development of participatory design, from a single perspective, as a start toward a more complete understanding.

THE PRACTITIONER-INFORMANT

Our project began in the summer of 1994. Stuart Laughton, a Virginia Tech graduate student at the time, initiated an investigation of how teachers could contribute to the participatory design of educational software. He worked with two teachers from the Montgomery County school division, one a middle school physical science teacher, the other a high school physics teacher. In this investigation we used ethnographic interviews as a means of understanding the teachers' concerns and requirements, and scenarios as a means of conveying and developing visions of how the new software could impact teaching and learning interactions. The focus of the research was on bridging the communication gap between classroom expertise and software development expertise.

This effort was successful, not only in producing several educational tools for the teachers, but in demonstrating that the teachers could play a creative and effective role in the design process. Specifically, it showed how the techniques of ethnographic interviewing and scenario-based design could facilitate cooperative design interactions involving teachers and software developers (Laughton, 1996).

The teachers Laughton had worked with also became part of the large team that developed a proposal for the U.S. National Science Foundation (NSF) in 1995. They provided sanity checks for plans to develop a virtual school networking infrastructure that could leverage teachers, students, and other resources in a sparsely populated region in southwestern Virginia. But the teachers' role was somewhat peripheral. There is a revealing asymmetry in this: although the university researchers could take the initiative to enter the teachers' context and establish a genuine two-way cooperation, the teachers were less able to reciprocate in "our" project-planning and grant-writing activity.

This asymmetry was over-determined. The teachers did not understand the culture of projects and grants as it exists in research universities. The project proposal we constructed was fairly typical of its idiom, which means we spent a lot of time discussing how to position our work with respect to national priorities, how to manage various threads of dependency among research actions and subgoals, and how to allocate and coordinate specific technical roles and responsibilities among various departments and faculty members. In the teachers' culture, grants are usually far smaller and more limited projects with budgets that barely cover the purchase of materials. Their proposals are generally one-to-three page workplans.

The university researchers are used to doing whatever is necessary and appropriate to plan and carry out research. This often involves learning about other people's work and activity, including visiting and even living in other sites and circumstances. Learning as much as we possibly could about the teachers and their work practices was a normal part of our research activity, and essential to this particular project. In contrast, understanding the university research model and the various individual researchers was not something that is normal for the teachers to try to do in educational research relationships. After all, the teachers are usually the subjects of the research, or part of the research manipulation; they are rarely seen by researchers as partners. And finally, understanding us was not something that the teachers were encouraged or supported in doing by the school system.

We later learned that at this point in time the teachers were both amazed and shocked by aspects of our virtual school proposal. They could barely believe that computer networking could support real-time collaborative class-room activities effectively, for example, allowing students to jointly carry out simulation experiments and writing projects. Figure 1 is the vision scenario for the virtual school that guided the development of our NSF proposal.

Perhaps more significantly, the teachers could barely believe that anyone would *want* to create a virtual school. However, these strong reactions were not conveyed to the university researchers at the time. Instead the teachers continued to serve as supportive domain experts. In part the teachers believed that they had relatively little to contribute, and that the researchers knew what they were doing. Of course, the teachers were confident of their own expertise as public school educators, but they did not see that expertise as a critical determinant in the virtual school vision. In this, they—and implicitly we—

Figure 1: The Marissa Scenario (Fall 1994) was our Initial Vision of the Virtual School

- Marissa, a 10th-grade physics student, is studying gravity and its role in planetary motion. She goes to the virtual science lab and navigates to the gravity room.

- In the gravity room she discovers two other students, Randy and David, already working with the Alternate Reality Kit, which allows students to alter various physical parameters (such as the universal gravitational constant) and then observe effects in a simulation world.

- The three students, each of whom is from a different school in the county, discuss possible experiments by typing messages from their respective personal computers. Together they build and analyze several solar systems, eventually focusing on the question of how comets can disrupt otherwise stable systems.

- They capture data from their experiments and display it with several visualization tools, then write a brief report of their experiments, sending it for comments to Don, another student in Marissa's class, and Ms. Gould, Randy's physics teacher.

reflected the values of contemporary society: somewhat skeptical of public education and public school teachers, while at the same time accepting of computer technology tout court.

The LiNC project ramped up in the spring of 1996 with an influx of graduate student research assistants funded by the NSF grant. We focused a great deal of effort on understanding needs and opportunities in the classrooms. University faculty and students became regular visitors in the classrooms of the four teachers who worked with us, videotaping classroom activities, and interviewing teachers and students. This extensive direct presence in the classrooms was one way in which we hoped to expand upon Laughton's work, which had relied on interviews with teachers outside the context of classroom activity.

We initiated a series of bi-weekly project meetings involving the teachers, the university faculty, and the central graduate student researchers. The topics of these meetings through the spring of 1996 was always dominated by the ongoing collection of materials and observations from the classrooms. Although our interaction with the teachers became far more regular and intensive in this period, their role was largely the same as it had been from the start: they provided information and interpretations based on their domain expertise and in response to requests from us. The teachers remained very cooperative and responsive, but we had to actively prompt and evoke their expertise. Their primary concern seemed to be that we not diminish learning opportunities for their students. They were interested in the project, willing to talk about trying things out, as long as it did not distract from their "real" goals and needs too much.

In the spring of 1996, George Chin, a Virginia Tech graduate student at the time, conducted a series of structured interviews focused on the teachers' practices regarding collaborative activities and their initial attitudes towards the project.

Figure 2 presents responses of four teachers to one of the interview items that specifically queried their expectations about project roles. Even after more than a year of working with us to develop the NSF project, which centrally emphasized teachers as designers, and the need for participatory approaches to the design of educational technology, the teachers still felt that their role was chiefly to test, or to facilitate testing with students. This is particularly striking since two of these four teachers are the same people who worked with Laughton. They had already participated in the design, not merely the testing, of new educational technology.

A major and long-lived challenge during this stage in the project and in the teachers' development as designers was to convince them that we truly wanted their ideas and not merely their compliance. One issue was the establishment of trust and mutual understanding. In Figure 2, T4 clearly is suspicious about the project's true goals. T4's reaction can be dismissed as extreme, but it is important to recognize that this sort of reaction is awkward to articulate. Perhaps what is significant is that T4 was willing to say out loud what others might have felt and repressed. At the stage of practitioner-informant, in which the main role of the user is to provide domain information and expert interpretations, it is easy to mistake users who are just "going

Figure 2: Responses of Four Teachers to an Interview Question (Spring 1996)

Prior to the start of the project, what role did you anticipate for yourself on the LiNC project?
T1:   I think I was expecting to be more of a guinea pig – you build it and I test it – you pick my brain and leave.
T2:   I did not truly understand the LiNC project, but thought I would be asked to try out programs with my students written by tech people.
T3:   I thought the programs would be developed and we would test them with the students and evaluate them – make suggestions for changes if need be.
T4:   Initial expectations were to function as contact with students. I thought we'd be involved mostly with trial runs of software and possibly some data collection. The possibility that this was a double-blind experiment was also present.

along" with participatory design, for users who are truly engaged and committed to a collaboration.

A second, more prosaic issue was the development of skills that would support critical evaluation of design ideas. In the early stages of our collaboration, the teachers' stance with respect to design proposals can be summarized as positive, with some skepticism about feasibility and effectiveness. For example, they accepted the Marissa scenario (Figure 1) and our subsequent design proposal involving a shared lab notebook, but both their support for these ideas and the qualifications of that support were somewhat vague. In retrospect, it seems clear that the teachers were not able to use the textual descriptions to envision these proposals in their own context. None had had much relevant experience; they were tentative, uncertain, and intimidated. When they subsequently had the opportunity to experience the proposals in analysis exercises and classroom prototypes, they were able to critique and extend the design in specific ways.

Although the teachers' interaction with the university researchers was most salient to us, they were at the same time also developing working relationships with one another. We were surprised to learn that including two high school-level physics teachers in our project in effect included all the county's high school physics teachers: there were only two, and one taught physics only part time. No one in the school system had mentioned this to us during the development of the grant proposal. We were also surprised to find that most of the teachers had not worked closely before, and knew one another only casually. This is a further manifestation of our own initial naiveté with respect to the culture of schools.

The teachers exchanged perspectives on teaching styles and pedagogical objectives during the early months of the project. Indeed, this exchange became a central topic in the project as it became clear that it entailed the requirement that our software be sufficiently flexible to support a variety of teaching styles and strategies. More specifically, the teachers had differing perspectives on collaboration among teachers and their classes. None felt that such collaborations would be sufficiently easy for them to manage or beneficial for their students so as to be immediately self-justifying. To varying degrees and in varying ways, they were intrigued, but not fully convinced or committed to the vision in Figure 1.

Later, we learned that two of the teachers had been slightly coerced into joining our project by the school administration. In retrospect, it is hardly shocking to find that expert practitioners might not be chomping at the bit to join a technology development project whose objectives would have the effect of discombobulating their own established practices. Indeed, the ambivalence and tension the teachers felt is absolutely appropriate. What was unfortunate is that this issue remained submerged for the most part.

Powerful organizational forces impinged upon our participatory objectives from the start. Laughton's investigation was an independent research project; it was relatively small in scope and depended on the teachers' personal commitment, indeed on their personal time. Our NSF grant provided far better resources; it meant, for example, that part of the teachers' time was compensated. Although several teachers later remarked that this helped them to believe that their participation was really valued, it inevitably also diluted "pure" intrinsic motivation with material rewards. The larger, better-resourced project also had a greater scope and intensity of commitments and responsibilities, with more coordination and management overheads—schedules, dependencies, reminders, requests, meetings, and so on.

The grant comprised a legal relationship between Virginia Tech and the Montgomery County school division. Thus, the teachers, as well as the university faculty who were principal investigators, became institutional representatives and the work became official work. The management structure of National Science Foundation grants differentiates among "principal investigators," who have final financial and management responsibility; "co-principal investigators," who share in overall decision-making; and "investigators," who usually have narrower technical roles. The number of co-principal investigators is limited (usually to four). One school administrator was among our co-principal investigators; the teachers were classified as "investigators." In context, this is somewhat radical: teachers and administrators are often left out of grant management teams entirely.

However, our management structure reified a power structure in which the university faculty and one school administrator were the "principal investigators," with financial and technical management responsibility, and the teachers were "investigators" who reported to them. This relationship validated the assumption on the part of the teachers that they were supporting our effort, rather than collaborating in a shared endeavor. Indeed, making project activities part of the teachers' official work emphasized that their role was to meet expectations of the school administration. In our initial euphoria about having significant resources for the project, it was easy to underestimate the downsides of having such resources (Greene & Lepper, 1979).

THE ANALYST

In July 1996, we held a two-week workshop for all project members. One of the central objectives was to analyze the ethnographic data that had been collected during the preceding spring. In particular, we made a detailed analysis of several videotaped classroom interactions. As a group (four teachers, four human-computer interaction designers, four software technologists), we used claims analysis (Carroll & Rosson, 1992) to identify salient features in these scenarios, and the desirable and undesirable consequences of these features for students. This kind of work is exciting but demanding. It is directed brainstorming in which lines of causal reasoning are rapidly improvised, questioned, and refined. The teachers, of course, knew a lot already about classroom matters. However, they were not used to explicitly identifying tradeoffs for human activity in classroom situations. As one teacher commented: "It intruded on the way I design activities—I like to brainstorm and think out loud, [but] every time you say something, it gets analyzed." The teachers seemed exhausted after these sessions.

Nevertheless, the teachers were remarkably effective in these participatory analysis sessions. They were at least as productive as any other constituency in the project team at identifying teaching and learning issues, key situational features, and tradeoff relations in consequences for students. An example claims analysis is a discussion we had about student leadership in groups. We analyzed videotape of a group activity in which students measured kinetic energy for collisions involving model trains. One issue we identified was leadership style. We contrasted a consensus-building style, in which the leader ensures that all ideas are considered and enhances group dynamics and the self-esteem of members, with an individual initiative-taking style, which is efficient, challenging, and provides opportunities for group members to play leadership and supporting roles.

Our claims analysis identified upsides and downside consequences of each style, but focused on the efficiency of initiative-taking in group leadership. At this point in the discussion, the teachers emphasized that while task-oriented productivity is important, a more critical consideration is that all group members have the opportunity to hypothesize and test their individual ideas, and to participate fully in the group activity. This led to a more complete tradeoff analysis of student leadership, and had specific ramifications for issues of floor control and group formation in the virtual school environment.

In Figure 3, we have analyzed two days of the workshop during which a total of 32 features and 220 associated consequences were generated. We associated each claim feature and consequence with the participant who originally identified it. Of all the claim features generated, 48% originated from teachers. Of the consequences generated, 48% originated from teachers. The corresponding figures were lower for both the software technologists (12% and 13%, respectively) and for the human-computer interaction designers (36% and 34%, respectively; see Chin, Rosson & Carroll, 1997).

Figure 3: Contributions to Claims Analyses by Teachers, Software Technologists, and HCI Designers (from Chin et al., 1997)

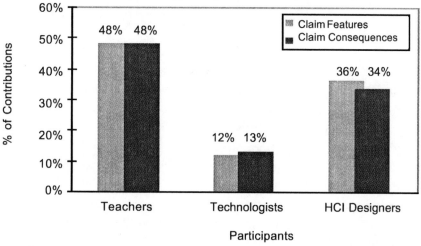

We also noticed that teachers were likely to contribute in the discussion of a claim schema even if a teacher did not originate the claim. We further examined the videotape to see for which features and consequences teachers had significant input. We considered a participant to have significant input if s/he originates, modifies, extends, or elaborates a feature or consequence. In the discussion of a lab notebook feature, for example, each teacher provided input into the discussion by describing how students use lab notebooks in his/her class. General discussions would often lead to a more rich and comprehensive view of the feature or consequence. From our evaluation, we found that teachers provided significant input to 88% of the features and 68% of the consequences (Chin, Rosson & Carroll, 1997).

One of the immediate and long-lasting changes in the project dynamics arising from the workshop was that the teachers became more active advocates for the importance of classroom situations. The teachers already believed that understanding and addressing real classroom issues was critical to the project, and recognized that they were in the best position to recognize and articulate these issues. What changed in the summer of 1996 is that they became far more willing to proactively share that perspective with other members of the project.

The only way to become an analyst is to analyze. In the workshop, we not only emphasized what we could see happening in a classroom activity, but also how we made sense of it. Teachers were confronted by a situation in which they had to transcend the role of informant, to make proposals about why some aspect of a learning situation might be good or bad. Analysts value the skills and knowledge of practitioner-informants, but at the same time it is the analysts who are in control; analysis, not raw data, drives design. By publicly objectifying their own knowledge in the workshop, the teachers appropriated the license not merely to testify about events in the classroom, but to make sense of those events with respect to the project's goals.

The teachers were even affected *as teachers* by this analytic work. For example, during the workshop, the teachers articulated some rationale for assigning students to groups—students with complementary skills and leadership styles can be grouped together, known personality conflicts can be avoided, natural mentoring relationships can be set up. Prior to this analytic work, the teachers had been quite relaxed about group formation, allowing students to choose their own partners (generally friends). However, in the year following the workshop, the teachers became much more proactive in creating groups, requesting and using online tools for group assignment.

Both informants and analysts must understand the problem domain. However, analysts must additionally understand the problem domain in the context of system capabilities. Through the course of the project, the teachers have learned a great deal about the various networking mechanisms incorporated in the virtual school software (text chat, video conferencing, whiteboards, email, Web pages, shared editors). Structured interviews indicated that through the first three years of the project, they also developed an understanding of how computer technology can be used to support their own teaching objectives, and of how students can remotely collaborate (Chin, in preparation).

In the fall of 1996, we designed and carried out a series of classroom collaborative activities. For example, middle school students at different schools used text chat, synchronous audio, and video teleconferencing to collaborate on a melting/freezing point experiment. Each group was given one of two possible substances; collaborating groups compared measurements from their lab experiments in an attempt to determine which group had received which substance. The teachers played a central role in conceiving of and analyzing these activities. For example, they identified the opportunity of pooling data as an appropriate and intrinsically motivating application of networking among classrooms in the virtual school. They led the analysis of how students' groups might use various networking mechanisms to collaborate in these activities.

This was a process of reflection-in-action (Schon, 1983): the teachers analyzed the technology by "auditioning" it in classroom activities. They tried to predict educational benefits and assess them by formulating activities involving sharing of data, equipment, and expertise.

THE DESIGNER

During the early spring of 1997, the teachers participated in a series of paper prototyping sessions. Scenario descriptions of classroom interactions were used as task-oriented representations that could help to articulate features of the learning environment. This was real design work that actually directed subsequent development of our virtual school software. For example, the teachers prototyped a milestone-tracking capability to help manage student groups. They developed the idea that teachers would provide templates in the collaborative notebook tool to convey assignments to students. They analyzed the problem of student and group authentication and developed a group-logon design. They also designed a folder scheme for partitioning student work. These contributions moved the teachers beyond the analyst role; they were not just articulating the problem, they were suggesting solutions.

In April of 1997, the teachers met on their own and formulated an approach to classroom activity design that they called "projects." They had concluded that the pedagogical value of the relatively brief and technology-oriented classroom activities investigated in Fall 1996 was too limited, that the overhead of initiating these activities was too high relative to their value. They urged a different approach for the 1997-98 school year, one involving activities that extended over several weeks, even months.

This episode is truly a turning point in the LiNC project. This is not because the teachers wanted to focus on long-term, rather than short-term activities; other members of the team also wanted to focus on more realistic activities, and on more ambitious activities that would drive our software ideas more vigorously. What is significant is that the teachers took the initiative to develop and articulate a central design concept to the group as a whole, and that this design concept entailed more responsibility and more work *for them*. There is no way to see their proposal as less than fundamental to the project's design strategy. Rather than responding to our visions (e.g., Figure 1), they were contributing a vision; rather than agreeing to a workplan, they were providing a strategy for the workplan. Perhaps most importantly, through this episode, the teachers embraced the virtual school as a major tool in their own pedagogical planning. This sharply contrasts with the earlier principle of cooperating as long as the project did not diminish learning opportunities for their students.

The teachers' transition to activity designers in the project was a sharp punctuation in the project's course of development. After this point, the teachers regularly met as a subgroup within the larger project. Their efforts to understand one another's teaching styles and pedagogical objectives became far more pointed and considered, as they tried to develop an integrated curriculum with common objectives, timing, scale, and grading. It was understood that the design of the classroom activities belonged to them, and that this was the primary source of requirements for the software design efforts. To a great extent, the teachers' planning drove other aspects of project activity.

The teachers' paper prototype design work was scaffolded in the sense that their efforts were supported and guided by experienced software designers on the project team. Nevertheless, the ideas came from the teachers. When this design was subsequently presented to the full project team, there was a spirited discussion of the specific features that had been proposed. Afterward, the teachers felt their design had been attacked, that they were put on the defensive. This is not a positive result; designers should not be defensive about their proposals, and their colleagues should be careful to avoid making them feel defensive. But what is equally notable is that the teachers felt ownership of the design, and wanted to defend it. They became embroiled in the typical give and take of design work.

Prior to this point, the teachers, as designers, had been coddled to some extent. Their ideas and perspectives were received with gratitude, generally in design sessions designated for teacher input, like the paper prototyping sessions. After this point, the teachers were treated much more normally; they neither received nor seemed to need or want special handling.

This has led to a productively eclectic design framework. Some members of our project start from architectural considerations about collaborative software, albeit constrained by classroom activity requirements and overall deign concepts. Some start from scenarios of project interactions for individual students and groups. The teachers, as designers, tend to start from classroom activities, pedagogical objectives, curriculum plans, and so on. What is true now, and was less true in the past, is that we are able to move convergently towards common goals from these diverse starting points. A key factor seems to be that even though different people take different approaches and represent different knowledge and skill, everyone understands everyone else well enough to see how we complement one another, and how things can fit together.

During the 1997-98 school year, the teachers introduced various innovative classroom activities. In one activity high school and middle school students collaborated on the design of a robot; the middle school students designed a grasping arm, and the high school students designed a mobile base. Many of these longer-term projects involved the development of mentoring relationships by community members in areas such as the optics of photography, mechanics in the context of amusement parks, the astrophysics of black holes, the engineering principles of bridge building, and the aerodynamics of kites and model planes. In some cases, the mentoring was carried out using combinations of video conferencing, email, and chat, raising many issues for our developing virtual school software, and indeed even for the concept of what the virtual school is intended to be. Our original concept had not developed the concept of community participation in the schools, but the teachers' initiatives helped to re-emphasize this theme in the project throughout the year.

The software we developed strongly reflects the design concepts championed by the teachers. Our original plan emphasized support for high-bandwidth, real-time interactions; our vision was of a graphically enhanced multi-user domain. Early development work focused on creating a shared whiteboard that would allow students to collaborate on simulation experiments (e.g., Koenemann, Carroll, Shaffer, Rosson & Abrams, 1999). However, the teachers' emphasis on long-term projects led us to reweigh goals having to do with maintaining work context. Our current virtual school is a Java-based networked learning environment, emphasizing support for the *coordination* of synchronous and asynchronous collaboration, including planning, note taking, experimentation, data analysis, and report writing (Isenhour, Carroll, Neale, Rosson & Dunlap, 2000). The central tool is a collaborative notebook that allows students to organize projects into shared and personal pages; it can be accessed collaboratively or individually by remote or proximal students.

In July 1998, the teachers circulated a detailed specification for a fall collaboration activity, which would last for two weeks, and which would orient students to the virtual school software; this would be followed by a long-term project, which would run from mid-November through late April. In retrospect, this phased use of the virtual school can be seen as a sophisticated response to the ongoing software development process. Through the summer, the overall system had been coming together, and the teachers knew we expected them to use it in their classrooms. Yet at the same time, they felt the need to scaffold their use of the software, to be certain that it would effectively support curricular activities.

The specification of major classroom activities for the 1998-99 school year was generated entirely by the teachers, and included several specific new functions they needed in order to carry out the planned activities (see Figure 4). For example, the teachers described an "info" button for the collaborative notebook; the button would open a browser on teacher-defined help for using the notebook in the current project. They described a bibliography tool as a notebook page with fields, supporting entry of various sorts of reference materials, as well as student notes derived from the references. They described a planner tool as a notebook page displaying project checkpoints and due dates. The teachers also requested software support to allow students (and teachers) to access the virtual school from home.

The teachers described a "message" tool for the collaborative notebook that could be used to attach comments to notebook pages. The tool would be used to approve student work (that is, to convey to groups that they were on track) as well as to answer student queries. It would also convey at a glance to other teachers that a given notebook page had been approved. The teachers were explicit that they would grade student projects as a team and trust one another's assessments. Even planning to try such an arrangement is quite radical from the standpoint of the culture of schools (Dunlap, Neale & Carroll, 2000).

We are still in the midst of evaluating the software and activity design outcomes of the LiNC project, a complex matter in itself (Gibson, Neale, Carroll & VanMetre, 1999; Neale & Carroll, 1999). However, our design method objectives have been achieved. The teachers all function now as ordinary members of the design team. They are empowered and feel that they have both the capabilities and the right to participate in all facets of design work. One teacher recently summarized this:

"Actually, my role in LiNC has been much more than I expected. I like feeling like I am an expert at something and that my experience is valued. I like feeling comfortable talking to all other players as equals. I like to truly collaborate and I like to be treated with respect. Finally, I like honesty even if I disagree."

This is precisely what we wanted to achieve. It is not a state of user buy-in, but a state of mutual respect and engagement.

Figure 4: General Functionality and Specific Features Introduced by Teachers through their Design Scenarios

General Functionality	Specific Features
• long-term projects • mentoring by members of the community • integration of synchronous and asynchronous collaborative work • interaction with virtual school from home as well as school	• assignment templates presented as notebook pages • info button providing access to teacher-generated help • structured editor for bibliography entries • planning page with project checkpoints and due dates • teacher comment tool

THE COACH

In August of 1997, the LiNC group organized a training program for middle and high school science and mathematics teachers throughout the Montgomery County school division; this effort was supported by the federal Eisenhower Teacher Development Program administered in Virginia by the State Council of Higher Education. Twelve teachers spent two weeks learning about various networking communication and collaboration mechanisms, and developing ideas and materials for using these resources in their classrooms. The university faculty and graduate students from our project helped to organize and run the training program as lecturers and coaches; indeed, the program proposal we wrote assumed that the teaching would be handled by the university faculty and graduate students (as is typical for the Eisenhower program).

As we planned the Eisenhower program, the four teachers in the LiNC project assumed more and more responsibility for various aspects. They began by coordinating plans and schedules among the 12 teachers, who after all were their colleagues. Soon though, the teachers were added to the program schedule, to share personal classroom experiences from the preceding school year. Finally, their role expanded to include coaching the other teachers during the Eisenhower program, and managing the year-long follow-up program during the 1997-1998 school year.

This was not a deliberate plan, though perhaps it should have been. The teachers were clearly able to inspire their colleagues. And they also seemed to benefit from the exercise of externalizing and reconstructing their experience in order to convey it to others. This put them in the interesting role of helping other teachers embark on the same journey they themselves had taken. Participating in the Eisenhower workshop as technology specialists, facilitators, and coaches, and ultimately as organizers, allowed the LiNC teachers to more vividly appreciate their own development, to reflect upon their new expertise, their changed skills and practices as teachers.

The highest stage of intellectual development in Piaget's developmental theory is the formal operational stage in which people reflect upon their own thinking processes (Piaget & Inhelder, 1969). Coaching others is a natural way to evoke reflection on one's experience. As the teachers assumed responsibility for the training and development of their colleagues, they considered their use of collaborative technologies, and of LiNC tools in particular. In the two-and-a-half years since the Eisenhower program, there are many examples of the teachers becoming leaders within the Montgomery County schools.

For example, the teachers have helped to recruit and train new teachers for the LiNC project. One veteran teacher (interestingly the one who was least experienced with technology at the outset of the LiNC project) has formed a partnership with two other teachers. In a group discussion in the spring of 1999 (a Web-forum; Carroll, Neale & Isenhour, 2000), this teacher argued that the time had come for the teachers to take even more responsibility in developing new activities. Subsequently, she identified a set of new activities she felt would be good candidates for collaborative learning (involving lego constructions), and organized the effort to select and design classroom projects, place materials in virtual school notebooks, and carry out an extensive long-term collaboration during the 1999-2000 school year. Such teacher autonomy is essential to the sustainability of collaboration infrastructures like the virtual school, and indeed it is precisely the kind of outcome one almost never sees in educational technology interventions.

Another veteran teacher initiated contacts with another Virginia school division (Giles County), arranging an activity in which his students would use the virtual school's collaborative notebooks to mentor writing projects of younger students. We went along to the meetings and agreed to play a supportive role, but it was clearly the case that this initiative would have gone forward with or without us. The teacher, at this point, needs only the tools to implement his designs.

To operate at the coach level, people need to see beyond particular applications; they must appreciate the patterns of utility that motivate *types* of examples. Many teachers interested in classroom computing are familiar with word processors and web browsers, and can make creative use of these. However, few are familiar with the potential of computers as collaborative systems. Some of the new teachers joining the LiNC project were sophisticated with respect to the educational potential of multimedia, film, virtual museums, and graphics, but did not readily grasp the value of advanced communication tools and integrated collaboration. The veteran LiNC teachers do see this underlying pattern, which enables them to innovate and lead as coaches. This willingness and ability to conceive of new applications is a critical step in sustainability of a technology infrastructure and systemic reform of practices (as in educational reform). It shows that users have truly appropriated the technology as their own. This creative adaptation can be seen as the highest level of development.

Several of the teachers expressed interest in writing their own grants to continue aspects of the LiNC project. In Fall 1999, two teachers, one of the veteran teachers and one of the new teachers, submitted two proposals. Figure 5 summarizes the timeline of the LiNC project, indicating the approximate span of each stage.

Figure 5: Timeline of the LiNC Project

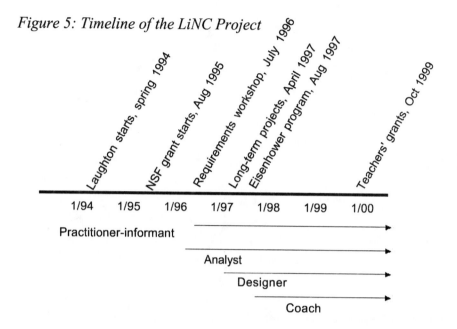

TRANSITIONS BETWEEN STAGES

Developmental theory explains transitions between stages as resolutions of conflict. Thus, the pre-operational child's conflicting perceptions of quantity based on single dimensions, such as height and width, are resolved in the abstraction of quantity as an invariant in the concrete operational stage. For development to take place, the child must have attained the requisite competencies to experience the triggering conflict, and then be able to reconceptualize the situation in such a way that the conflict dissolves.

This analytical schema seems to fit the transitions between the stages of cooperation we have described. The general mechanism seems to be that successive increases in knowledge, skill, and confidence empowered the teachers to resolve conflicts, by assuming successively greater scope of action and responsibility in the project. In the July 1996 workshop, the teachers faced the conflict that their pedagogical concerns and perspectives would be adequately represented and fully considered by the group only if they themselves represented those concerns. This went beyond the role they had played in the project up to then. But they were both motivated and competent to resolve this conflict by assuming the analyst role in the project.

Once the teachers were functioning as analysts in the project team, further conflicts and resolutions arose. In Spring 1997, the teachers experienced a conflict between their own analyses of requirements, and the current state of the virtual school software and development plans. They resolved these conflicts by formulating their own design proposals, ultimately a radical reorientation of the project's vision of classroom activity. Subsequently, the teachers recognized that they were the best qualified project members to administer the Eisenhower program, and more recently, that they are best qualified to pursue specific curricular extensions of the LiNC project.

The teachers' behavior also reflects development *within* the four general stages we have described. For example, during the requirements analysis workshop, scaffolding (examples, reflective prompts) was needed to engage the teachers in the novel and abstract activity of claims analysis. But as the project progressed, teachers spontaneously presented claims as a way to articulate personal positions, and frequently identified "upsides" or "downsides" as part of our design discussions. This of course is quite consonant with the general notion of learning as movement through a zone of proximal development (Vygotzky, 1978).

The designer stage also reflects several different levels of development. Initially, the teachers were able to collaborate with a research assistant in focused design sessions, co-writing scenarios of technology-mediated activities for their classroom. Later they banded together as a subgroup, pooling their goals and expertise to develop a scenario that specified a new vision of collaborative learning activities. Ultimately, each learned to function as an independent designer, with the result that they can now envision and specify activities optimized for their own teaching styles, objectives, and classroom environments. In their coach role, the teachers again worked first as a group in the Eisenhower workshop, but have now begun to recruit and mentor colleagues in a 1:1 fashion.

In sum, it appears that the transitions among stages were triggered by conflicts with respect to the teachers' role in the project. In each case, a series of scaffolded activities enabled them to attain the knowledge, skill, and confidence that led them to expand their role.

One natural follow-on question is whether and how the developmental process we described could be accelerated. Must it take five years for technologists to work effectively with teachers? In the case of cognitive development, the timing of stage transitions cannot be altered substantially because the capacities for resolving the triggering conflicts depend on brain development; in other words, they are governed by sequencing of physical development. In our case, the relevant capacities are not biological, but they are quite fundamental. Trust, empathy, and commitment are critical, and cannot be manufactured; they emerge from significant shared experience—joy and insight, as well as confrontation of external threats and resolution of interpersonal conflicts.

Some things we did more or less inadvertently, or at least intuitively, seemed to facilitate teachers' development as autonomous members of the project team. For example, at the outset of the project, one student research assistant took the initiative to identify and articulate teacher concerns to the rest of the group. This clearly helped the teachers to assume this role for themselves. A further technique we think might have been useful, but which we did not employ, would be to designate a "lead teacher." Especially in the early stages of the project, teacher concerns might have come to light too slowly because no one was specifically designated as responsible for representing those concerns to other constituencies.

Further efficiencies are definitely possible. We believe that we could accelerate the practitioner-informant stage by at least one year, and possibly a year-and-a-half. However, we are concerned that further compression would compromise the coordination of participatory and ethnographically driven approaches to requirements development—to a great extent a project such as this is tied to the natural rhythms of the school year. Other stages could be structured more deliberately, to ensure that teachers attain prerequisite competencies, and that they directly encounter and resolve role conflicts. In the LiNC project, the transitions among states was more or less organically driven by project needs, and by our evolving ideas for how to broaden the framework for participatory development. But trusting fortune in exploratory technology development can be bumpy: we believe that with experience, long-term projects can be managed to better align project needs and human development opportunities, as a sort of workplace "curriculum." We can imagine an overall speed up on the order of a factor of two.

We see this case analysis as positive and hopeful. If technologists and teachers can cooperate more effectively, can develop the knowledge, skills, and sensibilities to combine their different expertise more successfully, perhaps educational technology can become more effective. Perhaps it can have a more positive and profound impact on education. Other recent work seems to support similar themes. Davies (1991) describes the importance of teachers working together to articulate and analyze new strategies for schooling—and receiving stipends for their research efforts. Krasnow (1990) describes the new thinking and reflection produced in schools by empowering teacher-researchers. Shields (1994) emphasizes that research should study comprehensive relationships among parents, communities, and schools, as opposed to quantifying piecemeal relationships (like the correlation between test scores and parental attendance on school council). Wadsworth (1997) emphasizes that the engagement of parents, teachers, and community takes place through action—agreeing on needs, committing to actions, and reporting results, not through new ways to talk about problems.

LESSONS LEARNED

We originally committed to a long-term participatory design method because we conjectured that such an approach would be appropriate, if not crucial, for success in this educational technology setting. This appears to have been correct. We believe we could not have succeeded to the extent we have, had we not made this commitment. Working from the national agenda for school reform, educational technology, and science education (American Association for the Advancement of Science, 1993; Goals 2000: Educate America Act, 1994; National Science Teachers Association, 1992) and from our own vision of a virtual school (Figure 1), we would have built the wrong system, we would not have had effective support from teachers, and little or nothing would have been sustained after the initial project funding ended.

Participatory design is fundamentally a process of mutual learning, and thus of personal development for participants. But it is often exemplified by rather singular and ephemeral learning interactions. Our study expands the scope of the design participants' personal development by examining a case of long-term cooperative design interaction, and by describing a developmental sequence of roles with constituent capacities and responsibilities.

Much research on participatory design has focused on relatively short-term collaborative relationships. This is especially true in North America; for example, the well-known PICTIVE technique is directed at brief user interface design interactions of perhaps one hour (Muller, 1992). Such methods are both effective and democratic, but it seems unlikely that the experience of manipulating a user interface mock-up during a brief participatory session can have a significant developmental effect on a person's knowledge, skills, self-confidence, or other professional capacities.

Our case study is different in that user interface design per se has been a secondary issue. We have used brief participatory exercises since 1994, but this level of engagement is more a starting point than the objective of our work. More specifically, we wanted the teachers to have a significant voice in designing the functionality and the use of the virtual school, not merely its appearance. We needed to learn about pedagogical goals and practices, classroom management, school system politics, the relationship of community and the schools, and so forth.

Where participatory design investigations *have* focused on longer-term interactions, chiefly in Europe, these often involve extremely well-organized user groups with well-defined roles and prerogatives in the design process. In many cases, the users are represented by labor unions whose personnel provide legal representation of user interests in the design process. In these cases there is sometimes a clear demarcation, even conflict, between the user (union) interests and management's technology strategy. Indeed, this is an important element of the context for many of these studies. Because the user role in many of these studies is both specified a priori and representative (versus individual), the personal development of user-designers is not a central issue. These case studies also typically involve situations in which the development and deployment of new information technology is a given, and the challenge is to define appropriate technology for the users and their activities (Bødker, Ehn, Kammersgaard, Kyng & Sundblad, 1987).

In the educational domain, the deployment of new information technology is far from a given. Indeed, the introduction of new technology has historically almost always failed in school settings. One of the key questions for us was whether a concept for appropriate technological support could be developed at all.

The users in our domain are very loosely organized. As mentioned earlier, teachers traditionally work in isolation from peers; they manage their own work practices and environments (classrooms). The notion of "user community" in this domain is almost ironic. Teachers' unions in the U.S. are also extremely weak, and play no role in the introduction of classroom technology. Indeed, school administrations in the U.S. rarely have technology strategies at all. Thus, unlike the European case studies, the issue is almost never one of recognized conflict, but rather finding a direction at all.

The teachers in our team do not represent other teachers; they are individuals who, as members of our team, have become teacher-designers. This is precisely why their personal development as designers is a central issue in our study. Of course, we do hope that they are representative teachers—allowing us to generalize our investigation to other teachers participating in similar development projects—but this is a separate issue. The point is that in our project, and unlike many long-term participatory design efforts in Europe, the teachers act as individual professionals, just as university researchers do.

An interesting aspect of the teachers and their development is that the four original teachers are now among the most senior members of the LiNC team: only the two faculty participants have also been part of the project from the start, with students and post-docs joining and participating for shorter periods of time. Undoubtedly this has increased the teachers' sense of expertise and confidence, as they have seen numerous issues and ideas raised, addressed, incorporated, or discarded. More importantly, perhaps, they have seen these issues play out *in the context of their own work.* Thus these four individuals own a central element of the LiNC project's organizational memory—the activities of the classroom.

The stages we have described here are specific to our project; they emerged through specific things that we did, and are rooted in the specific goals of our project. At the same time, they suggest a schematic program for developing cooperative engagement more generally. Most participatory design work engages users at the practitioner-informant stage. This would seem to be an obvious and general starting point for any participatory design collaboration. In our project, the teachers transitioned to the analyst stage through their inclusion in a requirements analysis workshop and a significant process of iterative requirements development (Carroll, Rosson, Chin & Koenemann, 1998). This is perhaps not typical of participatory design practice, but it is a modest extension. Nevertheless, the teachers found it quite stimulating to be invited to objectify their own experience, to dissect it and not merely describe it.

CONCLUSIONS AND DIRECTIONS

In the fall of 1994, we created an envisionment scenario (Figure 1) that helped us win a large federal grant and energized local teachers with whom we shared it. But it did not address all of the relevant requirements and described what we later realized was the wrong system. The participatory process we engaged in allowed us to understand further requirements and to create a better system. Achieving the quality of participation required took time and effort, but was worth it.

Teachers' work is "invisible" in the sense that their work organizations (their school divisions) do not explicitly analyze its nature or support (Suchman, 1995). However, teaching is even more invisible than that of the legal personnel studied by Suchman, because it is only very loosely coupled to organizational workflow. As emphasized by Tyack and Cuban (1995), it is difficult for anyone to see what is happening in a given classroom. The personal control inherent in teachers' work is what makes participation in technology development so important. It is not just a matter of accurately describing the work, or even of designing appropriate support; the teachers also must accept and deploy "appropriate" solutions. When users have total discretion throughout the entire development cycle, a long-term participatory approach is essential.

We are planning further projects in a variety of community areas – developing networked access to a local natural history museum, support for new kinds of citizen participation in town government, and a regional approach to teacher professional development.

ACKNOWLEDGMENTS
We are grateful to Kathy Bunn, Laura Byrd, Peggy Davie, Jim Eales, Mark Freeman, Craig Ganoe, Alison Goforth, Jürgen Koenemann, Stuart Laughton,

Suzan Mauney, and Fred Rencsok for bringing such energy and creativity to the LiNC project. This work was partially supported by the Hitachi Foundation and the National Science Foundation (REC-9554206 and DGE-9553458). An earlier version of this chapter appeared in the *Proceedings of ACM DIS 2000* (Carroll, Chin, Rosson & Neale, 2000). Chin's current address is Battelle Pacific Northwest National Laboratory, P.O. Box 999, Richland, WA 99352.

REFERENCES

American Association for the Advancement of Science. (1993). *Benchmarks for Science Literacy*. New York: Oxford University Press.

Bentley, R., Hughes, J. A., Randall, D., Rodden, T., Sawyer, P., Shapiro, D. and Sommerville, I. (1992). Ethnographically informed systems design for air traffic control. In *Proceedings of CSCW '92*, 123-129. Toronto, Canada, October 31-November 4. New York: ACM Press.

Bødker, S., Ehn, P., Kammersgaard, J., Kyng, M. and Sundblad, Y. (1987). A utopian experience. In Bjerknes, G., Ehn, P. and Kyng, M. (Eds.), *Computers and Democracy: A Scandinavian Challenge*, 251-278. Brookfield, VT: Avebury.

Carroll, J. M. (Ed.). (1995). *Scenario-Based Design: Envisioning Work and Technology in System Development*. New York: John Wiley.

Carroll, J. M. (2000). *Making Use: Scenario-Based Design of Human-Computer Interactions*. Cambridge, MA: MIT Press.

Carroll, J. M., Chin, G., Rosson, M. B. and Neale, D. C. (2000). The development of cooperation: Five years of participatory design in the virtual school. In Boyarski, D. and Kellogg, W. (Eds.), *DIS'2000: Designing Interactive Systems*, 239-251. Brooklyn, New York, August 17-19. New York: Association for Computing Machinery.

Carroll, J. M., Neale, D. C. and Isenhour, P. L. (Submitted). *The Collaborative Critical Incident Tool: Supporting Reflection and Evaluation in a Web Community*.

Carroll, J. M. and Rosson, M. B. (1992). Getting around the task-artifact cycle: How to make claims and design by scenario. *ACM Transactions on Information Systems*, 10(2), 181-212.

Carroll, J. M., Rosson, M. B., Chin, G. and Koenemann, J. (1998). Requirements development in scenario-based design. *IEEE Transactions on Software Engineering*, 24(12), 1-15.

Chin, G. (In Preparation). *A Methodology for Integrating Ethnography, Scenarios, and Participatory Design*. PhD Dissertation, Computer Science Department, Virginia Tech, Blacksburg, VA.

Chin, G., Rosson, M. B. and Carroll, J. M. (1997). Participatory analysis: Shared development of requirements from scenarios. In *Proceedings of*

CHI'97: Conference on Human Factors in Computing Systems, 162-169. New York: ACM.

Cuban, L. (1986). *Teachers and Machines*. New York: Teachers College Press.

Davies, D. (1991). Schools reaching out: Family, school, and community partnerships for student success. *Phi Delta Kappan*, January, 72, 376-382.

Dunlap, D. R., Neale, D. C. and Carroll, J. M. (2000). Teacher collaboration in a networked community. *Educational Technology and Society*, 3(3), 442-454.

Gibson, S., Neale, D. C., Carroll, J. M. and VanMetre, C. A. (1999). Mentoring in a school environment. In *Proceedings of CSCL'99: Computer Supported Cooperative Learning*, 182-188. Mahwah, NJ: Lawrence Erlbaum.

Goals 2000: Educate America Act. (1994). Retrieved from the World Wide Web: http://www.ed.gov/CommInvite/.

Greene, D. and Lepper, M. R. (Eds.) (1979). *The Hidden Costs of Reward*. Hillsdale, NJ: Erlbaum.

Greenbaum, J. and Kyng, M. (Eds.). (1991). *Design at Work: Cooperative Design of Computer Systems*. Hillsdale, NJ: Erlbaum.

Hodas, S. (1993). Technology refusal and the organizational culture of schools. *Educational Policy Analysis Archives*, 1(10).

Isenhour, P. L., Carroll, J. M., Neale, D. C., Rosson, M. B. and Dunlap, D. R. (2000). The virtual school: An integrated collaborative environment for the classroom. *Educational Technology and Society*, 3(3), 74-86.

Koenemann, J., Carroll, J. M., Shaffer, C. A., Rosson, M. B. and Abrams, M. (1999). Designing collaborative applications for classroom use: The LiNC Project. In Druin, A. (Ed.), *The Design of Children's Technology*, 99-122. San Francisco, CA: Morgan-Kaufmann.

Krasnow, J. (1990). Building new parent-teacher partnerships: Teacher researcher teams stimulate reflection. *Equity and Choice*, Spring, 25-31.

Laughton, S. (1996). *The Design and Use of Internet-Mediated Communication Applications in Education: An Ethnographic Study*. PhD Dissertation, Computer Science Department, Virginia Tech, Blacksburg, VA.

Muller, M. J. (1992). Retrospective on a year of participatory design using the PICTIVE technique. In *Proceedings of CHI'92: Conference on Human Factors in Computing Systems*, 455-462. New York: ACM.

Muller, M. J., Haslwanter, J. H. and Dayton, T. (1997). Participatory practices in the software lifecycle. In Helander, M., Landauer, T. K. and Prabhu, P. (Eds.), *Handbook of Human-Computer Interaction* (2nd Ed.), 255-297. Amsterdam: Elsevier.

National Science Teachers Association. (1992). *Scope, Sequence and Coordination of Secondary School Science, Volume 1: The Content Core*. Washington, DC: National Science Teachers Association.

Neale, D. C. and Carroll, J. M. (1999). Multi-faceted evaluation for complex, distributed activities. In *Proceedings of CSCL '99: Computer-Supported Cooperative Learning*, 425-433. Mahwah, NJ: Lawrence Erlbaum.

Piaget, J. and Inhelder, B. (1969). *The Psychology of the Child*. New York: Basic Books.

Schon, D. A. (1983). *The Reflective Practitioner*. New York: Basic Books.

Shields, P. M. (1994). Bringing schools and communities together in preparation for the 21st century: Implications for the current educational reform movement for family and community involvement policies. In *Systemic Reform—Perspectives on Personalizing Education*, September.

Schuler, D. and Namioka, A. (Eds.). (1993). *Participatory Design: Principles and Practices*. Hillsdale, NJ: Erlbaum.

Suchman, L. A. (1995). Making work visible. *Communications of the ACM*, 38(9), 56-64.

Tyack, D. and Cuban, L. (1995). *Tinkering Toward Utopia: A Century of Public School Reform*. Cambridge, MA: Harvard University Press.

Vygotsky, L. S. (1978). *Mind in Society*. Cambridge, MA: Harvard University Press.

Wadsworth, D. (1997). Building a strategy for successful public engagement. *Phi Delta Kappan*, 78(10), 749-752.

Williams, M. G. (1994). Enabling school teachers to participate in the design of educational software. In *Proceedings of PDC '94*, 153-157.

Chapter VI

Cybercamp: A University/ Community Partnership for Universal Empowerment

Steven Hawley
Wright State University, USA

There is an ever-growing need for technology training for the many stakeholders (teachers and students) in our schools. There is an abyss created by technology, which is a medium that is moving forward rapidly within an institution that is bound by tradition. In this chapter, the reader is introduced to a program called Cybercamp, a means to bridge the abyss by having the producers and consumers of education build a bridge together. A partnership between the University of Cincinnati and numerous community organizations is presented, which provides for universal empowerment through technology training.

INTRODUCTION

Cybercamp was the result of work begun by two individuals from a university and a public school technology cooperative to address technology and its deployment toward the goal of universal access. In this chapter, you will meet the two individuals who developed this idea, understand their motives and feel their excitement as the entire approach became implemented. In addition, the existing conditions and the infrastructure required for the partnership are also presented, to help the reader who is interested in forming similar partnerships. We believe that technology in the schools is in reality a partnership between the students and the teachers. An interesting quote describes this:

"The test of a good teacher is not how many questions he can ask his pupils that they will answer readily, but how many questions he inspires them to ask him, which he finds it hard to answer."
(Rollins, 1997)

Since the 1960s, when universities had utilized computers for research, the proliferation of technology was restricted to large institutions that could afford the cost of implementation: business, government and universities. In the 1980s, primary and secondary schools were experimenting with technology, but wide-scale deployment was expensive and required more staff, something that was a luxury for most public and private schools. Two things occurred in the late 1980s-early 1990s. The personal computer became powerful enough to allow individuals to be able to effectively process information without being connected to a large mainframe-type computer. Computer networks such as the Internet, as well as network-based software, allowed for the sharing of information across the world in an inexpensive way. Information that was localized could now be shared with everyone. What was exclusive could potentially become inclusive.

The application of computer technology in schools had frequently begun as a series of programming courses for talented students taught by mathematics teachers. When software applications changed to allow "anyone" to manipulate a template to write (word processing), compute (spreadsheet), organize data (database) or present information (hypermedia), the mystery of technology had been changed to a mastery of tools to present information.

THE NEED FOR TRAINING

The learners became the learned when it came to technology. When it came to technology, students frequently had an insatiable desire to master the unknown, unlimited amounts of time and no fear of making mistakes. In some cases, the students became more familiar with the technology than the teachers. However, the level of familiarity with the technology was related to the level of access that students had to the technology. Students at schools in more economically advantaged areas might have access through school. Students from more economically advantaged families might have access to technology at home. However, the dream of universal access to technology was just a dream.

Schools realized that the use of new technology and the Internet could serve as a renaissance for learning because of the accessibility to vast stores of knowledge and its acquisition. The belief was that if students were exposed to a variety of different resources, they would be more successful. Teachers who were willing to unlock the vagaries and mysteries of the computer were rewarded with teaching assignments that allowed them to work with students and unparalleled responsibilities for managing technology in school systems with little or limited compensation initially. The reward was access to the latest technology and software.

However, the unfolding scenario did not lead to widespread training of the rest of the educational staff at any level: elementary, secondary or college and university. Those who already had access and were willing to spend the time reaped the rewards. However, training was frequently lacking. The cost of technology acquisition was very expensive, and frequently schools could not afford training. Even when technology training was provided, there was a large resistance to change in the school systems. For instance: "The Houston Independent School District, for example, during the mid-1980s provided an intensive, three-hundred-hour teacher training course in the effective use of technology....Yet graduates of the program...(experienced teachers) who practiced what they learned actually got negative grades on a new state-imposed teacher evaluation instrument that values 'teaching' according to the ability to stand in front of the blackboard and talk, rather than the ability...to employ modern, student-centered tools" (Perelman, 1992). Thus, the belief that the use of technology as one more tool to promote learning did not always "fit" into the existing patterns of teaching and instruction and the resulting organizational culture in the school systems.

The marketplace expanded with computer games that brought young people to the television screen for hundreds of hours to explore fictional landscapes and environments and to work on their fine motor skills to manipulate their pieces on a television screen. They could become empowered by mastery of vicarious experiences that allowed them to make independent decisions over time. The response from education was to decry this phenomenon as a harmful substitute to being outside to get more physical exercise and spending more time with parents, both of whom were working in ever-increasing numbers to sustain a meaningful standard of living.

Young people moved into the computer world to learn about how to access it and make it their own. Electronic mail and chat rooms made individuals accessible through their minds and their ability to communicate. No longer were they identifiable first by their skin color, ethnic background, or other physical characteristics. They could reveal themselves as they wished.

"What attracts me to the computer are the possibilities of 'conversation' among the multiple windows on my screen and the way an instantly responsive machine allays my anxieties about perfection. But other people are drawn by other sirens. Some are captured by virtual worlds that appear to be unsullied by the messiness of the real. Some are enthralled by the sense of mind-building-mind or merging with the mind of the computer. If one is afraid of intimacy yet afraid of being alone, even a stand-alone (not networked) computer offers an apparent solution. Interactive and reactive, the computer offers the illusion of companionship without the demands of friendship. One can be a loner yet never be alone." (Turkle, 1995)

Self-empowerment was possible in a landscape where the possession of knowledge was power, something that youth had seen adult generations do in different ways in their daily lives.

In summary, the use of technology expanded the horizons of young people who, in their zeal to learn, accepted the challenge of mastery. There was a cost to implementing technology but the greater cost was the time and willingness it would take for existing leaders and educators to master the resource so that it would be suitable for the effective inclusion of technology into the curriculum. This would be greatly enhanced by the community's demand of schools to address the acquisition of information that existed in many workplaces. However, educational leaders at all levels had difficulty realizing that what they were addressing was an expanding, ever-changing phenomenon, unlike the purchase of a book which is then used for several years. The latter is easier to manage.

CURRENTLY EXISTING INFRASTRUCTURE

The expansion of knowledge acquisition through technology brought about many efforts to develop plans to shape and manage it. Many of the plans incorporated the main concept of the Internet: the sharing of resources. When resources are shared, one becomes empowered to the degree that one shares what one has with someone else so that the synergy results in greater knowledge and more widespread application and personal networking. However, managing such sharing can be a challenge. Furthermore, the costs of acquiring the technology was a roadblock. In many cases, public and private education did not have the resources that business and industry had, so technology would be implemented slower to these learners. Since education is a guaranteed right of state government, the education establishment sought to have funding devoted to this initiative. These initial efforts built on existing initiatives within the educational marketplace.

A Preliminary Effort for Collaboration

One effort for coordination was the Ohio Valley Network. The Ohio Valley Network (OV-NET) is a group of agencies (e.g., data acquisition sites, colleges and universities, cable providers, educational television stations, freenets) in Southwestern Ohio who were working together to establish universal access to the information infrastructure highway. This group was founded in December of 1993 to bring together agencies with a common agenda to increase connectivity and to share resources to save money (Ohio Valley Network, 1994). The Ohio Valley Network was a fledgling effort originally brought about by a salesperson of a large computer hardware company. He realized that the institutions (colleges, universities, data acquisition sites) that are listed above all were his clients and that technology was set to expand at an exponential rate with the Internet. There had been a federal mandate to address universal access to technology for all families across the United States from President Clinton. It would manifest itself in the creation and implementation of the Universal Service Fund, which was passed as a part of the Telecommunication Act of 1996 (P.L. 104-104). This service fund would help defray the costs of schools, libraries and rural health care institutions connecting to the Internet (Lazar and Norcio, 2000). Because of these changes in the policy environment, more coordination between these community organizations would be helpful.

In 1979, the State of Ohio had created a system of 24 networked regional sites for the Department of Education to provide school districts with mainframe capabilities to process student and financial data. These regional sites were called data acquisition sites and had mainframe computers available to process large amounts of information for the 614 school districts across the state. In addition, the colleges and universities in the region had their own disparate networks related to their internal specialties and needs. At the time, cable providers were looking to expand into new markets. Educational television stations offered resources to schools and needed a new direction. Freenets, community networks that provided resources to people free of charge, were in place at this time in larger cities (e.g., Cleveland, Columbus, Dayton) to share community resources. A plan was drawn up by the OV-NET group to examine the opportunity to provide universal resources across the region. Unfortunately, after two years of meetings with the OV-NET group, there was little progress. Due to some political factors, the OV-NET initiative never really reached fruition. A golden opportunity for partnerships was lost. However, what emerged from this effort was a relationship between this author, who then was serving as the director of a large data acquisition site (the Hamiton/Clermont Cooperative Association of Boards of Education: H/CCA), and the Director of Academic Computing at the University of Cincinnati. We both managed large computer systems with networks that connected school systems or campuses. The future demand that would be placed on our respective systems that came about as a result of the development of graphic capabilities of the Internet gave us an opportunity to explore how we might share resources. We began our work together by meeting with each other's respective groups on cooperative purchasing, networking and telecommunications. This OV-NET group met several times over a two-year period.

State Policy Environment

The State of Ohio, seeing the importance of universal access to technology across its 614 school districts, began working on plans for technology access. At this time, legislators were increasingly dismayed at inconsistent test results among students and that common educational standards across grade levels and subjects were virtually non-existent for the "Ohio" student. What was being taught in the fourth grade in one part of the state was not consistent with what learners were exposed to at the same grade level in another location. State curricula and testing programs were being proposed as a means to bring the situation under control. All of these initiatives took place in a state which adheres to the concept of local control.

However, in the area of technology, a standardized "one size fits all" model was enacted. The Ohio legislature created SchoolNet (http://www.ohioschoolnet.k12.oh.us), a government super-agency which would manage funds for technology and make it available to schools across the State of Ohio. In the first phase, five computers would be placed in every K-4 classroom across the state in an effort to bring a common focus for technology to all Ohio students. Vast sums of money would be appropriated by the State of Ohio, and the SchoolNet agency would see that initiatives, such as the placement of computers in every K-4 classroom, would be met.

As this group operated, it tended not to work as a partner with any local efforts that had already been developed by individual school districts to forge their own solutions. Rather, funding priority was given to schools that were making an effort to meet the standards. An incorrect assumption was made that if technology already existed in schools, it would have started at the secondary level (Grades 9-12). While this might have been true in suburban schools, many urban and rural locations had not developed the area of technology. They had limited resources and served communities where technology had never previously been a priority. Thus urban and rural schools entered the world of technology significantly behind their suburban counterparts.

Differences Across the School Districts

The federal and state actions mentioned above all occurred in the mid-1990s. School districts were being asked to implement technology in prescribed ways using a blend of state resources (with guidelines) and their own monies. The Universal Service Fund (the federal government program to assist in the costs of connecting to the Internet) was not in place yet. Hardware and software was starting to be delivered and installed. However, there was no plan in place (and limited funding) for sustained training and professional development of educators. And each Ohio school district was in a very different situation.

Urban school districts had few technological resources available for their students and had left the deployment of technology in the classroom to the discretion of the individual schools. The rural school districts had limited resources and few internal personnel to implement the scope of technological resources currently available. While the opportunity to afford the hardware had increased, local priorities limited the support of such an effort. The suburban districts were where the greatest application of technology had taken place. Individuals had stepped forward who have taken the time to learn how to navigate in the environment of technology. Those people had been reassigned to handle the implementation of the new directions undertaken by the state that were meshing with the demands of the home environment where parents and community members already had access to the information highway. Networks were being set up and educators found resources to enhance teaching and learning. Workshops given by curriculum experts were often devoted to sharing a cookbook of ideas rather than taking the time to learn how to master the tools of technology. At that point in time, educators were being asked if they wanted to become a part of this movement and allowed to bring their students to labs and other access points on an occasional basis. There was a sense of foreboding with the new state directives addressing greater access to technology and no widespread efforts to provide universal training to educators as a means to bridge the chasm to already technologically motivated students. Hardware was arriving to be deployed. What would happen next?

THE PARTNERSHIP BEGINS

Being the Director of a data acquisition site (H/CCA) offered a privileged opportunity to see schools address these changes in various different ways. Our site provided the access to the Internet. We required that each school district name an Internet Coordinator who would attend regular meetings to learn and to share progress. Those meetings sparked additional people to begin networking which would shape the scope of services within districts. It also sparked discussion leading to common policies for funding access to each location at the lowest price. The H/CCA cooperative enjoyed the lowest cost per student for the Internet for the years 1997-1999 when compared with other cooperatives across the state. As a non-profit cooperative, the availability of funds for accessibility for both non-public and public schools allowed for the purchase of higher capacity network hardware, a filtering software system and higher levels of connectivity to leverage the available financial resources.

Clearly more individuals needed to be trained to assist in the deployment of technology across the schools in the region. The infusion of technology was too rapid to be effective. There was a need for a program to fill the gaps and provide for training to make sure that the implementation of technology within the schools was successful. The Cybercamp program grew out of the need to provide training to implement technology, and more specifically, to "train the trainers." Educators were an important resource. At the same time, why not deploy students as additional resources to provide support for educators in the schools and classrooms? The students could provide expertise in technology under the direction of the Internet Coordinator to support the mastery of content provided by teachers and staff. Why not use the resources of the university to provide an opportunity for young people to learn in a campus environment? The university seemed to be a very appropriate community partner, as it could provide resources, allow students to flourish outside of their home school environment and even possibly promote future matriculation.

THE MEMBERS OF THE PARTNERSHIP

The Role of the University

The purpose of Cybercamp was to create a cadre of individuals who could support the growth of technology in public and private schools by supporting its application with educators who were gaining access to it. This would be performed by successfully blending the needs for educators to learn about technology, in conjunction with the motivation of students who either knew or wanted to know more about its application. The University of Cincinnati seemed to be an appropriate host. This was especially true since the Director of Academic Computing at the University of Cincinnati was a high-level supporter of such a partnership.

The University of Cincinnati is a metropolitan university offering a wide variety of programs for students. There are 33,180 students on four campuses spread across 17 colleges. In its mission statement, the University of Cincinnati is designed to serve a diverse student body with a broad range of interests and goals. It is a place of opportunity (http://www.uc.edu/ucinfo/). Within the University of Cincinnati campus, there are a great number of individuals and departments which offered to take part and contribute to the Cybercamp program. Administrative support was sought and obtained from four components of the university. The Center for Information Technology Services could provide the computer lab space, along with their technology expertise for support and instruction. The Office of Student Affairs and Human Resources offered to provide financial backing, in the form of scholarships for students to attend the Cybercamp program. University College, a program for students needing courses before matriculating the regular classroom departments, offered to provide labs and personnel. The University of Cincinnati Bookstore offered to provide supplies and software.

Overall, the Cybercamp program would have access to computer labs containing the Windows and Macintosh platforms, an opportunity to visit emerging video technologies in the long-distance learning labs and access to university staff who would help in the training process. In summary, the University of Cincinnati provided an excellent atmosphere in which the Cybercamp program could flourish.

The Role of the School System

The Hamilton/Clermont Cooperative Association of Boards of Education (H/CCA) is a consortium of 24 public school districts in Southwestern Ohio. Six more public districts and non-public schools participated as associate members (those who pay for services but do not vote on governance issues). One hundred other districts and schools purchased services from the consortium. The member districts governed the consortium with normal business conducted by an Executive Committee made up of seven of the member districts which convened about every six weeks throughout the school year.

The members of the consortium offered to provide technical expertise through the staffing and organization of the program. School district technology coordinators would assist in all facets of the training process to ensure quality control. The Cybercamp program was developed with their input, implementation and evaluation. H/CCA data acquisition staff would also assist in the teaching to provide common standards to deploy technology across all the schools represented. Previously trained students would also be hired to provide expertise and support to assist in the learning process. The cost of staff and students during the Cybercamp program were paid for by the fees charged for the week-long experience and any grants which would be obtained.

THE ASSUMPTIONS OF CYBERCAMP

From the outset, a set of assumptions evolved through the work of the two main coordinators of Cybercamp (the author of this chapter and the Director of Academic Computing from the University of Cincinnati). These evolved from the input of university staff and school district technology coordinators as mentioned above.

- Everyone can succeed.
- Technology ought to be accessible to everyone.
- Once technology and its applications are learned, they must be applied to educational activities that enable participants to be successful.
- Learning results from networking with others. Teamwork is essential if problem solving and demonstration of knowledge is required.
- Participants must learn standards and be able to be evaluated and to evaluate themselves. They must, therefore, have many opportunities for evaluation to take place.
- There is a set of skills related to technology, both hardware and software, which must be demonstrated. Mastery comes with continual application.
- Communication with the stakeholders (e.g., schools, educators, parents) in education is constant and ongoing. This means communication will occur throughout the training as well as after the training has taken place so that support is felt by each participant. This communication will occur using a variety of media so that the stakeholders and participants will be able to share in the progress made and outcomes accomplished.
- Participants will learn from a team of providers who are certified educators and qualified students.
- The staff must be able to work together as a team. Knowledge of technology is all right, but the ability to communicate and to empower others was more important.

For the Cybercamp program, the approach that would be taken was to "train the trainers" (the trainers being junior high and high school students). That is, those who participated in Cybercamp would return to their schools to impart their knowledge to others to allow more universal access to technology. Students from urban, rural and suburban areas needed to work together to respect one another for what they do rather than who they are. In addition, those trained would also be able to assist community agencies, religious groups and businesses.

THE CYBERCAMP PROGRAM

The cornerstone of the Cybercamp model was training and support. This occurred according to the assumptions stated in an earlier section. In the first two years of the program, week-long summer experiences brought together educators and youth from the metropolitan Cincinnati region in Southwestern

Ohio to be trained by a team of adults and students. Cybercamp took the form of a 40-hour, five-day workshop which had long and short days. A manual of activities and content to be learned was given to each participant on the first day. The key components of the program are listed in Table 1.

GROWTH OF THE CYBERCAMP PROGRAM

In 1996 and 1997 the Cybercamp program was conducted on the main campus of the University of Cincinnati for students. In 1997, students from Cincinnati Public Schools (e.g., Hughes and Taft High Schools) also participated along with high school students from suburban and rural high schools.

The majority of the cost of the program was paid for by the schools represented (70%). The remaining portion came from the University of Cincinnati and H/CCA. The student participants were selected by school personnel based on individual school criteria, so that each one could return to the school to implement technology in the upcoming year.

Evaluating the Cybercamp Program

The First Year (1996)

The first year of the Cybercamp program (1996) was considered to be a pilot test. Several questions had to be answered:

- Could an experience be designed in which everyone (e.g., participants, staff, youth counselors) could learn from each other?
- If the entire staff were hand selected, would they be able to work together?
- Would parents believe that their financial investment of $200 per student in Cybercamp was worthwhile?
- Could parents appreciate their offspring's investment in technology?
- Could a major university work with an organization representing schools?
- If students were trained, would they be utilized in the development of their school's approach to technology implementation?

There was no formal research done on the above topics. However, the answer to the above questions was a resounding YES from participants and schools who sent students to the program. A great deal of positive feedback had been received during and following the program from parents, students, educators in their schools and school district technology coordinators. Forty percent of the students in the first-year program were hired by their districts to load software and maintain computer labs as well as assist with training efforts.

Table 1: The Overall Program Schedule for Cybercamp

Day 1	A battery of pre-tests was given: a survey of participant attitudes about technology, a self-assessment of actual knowledge of specific tools and a content pre-test to determine familiarity with those tools to be covered. The latter was used to group participants. (Kysilka, 1997)
Day 1	Grouping of participants was by skill level so that teaching groups were no larger than 15. Both an adult and student instructor were assigned to each group. Students were then grouped into three or four from different schools to work together within the larger groups throughout the workshop.
Day 1-2	The first two days of the experience were devoted to learning the tools of technology which would later be demonstrated. Also each group worked together to select a topic which they could present utilizing the tools learned. For example, the first two days in 1996 were devoted to empowerment, group dynamics, electronic mail, PowerPoint, Web page construction, a demonstration of the use of a long distance learning lab and searching the Internet. In 1997, the first two days were devoted to searching the Internet, electronic mail, group dynamics, PowerPoint and Web page construction.
Day 2	The groups began to assess their own capabilities through individual and group "fun" activities. An Internet treasure hunt occurred on the second day where individuals went around the world using the computer to come up with answers in a fixed time limit. A simulation game was used later in the week to allow users to work against other team members.
Day 2	At the end of the second day, a guest speaker talked about individual responsibilities on the Internet. A member of the Regional Computer Crime Task Force provided a seminar on Cybercrime.
Day 3-4	A research project comprised the third and fourth day's content. Each group's topic was developed into a presentation using the tools learned earlier in the week. Participants could use the studio to have their presentation videotaped if desired.
Day 4	At the end of the fourth day, evaluation took place. The first form of evaluation was of each other's work according to a set of pre-determined criteria. Individuals were judged by their peers on the Web page they had created, and each group was evaluated by the other groups on the project they had prepared. In the evening, parents and educators were invited to an open house where all groups presented their projects in roundtable formats. Web pages were put on the Internet to be viewed at computer stations. The guests viewed all of the work that had been done.
Day 5	The last day was an opportunity to work together as teams in virtual reality settings that were fun. Virtual trivia allowed participants to recall specific information using technology. Virtual sports allowed participants to demonstrate their athletic skills in a virtual setting (e.g., golf, soccer, football).
Whole Week	Communication was maintained through the use of electronic mail. Participants responded to specific messages throughout the week to practice their skills.
Whole Week	An Olympiad took place throughout the week where the participants worked by themselves and as a team to gain points for prizes awarded on the last day. The prizes were items chosen to enable the participants to continue their learning beyond Cybercamp. Activities which formed the Olympiad included the Treasure Hunt, the simulation game, the Web page evaluation, the project evaluation, and the activities on the last day. Group scores were maintained and the overall individual performer was also identified

It is estimated that each Cybercamp participant had an effect on 50 students and educators in the subsequent school year, making the outreach to 4,000 people in the schools. Four of the seniors (25%), upon graduation, chose to attend the University of Cincinnati. Parents and teachers learned a great deal from the participants. A timeline for the growth of the Cybercamp program is in Table 2.

Evaluation of the 1997 Cybercamp Program

In 1997, Dr. Marcella Kysilka from the University of Central Florida did a more formal evaluation study of the Cybercamp program. Here are some of the conclusions of her research:

- "Students completed all the tasks, thus learning the skills Cybercamp was designed to teach.
- All during the camp, students were actively engaged in learning.
- The minority students were very involved in learning, and even though they had less access to computers at school or at home, indicated that they intended to use computers once Cybercamp was completed.
- Parents thought the program was successful. They were very interested in seeing all of the presentations and moved from station to station and were very conscientious in viewing the work of students who did not have parents present.
- The staff members worked diligently throughout Cybercamp. They were readily available to help students complete tasks. They answered students' questions willingly and spent time helping the students learn to solve their own problems." (Kysilka, 1997)

Current Status of the Cybercamp Program

In the summer of 1998, two Cybercamp programs occurred. One cybercamp program was held at Owens Community College. Youth who had

Table 2: Timeline for the Growth of the Cybercamp Program

1996	Cybercamp Program for students at the University of Cincinnati
1997	Cybercamp Program for educators at Cincinnati Hills Christian Academy AND for students at the University of Cincinnati
1998	Cybercamp Program for students at Owens Community College in northeast Ohio; Cybercamp Program for students at Winton Woods High School (suburban Cincinnati)
1999	Cybercamp program evolves into Cyberstars program during and after school
2000 and 2001	Cybercamp program is used to train future Cyberstars to build hardware and support software in schools

worked as counselors and teachers in Southwest Ohio in 1996-97 accompanied the author to present a program using the technical staff from local school districts and Owens Community College. The college offered the facilities and visited often to observe what was going on.

The 1998 Cybercamp program in Cincinnati occurred much as the first two years but took place at one of the local high schools. Unfortunately, the University of Cincinnati had already scheduled their facilities due to internal expansion of their offerings. However, the university continued to contribute financial support for student scholarships in the program. Additional support was provided by gifts from business and industry (e.g., computer and communications companies). Representatives had seen the positive contributions made by youth in the first two years and stepped up to offer funds to support scholarships and/or sponsor specific activities in the program. The focus of the program changed to include an emphasis on hardware, as schools needed to have individuals who would better support their expanding technology efforts.

In the past three years, the Cybercamp program has grown in different ways. Both of the originators remain with universities in teaching roles. In 1999, the Cybercamp program evolved into a Cyberstars program offered during and after the school day. It involves urban youth learning to work with and maintain hardware, software and networking to provide expanded access within the urban environment. At the same time a contingent of students is using video and other communication technologies to record the experience. The program has evolved from a youth counseling effort into one of mentoring, counseling and teaching to promote empowerment of urban youth.

This evolution has come about with the support of community agencies which have provided financial support through internships for qualified youth. These partnerships have resulted in the Community Access to Technology initiative which allows business, governmental agencies and/or individuals to contribute their hardware to a central location for refurbishing and placement in schools and community agencies. Experienced Cyberstars are now developing the workshops to train their peers to serve as future Cyberstars.

Through this new program, urban youth have rebuilt 2,000 donated computers and placed them in schools and agencies. Some of these youth have participated as technology assistants in Wright State University classes to help with the instruction of technological skills. The initial collaborative effort has changed to include community agencies that serve youth, the urban school district, representatives of business and industry. The partnerships are rapidly evolving as the agencies expand their focus to include empowered urban youth. Students are now being offered internships and full-time jobs as a result of the Cyberstars program with technology companies.

THE FUTURE

Beginning in August of 2001, the Cincinnati Public Schools will be opening a Virtual High School designed to empower youth who have dropped out or who wish to obtain their secondary education in a different way. A two-year pilot program, with Cyberstars taking technology-based courses, took place from 1999-2001 to took place from 1999-2001. The results were that attendance in technology-supported content classes went up 30% and students passed 94% of all courses offered in that format.

The Cyberstars program will evolve into a community service program designed to provide student empowerment across the curriculum with special emphasis on technology. In the Virtual High School, all students will take courses at their own pace to meet district standards with a staff of certified educators and qualified students. Teaching staff will be available online or at a center to provide individual and small-group teaching. For those who wish to take a greater role in technology beyond the virtual coursework, they can take coursework and then practice their knowledge through community service and internships. Greater Cincinnati sits ready to accept them in the workforce once trained.

SUMMARY

Collaboration is a relationship where individuals and agencies share the responsibility for leadership, implementation, evaluation and moving ahead. The partnership that evolved from the initial meetings sponsored by a vendor has strengthened and evolved over the past eight years. The initial Cybercamp idea has changed because the needs have changed, and the policy environment has changed. A partnership takes time to develop and additional time to nurture if it is to flourish. In any arrangement, all must perceive themselves "winners" if such a relationship is sustainable. The principal rewards are not always financial in nature. The experience of working with the University of Cincinnati and the schools of Southwestern Ohio offered both institutions an opportunity to solve a problem. The program was designed to offer local students a glimpse into the urban university experience while pursuing a highly motivational and rewarding set of activities. It expanded the university's offering to the community beyond the regular sports camps, which were and continue to be successful. For the school systems, trained youth would provide an inexpensive support system to support their efforts to implement technology in their districts. Some chose to offer credit for that expertise and others created jobs for youth. However, the empowered students were motivated to carry on the message of universal access to their teachers and their peers. The cost of any venture must always be assessed in terms of time, facilities and money. Any program ought to be self-sustaining and partners must see a clear payoff for their participation. No one agency should be doing a disproportionate amount of the work.

Collaboration is hard work. It requires sustained communication within an atmosphere that creates win-win opportunities for everyone who takes part. Of the Cybercamp participants, the students emerged from this intensive experience with a positive attitude about their contributions to technology. The schools they represented were also the beneficiaries by gaining a student technical staff they could use to further their own programs. For the two of us who started this enterprise, it has empowered us to reach out to urban youth to create more opportunities to bridge the digital divide. Now that we are there, we can reach back to our institutional affiliations to forge new partnerships.

REFERENCES

Kysilka, M. (1997). *Final Evaluation Report*, Cybercamp 1997. Cincinnati, OH: H/CCA.

Lazar, J. and Norcio, A. (2000). Service-research: Community partnerships for research and training. *Journal of Informatics Education and Research*, 2(3), 21-25.

Ohio Valley Network. (1994). *OV-NET Internet Advisory Committee Conference*, Cincinnati: The University of Cincinnati.

Perelman, L. (1992). *Schools Out*, 225-226. New York: Avon Books.

Rollins, A. and Maggio, R. (1997). *Quotations on Education*, 30. Paramus, NJ: Prentice-Hall.

Turkle, S. (1995). *Life on the Screen*, 30. New York: Simon & Schuster.

Section III

Business Partnerships

Chapter VII

A Stage Model for Academic-Corporate Partnerships: Using an Advisory Council to Build Bridges Between an Academic IS Program and the Business Community

James R. Coakley
Oregon State University, USA

Craig K. Tyran
Western Washington University, USA

A strong partnership with the business community can serve as a critical factor for an information systems program in higher education. The purpose of this chapter will be to draw on 10 years of experience to discuss our insights and lessons learned with regard to the Corporate Partnership Program for Information Systems at Oregon State University. The chapter begins with an overview of a "Stages of Partnership Growth" model that provides a framework for understanding and managing the evolutionary stages of growth for the academic-corporate partnership. The model will be illustrated by examining the evolution of the information systems program at Oregon State University. An advisory council comprised of representatives from the business community has played a key role in the development of the information systems program at Oregon State University. Suggestions regarding the creation and maintenance of an advisory council are discussed.

INTRODUCTION

Over the past 10 years, the undergraduate information systems (IS) program in our College of Business at Oregon State University has undergone substantial development and growth. One of the key foundations for our IS program has been our "Corporate Partnership Program." The Corporate Partnership Program creates a strategic win-win situation between academia and the professional IS community in the Pacific Northwest region of the United States. The IS community that we work with encompasses a broad range of organizations including large Fortune 500 companies, small to medium-sized regional businesses, non-profit institutions, and municipal organizations. All of these organizations in our IS community share the same concern; they want to have a reliable source of highly qualified IS professionals. The Corporate Partnership Program supports the IS community by means of a formal alliance that enables our academic program to effectively meet the needs of industry and students.

The purpose of this chapter will be to draw on 10 years of experience to discuss a) our insights and lessons learned with regard to our Corporate Partnership Program, and b) the role of an advisory council in the evolution of our alliances with the business community. We believe that our experiences will be relevant to others, as there are presently many IS programs in colleges and universities that have been grappling with the issue of how to maintain a close connection with the business community. We begin this chapter with a brief overview of a "Stages of Partnership Growth" model that we have developed for academic-corporate partnerships. Next, we illustrate the Stages of Partnership Growth model by using our IS program as an example. In describing how our partnership with industry has evolved over the past 10 years, we will provide specific details regarding several aspects of our partnership program including the initiation and development of our IS Business Advisory Council.

BACKGROUND: A STAGES OF PARTNERSHIP GROWTH MODEL

Stages of growth models have long been used to describe evolutionary development in a variety of business areas including economics (Rostow, 1960), small business (Churchill and Lewis, 1983), and information systems management (Gibson and Nolan, 1974). In this section, we introduce a Stages of Partnership Growth model that provides a framework for understanding and managing the evolutionary stages of growth for the academic-corporate partnership. Classifying and describing the general pattern of growth for the partnership of an IS program with industry may at first seem to be a daunting task. Academic IS programs and potential industry partners can vary tremendously with respect to such factors as academic and corporate missions, organizational culture, personnel, and regional industrial and economic factors. However, as we reflect upon our experiences at Oregon State University, as well as at other institutions, we have been able to identify distinctly different stages associated with the development of the academic-corporate partnership and we have found that there are common characteristics and issues that may emerge during the development of such partnerships.

The Stages of Partnership Growth model for corporate partnerships that we have developed is depicted in Figure 1. Each stage in the model is defined by the nature of the alliances with business organizations, the curricular approach within the degree option, the opportunities for student experiences

Figure 1: Stages of Growth in a Corporate Partnership Program

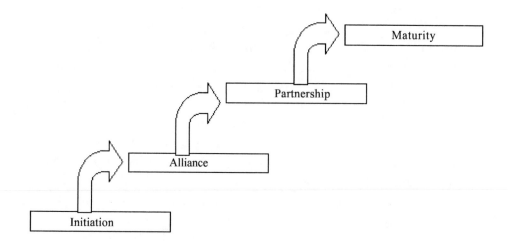

outside of the classroom, and the culture within the IS faculty. The model can provide value for those IS programs that wish to create a partnership program, as well as those which have a partnership program and are continuing to evolve. For IS programs that are interested in building bridges between academia and industry, the model can provide guidance for moving forward. For programs that are already involved with industry partnerships, the model can be used to help anticipate the future opportunities and challenges that may arise as partnerships grow and evolve.

Stage 1: Initiation

The initiation stage represents the nascent period of partnership. The relationships between the IS program and those in the business industry are in the early stage of development, typified by informal and often infrequent contacts. For example, IS faculty may interact with industry professionals during meetings of professional business societies. The primary basis for the curriculum is typically derived from published academic guidelines (e.g., the IS '97 guidelines (Association of Information Technology Professionals, 1997; Davis et al., 1997)), and minimal efforts are made to get input or guidance from the university's industry constituents. Discipline-related experience opportunities such as part time jobs and internships may exist for IS students, but are generally dependent on the individual student's initiative in identifying the opportunity. The culture of the IS faculty is oriented such that the faculty control the shape and direction of the curriculum with little input from external constituents.

Stage 2: Alliance

In the alliance stage, an IS program moves from loose, informal relationships with the business community to stronger alliances in which the academic program and business community begin to rely more closely on one another. The alliance is often formalized through creation of an advisory council. The advisory council becomes the forum for recurring meetings between the IS faculty and their business constituents for the purpose of reviewing the curricular programs and creating experience opportunities for the students. The IS faculty responds to the guidance and fine-tunes the curriculum such that it evolves as new technologies and paradigms emerge within industry. Curricular adjustments are made to better prepare students for experience opportunities between their junior and senior year. The IS faculty start to develop a more practical approach, both in classroom instruction and research.

Stage 3: Partnership

In the partnership stage, the alliances evolve into a partnership. There is a sense of shared ownership of the curriculum between faculty and business constituents. Industry representatives are actively involved in the design and delivery of classroom projects that integrate conceptual knowledge and applied skills. Business commits to support classroom activities by providing guest lectures on selected topics. Structured internship programs emerge, where faculty act as intermediaries to match student skills and needs with business opportunities. The faculty also begins to align their research agenda with the needs of their business constituents.

Stage 4: Maturity

In the maturity stage, joint ventures begin to emerge between the IS faculty and the business community, as well as among different entities in the business community. A joint venture is a common type of strategic alliance in which a new organization is created among business partners (Daft, 2001). In the context of the Stages of Growth model, a joint venture represents a more formal type of partnership involving the IS program and the business community. The joint venture will conduct its activities using its own assets and liabilities and have a separate decision-making identity. The opportunity for reduced competition and shared risk among sponsoring organizations is one of the major motivators for a joint venture. For example, a joint venture could entail the creation of a cooperative program to provide experience-building activities, such as internships, as an integral part of the IS curriculum. A joint venture of this type would involve the IS faculty as well as numerous partners from the business community. Industry participants would be motivated to join this type of venture to develop and attract a well-trained pool of IS graduates who have had the opportunity to enhance their educational coursework with practical experience. The costs for business organizations participating in this type of venture would be for ongoing resources such as people, equipment, and financial support. Also, the participants in the venture would agree to provide a specified number of opportunities for students regardless of the economic climate.

THE EVOLUTION OF THE CORPORATE PARTNERSHIP PROGRAM AT OSU

To illustrate the Stages of Partnership Growth model, we will use our IS program as a case example. In addition to describing the different stages of the model, we will also summarize the internal and external influences (i.e., triggers) that motivated us to transition from one stage to the next.

Academic Setting and Curriculum

At Oregon State University, the College of Business has approximately 1,500 undergraduate students, 60 MBA students, and 45 faculty positions. The College offers an undergraduate degree in business, but does not offer discipline majors. Although students cannot major in information systems, they can take a concentrated set of discipline-specific coursework in the IS area. The curriculum for the undergraduate IS program presently consists of five upper-division information systems courses taught in the College of Business, plus a project management course taught in the College of Business, and a programming course taught through the Department of Computer Science. More information regarding the IS curriculum may be found in Appendix A.

Stage 1: Initiation

The IS option at our college was created in 1989 within a Management Science Department. Within two years, 25 students were enrolled in IS option courses (see Figure 2). At this point in time, the IS program was in Stage One of the Stages of Partnership Growth model, which is the initiation stage. In our case, we were developing a curriculum based on the Data Processing Manage-

Figure 2: Comparison of the Number of Students Starting the IS Option vs. Program Capacity

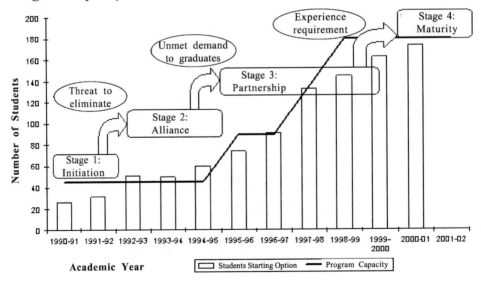

ment Association (1990) guidelines, and we had established informal relations with IS professionals within regional businesses (e.g., faculty were encouraged to attend local chapter meetings of the Society of Information Management). A small percentage of our students were obtaining summer internship experiences. However, these internships were typically general business experiences (e.g., sales or bookkeeping assistants) and were not focused on IS-related types of work activities. There were no formal activities coordinated by the IS program to assist students in finding full-time or intern positions. There were three tenure/tenure-track faculty positions in IS, and the culture of the IS faculty was not distinguishable from the culture of other faculty within the college.

The Trigger to Move to Stage 2: Threat to Eliminate Program

As with many state institutions at the time, our university was faced with declining student enrollments. In addition, a statewide tax-cutting initiative led to declining budgets throughout the university system. This period also marked the arrival of a new Dean for the College, whose first order of business (given the budget pressures) was to eliminate selected programs within the college, and reduce the overhead in the college by merging six departments into two. At this point in time, the view of the senior faculty and administration of the college was that an accredited College of Business should only provide degree options within the traditional business disciplines: Accounting, Finance, Management, and Marketing. This philosophy, combined with the small size of a relatively new program, marked the IS program for elimination.

Stage 2: Alliance

The administrative decision to eliminate the IS option incited an outcry from the business community and was the key event that prompted our Corporate Partnership Program to evolve to the alliance stage of growth. Even though the IS program at our college was still in its infancy, regional business representatives were hoping to depend on our program to serve as a pipeline for new IS graduates as they were forecasting a substantial increase in the demand for information systems business analysts. As a result, an alliance was formed between the IS faculty and industry to take actions to overturn the College's decision to eliminate the IS program. Ultimately, a group of industry leaders who supported the IS program were successful in convincing university leadership to retain the IS option within the college.

After the IS program was "saved" from elimination, the alliance between industry and the IS faculty continued to develop. Although the college had a "Business Advisory Council," this council did not have IS representation and did not represent the interests of the IS community. Hence, a separate IS Advisory Council (ISAC) comprised of Chief Information Officers (or equivalent positions) was created to support the IS program and serve as an advocate with respect to the college administration. The initial areas of support provided by this council included the following:

- *Curricular Review*: Given the limited number of courses available within the IS option (six courses totaling 24 quarter-based credit hours), the ISAC began a detailed review of the IS curriculum, which included numerous focus sessions with industry experts to develop relevant course projects. The result was an integrated junior-year sequence of courses, modeled after the systems development life cycle, with hands-on projects that related to the conceptual material in each course.

- *Student Career Orientation*: The ISAC began sponsoring numerous joint activities with industry to provide additional career orientation to the students outside of the classroom environment. These activities included student field trips and an IS Career Night. The Career Night was not a "recruiting fair;" rather, it was an opportunity for the IS students to interact with representatives from industry in a non-recruiting environment to learn about job opportunities and career options. In addition, the Career Night offered participating business organizations the opportunity to learn more about the IS program.

- *Program Growth*: The ISAC sent letters to high school counselors throughout the state of Oregon to inform them of the existence of the IS program in the College of Business, and to describe the differences between an IS program (aimed at producing business systems analysts) and the traditional types of computer science programs available at all of the universities in the state.

As a result of these actions, the response from industry and students was very favorable. The revised curriculum was widely accepted by industry, and the students in the program were actively recruited. The opportunities for IS-related job experience for the students were expanding (approximately 25% completed internships or on-campus experience positions), and most of the students (over 90%) were placed into full-time positions prior to graduation. The news regarding the career opportunities afforded by the IS program spread rapidly among prospective students, and the number of students in the IS option grew very quickly. Within a very short period of time, the number of students in the program exceeded the 45 students per year capacity that was based on student/teacher ratio guidelines for the American Association of Collegiate Schools of Business (AACSB) (see Figure 2, the "Alliance" phase).

The Trigger: Unmet Demand for IS Graduates

Although the number of students in the IS program was growing, the university as a whole continued to experience declining budgets and declining undergraduate enrollments. The college was not able to add new faculty positions, and there was concern among the administration and senior faculty outside the IS area that growth in the program would exceed industry demand. Contrary to the concerns of these people in the college, the IS community foresaw a growing need for well-trained IS professionals. Through pressure from the ISAC, a tenure-track line for IS was gained by reallocating a faculty position from another part of the college and the student capacity increased to 90 students per year. While this was considered a positive step by the ISAC, the increase in program capacity clearly did not meet the perceived need of the IS community.

In 1995, the ISAC generated a "white-paper" that forecast increased demand for IS graduates in the state of Oregon. Their immediate goal was to convince the college administration to increase the number of IS faculty positions, and thereby raise the capacity of the program. Based on projections from numerous organizations within Oregon that would be served by graduates of the program, they identified that a significant "supply gap" would exist if the program remained at the existing capacity constraints. This analysis focused specifically on the demand for "new college graduates." This supply gap, depicted in Figure 3, showed that the projected demand exceeded the

Figure 3: Forecast Demand for MIS Graduates (from 1995 IS Advisory Council White Paper)

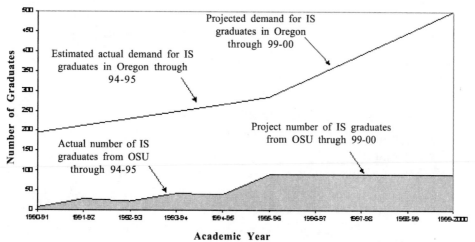

Academic Year

projected number of graduates from the IS option. As indicated in Figure 3, starting in the 1995-96 academic year, the projected number of graduates was set to 90 students per year, which was the program capacity at that time.[1]

Stage 3: Partnership

Our IS program is presently in the "Partnership" of the growth model. As indicated above, the ISAC White Paper triggered our move into this stage of the model. One of the reasons for this was that during the process of preparing its "White Paper," the ISAC contacted numerous Oregon businesses, which enhanced the visibility of the IS program and further enhanced the breadth and depth of our relationships with industry partners in the region. We consider the subsequent strength of our partnerships with the business community to be a significant factor in the recent growth and success of the IS program. Today, our IS program can be characterized as having formal alliances with business, a curricular approach that requires students to integrate related skills, extensive experience opportunities for the students outside of the classroom, and a faculty team that embraces change. Key aspects of our IS program at this stage include:

- An 18-member ISAC comprised of chief information officers (or the equivalent) from a wide variety of business organizations ranging from Fortune 500 companies to fledging "dot.coms."
- Established ongoing relationships with an additional 60 organizations.
- An IS program that has developed a strong reputation among industry leaders within the region as being a "business-driven" program, with faculty who are responsive to industry needs. The program has an integrated curriculum that is "lock-step" (must be taken in an appropriate sequence). Each course has a hands-on component, with subsequent courses building on previously learned skills. Our IS curriculum is described in Appendix A.
- An active internship program that offers a broad range of experience opportunities within the business community and across campus.

An Example of Partnership: Internship Programs

Our internship program provides an example of the partnership that exists between business and the IS faculty. Together, we decided that the goal of an internship should be to extend the discipline-related education of the student. Thus, we draw a clear distinction between an experience-building internship and a job that merely involves IS activities. The type of internship that is appropriate for a student depends on a student's background. For example, an appropriate first internship for a student might be an IS help-desk position. This type of position can help to develop interpersonal and problem-solving skills, as well as develop the student's understanding of organizational IS applications. If this same student were to seek an additional experience opportunity, returning to the same company in the same help-desk position would not be considered an internship since such a job may not extend the student's knowledge of the discipline, or extend their IS-related skills, even though it is IS-related work.

We categorize our experience-building opportunities into three types of business internship programs:

- **Structured Programs Within Companies**. Several companies have developed formal internship programs and recruit from numerous campuses for student interns. Some of these companies will visit campus to interview candidates. Others use a centralized application process, and only interview "finalists." These programs are very good experiences for the students. Most have pre-approved projects and programmed activities to extend the students' knowledge of the use of IT within business organizations. The role of the IS faculty in these partnerships is usually to advertise the opportunities to the students.

- **Unstructured Programs with Industry**. We have many companies who hire student interns every summer, but do not have a structured program. Our minimum requirement with these companies is that each student should have an assigned mentor and designated projects. They could be part of a larger team, or could be assigned to developing some of the "back-burner" applications that exist in all IT organizations. Within these programs, the IS faculty work with industry to define appropriate projects that can be completed by students who have taken the junior-year sequence of courses.

- **Cooperative Programs**. We participate in a cooperative internship program where the students are selected into the program, and then assigned to an internship with one of the participating companies. This approach is has been found to be very effective because it consolidates the selection and placement process. Instead of using a traditional recruiting approach where each company conducts its own independent recruiting process, a single process is held where representatives from the cooperative program form a panel and interview the students to determine which students will be accepted into the program. Once selected, the student is "guaranteed" an internship with one of the participating businesses (with appropriate conditions such as maintaining good academic standing, etc.). This relieves stress on the students, and saves time and expense for the participating businesses. Our experience is that most companies are looking for similar skill sets in the intern candidates. In fact, for the initial screening interviews, many companies send people from their personnel department to perform the screening of candidates. Once the pool of candidates is selected, a second round of interviews with business representatives is conducted to help the representatives determine which students may be the best match for their organization. The student candidates are ultimately allocated to the different organizations using a selection process where organizations sequentially pick students using a predefined order. The process is similar to that found in professional sports (e.g., the professional basketball draft conducted in the United States). While some organizations initially have reservations about this approach to recruiting, they are usually convinced of the viability of the approach once they participate in the process.

In all three of these intern programs, IS faculty act as intermediaries. The IS faculty have undertaken numerous supporting activities to facilitate the selection and placement of our students into experience opportunities. These include:

- **Resume and Interview Skills Workshop**. These are IS faculty-run workshops where we work with IS students to enhance their job search process. We discuss how to develop IS resumes and cover letters, the art of interviews (e.g., expectations of the interviewer, typical behavioral and technical questions, dress), what to expect during interview site visits, and how to evaluate offers. We also have a program where student resumes are reviewed by IS alumni.

- **Infrequent/New Internship Programs**. One of our biggest challenges has been convincing a company to take its first intern. In the past, individual faculty members have worked with organizations that are interested in creating an internship to identify suitable projects for a student intern and prepare the organization (vs. preparing the student) for the internship experience. Through the ISAC, we are now beginning to form a "mentor training" program where industry representatives who have previously served as mentors to interns share their experiences and offer guidance to those in other organizations on how to create rewarding internship opportunities for the student.

- **Selection and Placement of Students**. IS faculty facilitate the process of helping interested and qualified students get connected to the organizations that have job opportunities available.
  - *Career fair*: In the fall, we hold an informational career fair where students learn about full-time and internship positions. Over the past three years (1998-2000), an average of approximately 75 business representatives and 150 students have attended this event each year.

o *Resume book*: We collect resumes from the students seeking full-time and internship positions, and send these to our corporate partners.
o *Career-related postings*: We distribute information about job opportunities and campus visits to the IS students using e-mail (external agencies do not have access to student distribution lists).

Industry support has played a key role during the "Partnership" stage of our corporate partnership program. During this stage, the IS program grew from 90 students to over 150 IS students graduating per year. The IS program currently produces approximately 40% of the undergraduate graduates from the college and is twice the size of the next largest degree option. Over half of the IS students participate in at least one experience-building IS-related internship before they graduate. The curriculum, combined with internship experiences, produces IS graduates that are in high demand. The following quote from an individual involved with campus recruiting for a national firm illustrates the way many businesses view the IS program:

"I've spoken with many students at different schools and feel Oregon State is one of the top two in terms of well-rounded students. I directly attribute this to the time and effort professors devote to their students. I wish all schools would adopt your philosophy in providing opportunities for students to understand the importance of the soft skills (communication, team work, getting along with others)."

The Trigger: Mandatory Experience Requirement

We believe that we are now transitioning into the fourth stage of growth: the maturity stage. Our ISAC has challenged us to make the internship (or equivalent experience opportunity) a required part of our IS academic program. Such a requirement will have implications on both our external alliances and curriculum. An experience requirement places increased pressure on our alliances to assure an adequate number of experience opportunities within industry, even during economic slowdowns. Thus, our ISAC is becoming the "champion" to expand industry participation and form a joint venture for formal internship programs. The proposed venture would create a separate entity to support and manage the internship process. The venture would be financed and governed by the participating organizations. The role of the faculty in this venture would be to tailor course content within the curriculum as our student population gains practical work experience. In this way, the curriculum would supplement and extend the practical knowledge gained by the students through the internships. As we transition into this stage, we foresee an ever-increasing integration between our IS program and the business community, and anticipate that council members will play an even more active role in fostering support for the program.

A CRITICAL COMPONENT FOR SUCCESS: THE ADVISORY COUNCIL

We have found that the key component for our evolving partnership with the business community has been the advisory council. The creation of an advisory council provides the first step in formalizing alliances with business, and becomes the foundation for forging more fruitful relationships with business and government organizations within our region. In this section, we will provide insights into the tasks of establishing and maintaining an IS Advisory Council (ISAC). Selected issues are discussed below.

Establishing an IS Advisory Council

Taking the appropriate steps in the initial creation of the advisory council is critical to its future success. Key steps that we have identified include:

- **Define the Role of the Council**. Similar to a board of directors for a corporate or non-profit organization, there are many roles that an IS advisory council can perform (Redraw the line ..., 1995; Conger et al., 1998; McFarlan, 1999). The key roles that we have identified include:

  o *Strategic planning*. Establishing a vision, mission, and achievable goals and objectives were critical during the formulation of our IS program, and enabled us to maintain control of the program during our periods of rapid growth (30% per year from 1995 through 1998). The ISAC performs bi-annual reviews of our strategic plan.

  o *Curricular guidance*. In the fast-paced world of IS education, it is critical to receive guidance from industry on information technology (IT) trends. An effective IS curriculum must achieve a balance between conceptual theory and application. The primary curricular role of our advisory council has been to define the conceptual knowledge and skills needed by graduates for entry-level business analyst positions. This guidance has been crucial to maintaining a viable course-constrained undergraduate program, given the explosion in conceptual content within the IS discipline over the past 10 years. With respect to the "skills" component of the curriculum, the ISAC has helped us to define the broad set of technical and non-technical skills needed by our graduates, and how to sequence those skills throughout the curricular courses. Our ISAC currently performs yearly reviews of our curriculum.

o *Developing experience opportunities.* Most companies place a higher value on graduates who have attained some degree of actual discipline-related experience during their undergraduate education. The challenge, from a curricular perspective, is providing an adequate minimal set of conceptual knowledge and skills to the students such that they can participate in IT-related experience-building opportunities. The ISAC helped us define this minimal set and create our integrated junior-year sequence of courses that prepare students to participate in experience opportunities with industry. They also played a key role in developing our internship program, which was discussed in the previous section of the chapter.

o *Placement of graduates.* Most colleges and universities have a "Career Services" function that facilitates recruitment of graduates by business organizations. Our experience suggests that many organizations, especially organizations with smaller IT groups, do not participate in these university-wide activities. At the suggestion of the ISAC, we created two "recruiting-oriented" activities: an IS Career Night and an IS Resume Book. The ISAC helped to identify the organizations (and individual contacts within those organizations) that would benefit from participation in these activities.

o *Fund raising.* At many colleges and universities, fund raising attempts for an individual program quickly become mired in politics. Many business organizations have additional barriers that severely limit their ability to make "donations" to academic programs (benevolence committees, etc.). Our ISAC has helped us change our focus from "benevolence" to a "service provider" orientation. Our corporate partnership program is evolving to a "contract for services" concept that provides funding to support our activities.

o *Joint research projects.* The ISAC is also a forum where industry representatives can communicate to the IS faculty current issues and concerns deserving of scholarly study, and for faculty to discuss their research programs and the implications for practice. When appropriate, members of the ISAC can assist faculty with access to data.

o *Influence with university leadership.* As discussed earlier, our ISAC was created to serve as an advocate of the IS program to the university administration. The ISAC continues to provide a communication link to the College Business Advisory Council, and the administration within both the college and university, relative to the IS program's needs, directions, and activities.

o *Donation of materials*. Maintaining an IS program on the cutting edge of information technology requires significant resources. Our college administration has done an excellent job at maintaining the information technology infrastructure. Individual members of the ISAC have supplemented the infrastructure by providing specialized software, peripheral equipment (printers, laptops), and data to support course projects.

- **Charter**. A "charter" formalizes the relationship between industry and the academic unit. The charter provides guidance for membership, frequency of meetings, and several other aspects of the council. These guidelines are useful when the leadership changes in the council (e.g., a new chair) or within the academic unit (e.g., a new faculty leader). To aid others who may wish to establish or formalize their advisory council, we summarize the key features of the charter below. Also, we have included a copy of our charter in Appendix B.

  o *Purpose*: In our view, the purpose of the ISAC is to maintain and manage a partnership with industry that enables the IS program to implement its vision and attain its strategic objectives.

  o *Objectives and Activities*: The key objectives and activities of the ISAC should directly relate to the role that the council would play.

  o *Operation*: This section is used to clarify the operational process for the council. Ours is relatively brief, indicating that the council will meet twice per year, and that the chair and a designated faculty member will be responsible for planning and conducting the meetings.

  o *Membership, officers and committees*: Key issues in this section include membership, the process for gaining membership on the council, and designating the "voting" members.

Maintaining an IS Advisory Council (ISAC)

Once a council is formed, there are many "maintenance" considerations that must be addressed. These considerations include:

- **Individual vs. Corporate Membership**. When individuals on the advisory council change organizations, does their position stay with the company, or does it stay with the individual? We use both approaches, and this has become the primary reason for growth in the number of members on the council. Our experience suggests that when an active supporter of the program moves to a new organization, that individual will want to continue their association with the program, and will foster sponsorship within the new organization. Because this individual was an active supporter of the program, a broad alliance was formed with other individuals within the previous organization, and they are also interested in continuing the relationship. We have one long-term member who is now associated with his fourth organization since joining the council. With one company, we are now on our fourth representative who is filling the council position.

- **Size of the Advisory Board**. The size of our advisory council has been designed to be 15-20 people based on recommendations from the literature (e.g., McFarlan, 1999). We have found that a board that has 15-20 members is large enough to offer a diverse ranges of views and insights. However, a board of this size is small enough to be productive and engage all members of the board.

- **Selection of Membership**. In order to meet the needs of the business community, it is important to tap the appropriate people to join the council. Contributions to the IS program can come in many forms such as financial resources, influence, and time. We have found that some members, especially those in government organizations, are not able to tap into their organization's assets to offer substantial financial contributions (although many will make personal contributions). Hence, in a departure from the practices of many non-profit types of boards (McFarlan, 1999), we have not made financial support a condition of membership on our advisory council board. Rather, we have found it useful to assemble a balanced advisory council team based on a "time, talent, influence, and resources" criteria. In this way, we have assembled an advisory council of members who complement one another: while some members can provide organizational influence or monetary contributions, other members provide vital contributions in other ways such as by providing energy and time. We attempt to ensure that we have representation from all sectors of business: manufacturing vs. service, profit vs. non-profit, private vs. public, etc.

- **Faculty Accountability**. A partnership with industry is not a one-way street. Faculty cannot expect the industry members to continue their support of the program without faculty follow-up to council recommendations. As with other types of boards (Conger et al., 1998), we have found that members of our advisory council board expect their input to be considered in the development of the IS program. We have thus found it useful for the IS faculty to be accountable for providing a response to the council with regard to "action items" arising from the advisory council meetings. While not all recommendations from the council are accepted, it is important for the IS faculty to provide timely briefing sessions to apprise the advisory council of program modifications. If a recommendation cannot be implemented due to resource or political constraints, then the feedback to the council provides them the opportunity to re-assess the recommendation, and take appropriate actions to facilitate the implementation if needed.

CONCLUSIONS

Many IS programs in colleges and universities presently need to deal with two key issues: 1) the rapid changes in technology and industry practices, and 2) the growth of student enrollment in IS programs prompted by the transition to a digital economy. One of the ways for academics to address the challenges presented by these issues is to create and nurture a strong partnership with the business community. The business community can help IS faculty keep abreast of changes in the professional IS workplace and can offer practical insights and support related to managing the growth of IS programs. As discussed in this chapter, a critical success factor for developing alliances with the IS community is an advisory council. The advisory council can play a variety of roles with regard to supporting an IS program, including curricular guidance, student placement, and faculty support.

Once an IS program makes the decision to form and use an advisory council, the Stages of Partnership Growth model introduced in this chapter can provide guidance. For IS programs that are interested in building alliances and creating an advisory council, the growth model discussed in this chapter can allow a program to assess their situation and can provide a sense of direction for moving forward. For IS programs that have already established an advisory council, determining their current stage in the growth model can help them to identify ways to more effectively exploit academic-industry alliances. For programs that wish to move to a higher level on the Stages of Partnership Growth model, the model can be used to identify future opportunities and challenges.

As discussed above, our IS program has evolved tremendously over the past decade with regard to our relationships with the business community. In this chapter, our goal was to share our experiences and insights with regard to the creation and growth of our Corporate Partnership Program. We believe that the Stages of Partnership Growth model presented in this chapter, along with our illustrative experiences, will help others to learn about the evolutionary stages of using an advisory council to develop partnerships with industry.

APPENDIX A: INFORMATION SYSTEMS CURRICULUM AT OREGON STATE UNIVERSITY

At Oregon State University, the information systems (IS) program is an "option" within the College of Business. The goal of this program is to produce IS graduates who will be prepared to work as business systems analysts:

- Our students graduate with a degree in Business Administration, but also have an in-depth understanding of information management concepts.
- Case analyses and course projects promote critical thinking and problem-solving skills by encouraging students to design computer applications that create new business opportunities and solve business problems.
- Each student acquires relevant technical skills by designing and developing desktop business applications using Microsoft Access, enterprise-wide client-server business applications using Microsoft Visual Basic and SQL server, and enterprise-wide business applications using Oracle. Windows 2000 is used to provide hands-on network administration experience.
- The curriculum also emphasizes many of the "soft skills" needed to be successful in today's business environment: communication skills, interpersonal skills, and teamwork.

All IS option students complete the standard "Business Core" curriculum. This provides a strong foundation in business fundamentals, including accounting, finance, international business, management, marketing, and personal productivity tools (Office suite). IS option students also complete:

- An introductory-level programming class using C, C++, or JAVA to learn the fundamentals of newer third-generation programming languages, including language elements, structured programming constructs, and data structures.
- A specialized course in Project Management that deals with planning, scheduling, organizing, and controlling projects with primary emphasis on the project management process and tools. Students are required to develop a project plan using Microsoft Project.

The curriculum for the IS option presents an integrated set of courses modeled after the Systems Development Life Cycle to prepare these business students for entry-level positions in the information management career field. Each course is described below:

Introduction to Information Management (BA370). This is the first course in the junior-year sequence that is intended to introduce business students to the information management career field. The project initiation and systems study phases of the systems life cycle determines whether the organization has an opportunity or problem, and whether information technologies can be applied to enable the opportunity or solve the problem. This first course emphasizes how information technology can be applied to enhance decision-making and further competitive strategies within a business environment, and on the characteristics and roles of business information systems.

The hands-on component of the course requires each student to develop an integrated desktop business application program using Microsoft Access. To support the project, relational database design concepts are introduced. The project involves designing the database, developing customized forms and reports, and using Visual Basic for Applications code to implement event-based procedures within the application.

Business Systems Analysis and Design (BA371). The second course in the junior-year sequence explores systems analysis, design, control, and documentation of Business Information Systems applications. The course teaches both the process-oriented and data-oriented development methodologies. Students use computer-based tools and structured techniques that support analysis and design concepts. The hands-on component of the course extends the desktop application project started in BA370 to an enterprise-level client-server application using Visual Basic and SQL server.

Business Systems Development (BA372). The final course in the junior-year sequence focuses on development, testing, and implementation. Students are required to develop new modules and enhance existing modules within an enterprise-wide business application using Oracle development tools.

Business Telecommunications and Networking (BA479). This senior-level course introduces computer networking from the designer's perspective. The students explore hardware, software, methodologies, and characteristics of basic networking technologies. Students also become familiar with matching business communication needs with appropriate networking architectures. The hands-on component of the course provides experience with a network operating system (Microsoft 2000).

E-Business and Information Resource Management (BA483). This course is designed to address the integration and management of enterprise information resources, with an emphasis on electronic commerce. As a capstone senior-level course, students are expected to integrate material from other business courses, especially the business policy course. The course covers the entire spectrum of the systems life cycle. Students must analyze

Figure A-1: IS Option Courses in Relation to the Systems Development Life Cycle

Systems Development Life Cycle

Project Initiation	Systems Analysis	Systems Design	Application Development	Testing & Implementation

Courses in IS Curriculum

Intro to IM BA370	Sys Anal & Design BA371	Bus Systems Develop BA372

Networking BA479

E-Business & Information Resource Management BA483

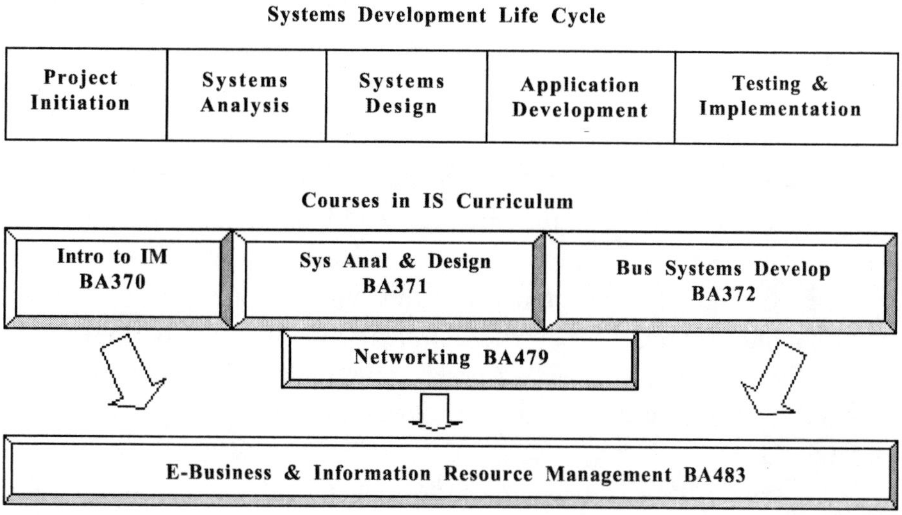

environmental influences on companies, and how they create and implement strategies for the exploitation of information, information technology, and E-Commerce. The students complete an integrative e-commerce project based on the conceptual framework of Porter's Value Chain. (See Tyran and Coakley, 2000, for a complete description of the project.)

APPENDIX B: CHARTER FOR INFORMATION SYSTEMS ADVISORY COUNCIL

Information Systems Advisory Council
College of Business
Oregon State University

Charter

SECTION I: PURPOSE

The primary purpose of the Information Systems Advisory Council is to provide an effective partnership among Information Systems professionals and the students and faculty of the Information Management Program at the College of Business at Oregon State University. The Council will provide advice and guidance pertinent to the maintenance and enhancement of a distinguished program, the continued relationship among information systems professionals, and achieving the mission of the Information Management Program.

SECTION II: OBJECTIVES AND ACTIVITIES

The Council shall assist the Information Management Program in the following ways:

1. Be an advocate of the program to the University administration, other units on campus, students, prospective students, prospective employers, prospective faculty, and others. Provide a communication link to the University administration relative to the Program's needs, directions, and activities.

2. Advise and counsel the Dean, Department Chair, Faculty, and students regarding the Information Management Program.

3. Enhance the quality of the student experience through involvement in curriculum design, facility enhancement, scholarships, internships, and other interactions with faculty and students.

4. Communicate to the information management faculty current issues and concerns deserving of scholarly study. Serve as a forum for faculty to discuss their research programs and the implications for practice. When appropriate, assist faculty with access to data.

5. Participate actively on the Business Advisory Council to ensure the needs of the Information Systems community are represented.

6. Support other activities recognized by the Council as worthy of the energies of its members.

SECTION III: OPERATION

The Council will meet at least two times each year. Meetings will be called by the Council Chair and the responsible faculty member from the Oregon State University Information Management Program. These two people will be responsible for establishing a meeting agenda and providing notice of the agenda to the other members prior to a meeting. Minutes of the meetings will be kept and provided to all Council members.

SECTION IV: MEMBERSHIP, OFFICERS, AND COMMITTEES

1. The Information Systems Advisory Council will consist of not fewer than 12 information systems professionals that reflect a cross-section of Oregon employers.
2. *Ex officio* members will include the Information Management faculty, the Dean of the College of Business, and the Chair of the Department administering the Information Management Program.
3. Members may be nominated by other council members or by the responsible faculty member in charge of the Information Management Program in the College of Business at Oregon State University.
4. The term of professional membership will be three years. Members may be re-appointed at the discretion of the Council and the responsible faculty member from the Information Management Program.
5. The Chair will be nominated and elected by members of the Council. The Chair will normally serve a three-year term.
6. The Council Chair will appoint committees as needed. Faculty members may be asked to serve on committees.

ENDNOTE

1 The reader may note that there are numeric differences between the number of students starting the program within an academic year (Figure 2), and the number of students graduating from the program (Figure 3). Since the time required to complete the option courses and other graduation requirements varies, the number of students graduating from the program each year fluctuates.

REFERENCES

Association of Information Technology Professionals. (1997). *IS '97: Model Curriculum and Guidelines for Undergraduate Degree Programs in Information Systems*. Retrieved May 29, 2000, from the World Wide Web: http://www.is2000.org/is2k/review/review.asp.

Churchill, N. C. and Lewis, V. L. (1983). The five stages of small business growth. *Harvard Business Review*, 61(3), 30-39.

Conger, J. A., Finegold, D. and Lawler, E. E. (1998). Appraising boardroom performance. *Harvard Business Review*, 76(1), 136-148.

Daft, R. L. (2001). *Organization Theory and Design, 7th Edition.* Cincinnati, OH: South-Western Publishing.

Data Processing Management Association. (1990). *DPMA Model Curriculum for a Four-Year Undergraduate Degree.* DPMA.

Davis, G. B., Gorgone, J. T., Couger, J. D., Feinstein, D. L. and Longenecker, Jr., H. E. (1997). IS '97: Model curriculum and guidelines for undergraduate degree programs in information systems. *Database*, 28(1), 1-94.

Gibson, C. F. and Nolan, R. L. (1974). Managing the four stages of EDP growth. *Harvard Business Review*, 52(1), 76-88.

McFarlan, F. W. (1999). Working on nonprofit boards: Don't assume the shoe fits. *Harvard Business Review*, 77(6), 64-76.

Redraw the line between the board and the CEO. (1995). *Harvard Business Review*, 73(2), 153-161.

Rostow, W. W. (1960). *The Stages of Economic Growth, A Non-Communist Manifesto.* Cambridge, England: University Press.

Tyran, C. K. and Coakley, J. R. (2000). The e-commerce course project: Creating educational linkages with the value chain. *Journal of Informatics Education and Research*, 2(2), 59-70.

Chapter VIII

The Development of IT/ Community Partnerships at a Small Regional University

John Borton and Kathy S. Lassila
University of Southern Colorado, USA

Lacking the resources and national recognition of large universities, small regional universities and state colleges must employ different strategies in the formation of IT partnerships with community organizations. Opportunities for mutually beneficial relationships with K-12 students and parents, current CIS students and alumni, CIS faculty, local businesses, the local IT industry, government agencies, non-profit organizations, and current and prospective employers of program graduates are plentiful. These relationships can lead to stronger curriculum, improved student job opportunities, increased enrollments, high quality adjunct faculty, private funding sources, and enhanced reputation of the IT program and the university within the region.

INTRODUCTION

Partnerships between information technology (IT) academic programs and community organizations have, in varying degrees, been part of the university landscape since the inception of IT degrees. Large urban universities and research institutions leverage their national reputations and resource base in the formation of IT partnerships, frequently resulting in large corporate donations to support program development, facilities, faculty and students within IT academic programs (Tobias, 2001). Smaller regional universities and state colleges must employ different strategies in the formation of IT partnerships with community organizations. The activities involved in these relationships may differ from those of larger academic institutions, but the benefits and advantages to all involved parties are equally valuable.

This chapter describes a "Partners in Excellence" plan that has evolved over a 23-year period into a comprehensive program of community interactions for a computer information systems (CIS) undergraduate degree program at a small regional university. Partners in Excellence involves a variety of community constituents: K-12 students and parents, current CIS students and alumni, CIS faculty, local businesses, the local IT industry, government agencies, non-profit organizations, and current and prospective employers of CIS program graduates. The CIS degree program receives benefits from Partners in Excellence through increased enrollments, on-going development of curricula and pedagogy, enhanced reputation in the community, donations from local organizations, and from contributing to university goals for service to the surrounding community. Community constituents receive a wide variety of advantages from their interactions with the CIS program, including IT services they would not have access to without the Partners in Excellence plan.

Following a review of some of the existing partnerships between IT academic programs and community organizations documented in the literature, the Partners in Excellence framework is presented and discussed. Future directions for the Partners in Excellence program are also included. The chapter concludes with guidelines for IT programs at small regional universities and state colleges who wish to develop stronger community partnerships.

BACKGROUND LITERATURE

Over the past two decades, a number of factors have driven the demand for closer relationships between IT academic programs and community organizations, and both groups have requested or initiated collaborations. The primary focus of IT academic program collaboration with industry has centered on curricula issues. Prior research reported that inadequate formal education and training in IS, for both developers and users, was the cause for the majority of the cases of non-acceptance or resistance to information system implementation and other causes of information system failure (Yaffe, 1989). These early researchers proposed curriculum changes developed as a joint venture between academic institutions and industry, both private and public sector, as the solution. However, conflict within universities over what kind of, and how much, input industry should have to program curricula exists (Kass, 1992). The fundamental issue is whether an academic program should be demand driven or should focus instead on the current state of the art and theory of the field (Quarstein, Ramakrishna & Vijayaraman, 1994). Varying degrees of industry influence on curriculum development are evident.

Industry continues to press for a university response to the technological needs of information-intensive industries (Kass, 1992). In response to industry pressure, many universities have established forums to foster dialogue between industry needs and academic results (Wells & Sevilla, 2001). A common approach to influencing curriculum is the traditional route of having industry members sit on university advisory councils. These meetings are often unsuccessful, with industry annoyed at academia for not focussing on practical subjects, while academia views industry as narrow and shallow. Shared learning repositories, which help develop a joint vision between industry and academic institutions, have been proposed as a solution by some researchers (Wells & Sevilla, 2001).

Industry advocates continue to call for universities to better prepare IT students for the real world characterized by technological change (Tobias, 2001). The capacity of industry to upgrade applications and technologies typically exceeds the time required for academic institutions to identify changes and create new or revised courses and programs for delivery to the public. Some universities have responded by formalizing programs where students work directly with corporations prior to graduation, or corporate CEOs visit university classes and teach courses in the IT curriculum (Tobias, 2001).

Other researchers have more specifically identified the gap between industry needs and academic preparation of new graduates (Trauth, Farwell & Lee, 1993; Lee, Trauth & Farwell, 1995). Industry cites the need for a balance between technical and business knowledge and problems with relevance of IS curricula. The absence of a shared vision between IT academic programs and universities on the appropriate skill mix for IS professionals is blamed for the gap. Universities have responded to community pressure by developing communication channels with industry to identify desired skill mixes, revise curricula and attempt to close the gap (Lee, Trauth & Farwell, 1995; Wells & Sevilla, 2001).

In recent years industry has increasingly turned to academic institutions to aid in easing the enormous demand for IT workers. Some innovative collaborations have spawned crash courses in IT skills to retrain existing professionals or displaced workers for careers in computer-related fields (Wells, 1999). These programs offer a combination of academic and hands-on training through paid internships with local IT companies.

IT academic programs have also called on the community in times of need. Lemos (1985) called on industry to become involved in attracting and retaining IS educators in the early to mid-1980s. He urged industry to develop employment plans for faculty when school was not in session, to support legislative issues impacting higher education, to refrain from stealing IS faculty and graduate students for industry positions, and to provide support for IS doctoral students. IT programs have also called on industry to play a role in attracting new students to IT programs (Rifkin, 1987). To appeal to prospective students, industry can demonstrate the need for IS graduates and document their strong income earning potential.

In summary, the literature reviewed showed that both the IT industry and academic institutions request and initiate collaborations with each other for a variety of reasons, and these collaborations may take different forms. Industry seeks collaborations with universities to: produce graduates with the right skills, produce more graduates to meet rising demand in high tech industries, and to help retrain existing and displaced workers. IT academic programs seek collaborations with industry to: gain input to curricula development, provide "real-world" and hands-on experience for students, help meet the demand for IT educators and help finance on-going program development in a rapidly changing technological environment.

Little distinction between large and small academic institutions and their approach to forming community partnerships was noted in the literature. This may imply that the factors driving collaboration and the resulting activities apply equally to all IT academic programs regardless of size, or that no attention has been paid to the difference in institutional size in the investigation of collaborative activities. The following section examines the context of a CIS program at a small regional university and then presents the development of a comprehensive community interaction program well-suited to the context.

PARTNERS IN EXCELLENCE PROGRAM

Computer Information Systems at the University of Southern Colorado

The University of Southern Colorado (USC) is a small regional university located in Pueblo, Colorado, a town of 100,000 that serves the local community and the surrounding rural communities in Southeastern Colorado. Achieving university status in 1975, USC's enrollments have been tied very closely to the local economy throughout its short history. Pueblo is a traditionally blue-collar community that, for decades, based its economy on the successes of the local steel-mill. In the mid-80s the steel mill shut down having a major impact on Pueblo's economy. The community began the process of rebuilding and expanding its economic base, and formed a regional economic development organization to attract new business and industry to the area. Growth has been slow, and the economy remains heavily grounded in manufacturing and small business.

The University of Southern Colorado is a member of the Colorado State University System. The 275-acre campus enrolls approximately 4,000 students in 29 undergraduate and six graduate programs, with approximately 500 full-time faculty and staff. The University community is committed to diversity, and has made educational equity for students a high priority. The Computer Information Systems program currently has 312 majors and 45 minors, serviced by five full-time, tenure-track faculty members and six part-time instructors. The University of Southern Colorado is accredited at the bachelor and master level by the Commission on Institutions of Higher Education of the North Central Association of Colleges and Schools.

USC's closest urban center is Colorado Springs, located approximately 50 miles from Pueblo. It has experienced a surge of growth, particularly in the high tech industry. Key companies in Colorado Springs who employ CIS program graduates include MCIWorldCom, Compaq, Oracle, Lockheed Martin, Intel and Agilent Technologies. Denver is located approximately 90 miles north of Pueblo, and is home to many Fortune 500 companies who also employ USC CIS program graduates.

The Computer Information Systems (CIS) department is part of USC's College of Education, Engineering and Professional Studies. The current CIS program at USC came into existence in 1994, when the previous four-year program and its three options (information system applications, computer science and computer engineering) were reformulated into the existing CIS program based on input from a departmental industry advisory board. The current curriculum has a strong business application orientation, but with 48 semester credits required in the major, is technically more demanding than typical IS programs found in business schools. The current CIS curriculum is summarized in Table 1.

From 1994 to 2001, while USC's overall enrollment was in a steady decline, enrollments in the CIS program tripled, from a low of 105 majors to a high of over 300 majors. While part of the CIS enrollment increase can be

Table 1: USC Bachelor of Science in Computer Information Systems

CIS REQUIRED COURSES (39 credits): Intro to Computer Information Systems Intro to Programming and Design w/Visual Basic Intro to Object-Oriented Programming w/C++ Advanced C++ Programming UNIX Object-Oriented Systems Analysis/Design using UML Web Application Development (D/HTML, Javascript, XML) PC Architecture Network Concepts w/NT Server Database Design w/Access and ERDs Senior Professional Project (team-based, community effort) Senior Seminar (Intro to IT profession)	**REQUIRED RELATED COURSES FOR CIS (9 credits):** Statistics or Calculus Management Accounting or Upper Division Management **MINOR SUBJECT AREA (20-24 credits):** Business Administration, Mathematics, or Electrical Engineering Technology are recommended; any minor offered by the university is accepted.
CIS ELECTIVE COURSES (9 credits from below): Advanced Operating System Design and Internals Internet Programming with Java Internet Server-Side Programming with ASP Network Enterprise Administration (Novell, NT, UNIX) Advanced Database Administration with Oracle Knowledge-Based Systems Advanced Visual Basic Programming Current Topics (Based on faculty and advisory board) Internships/Cooperative Education	**GENERAL EDUCATION (36 credits):** Includes Computer Literacy Skills (MS Office) **FREE ELECTIVES (4-7 credits)** **120 TOTAL SEMESTER CREDIT HOURS REQUIRED**

attributed to a nationwide trend toward increased enrollments in computer-based programs, the CIS faculty argue that the balance of the improvement was a result of increased involvement with, and responsiveness to, the needs of the regional community. During the timeframe of the enrollment increase, the CIS department worked to develop and nurture a variety of community partnerships, which are described in the CIS Partners in Excellence Model that follows.

CIS Partners in Excellence Model

The Partners in Excellence program evolved over a multi-year period. Almost since its inception, the CIS department worked closely with an industry advisory board. Initially, the CIS faculty began to focus on industry relationships in an attempt to reverse the downward trend in enrollments that prompted the implementation of the new curriculum in 1994. In 1998, during the process of developing a grant proposal to fund enhancement of the CIS program, the variety and strength of the partnerships developed with the local community came sharply into focus. It was clear these partnerships had allowed the program to grow and improve to meet the needs of the CIS students while meeting the needs of our community constituents. The partnerships with the community became a guiding theme for the CIS department referred to as "Partners in Excel-

Figure 1: CIS Partners in Excellence Program

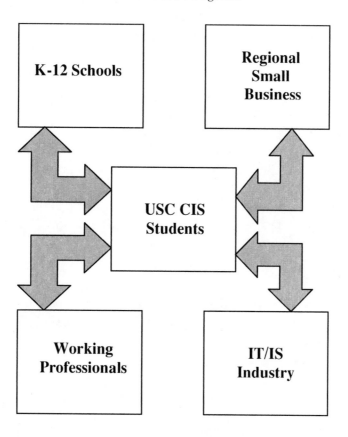

lence." The CIS Partners in Excellence program develops and sustains linkages with community entities at all levels. Figure 1 depicts these linkages which are discussed below in detail.

K-12 Partnerships

K-12 partnerships have been developed across the region through the following activities: faculty guest speakers at school career days; college student tutoring of middle and high school math students; sponsorship of two summer computer camps for high school students (with 72+ high school student and teacher participants); and hosting of an annual web site design contest for middle and high school students (with over 100 participants annually).

Early in 1994, in a step toward boosting enrollments, the CIS faculty initiated a survey of regional high school students to discover what college-bound students were looking for in post-secondary education. Over 300 high school students in Pueblo and two surrounding cities were surveyed. The survey showed that the top three items that determine a student's choice in majors and schools were: job opportunities upon graduation, job salaries and schools offering the curriculum students wish to pursue.

The following academic year, the CIS faculty initiated a concerted marketing campaign to attract students to the program. A $5,000 advertising budget was used to run several small ads in local newspapers headlining the average starting salary of program graduates and including a summary of the program curriculum. Faculty visited the local high schools and talked about career opportunities in the computer industry and the high school courses required to complete the CIS degree program in a four-year time frame. Recent high school graduates, who were in the CIS program, accompanied faculty and talked to students about the transition from high school to college, course loads and social life at the University. Faculty accompanied by current CIS students also attended high-school career days and other activities to get the word out to high-school students, parents, counselors and teachers. Although CIS faculty contact in the high schools was important for recruitment, the inclusion of current CIS students added an element of reality and personal identification to the discussion of CIS academic and career opportunities. The following year, the department realized a 30% increase in enrollments, primarily in the freshman classes.

An opportunity arose through an existing university program to involve CIS students in a program to tutor middle school and high school students in mathematics. This type of contact was good not only for the high school students being tutored, but gave the college students a sense of community and involvement that prior studies showed would boost retention. As a by-product of the program, students receiving the tutoring became interested in and more aware of academic opportunities in the computer field. The CIS students not only talked about mathematics, but other subjects they were taking in the CIS program as well. Overall, the tutoring program had very positive short- and long-term benefits for all students involved, the local community and the CIS program.

In 1997, the CIS department sponsored the first annual web-design contest for middle and high school students. The contest draws an average of 100 students in teams from across the state of Colorado each year. Students design web sites for their school or for an activity within the school. Student contestants are provided access to the university web-server through an access-port donated by a local ISP service provider which partners with the CIS department as a co-sponsor of the contest. The contest provides another way to involve current CIS students in department-related activities outside of the classroom. Students in the CIS program provide contest judging and technical assistance to contestants. A preliminary contest round is held in which contestants are provided tips for improving the web site and/or technical advice. The contest finals are held on a Saturday at the local shopping mall, and student entries are judged using a large-screen computer projection unit so that the sites may be viewed by anyone in the community who is interested. Winning teams are awarded prizes sponsored by local businesses. The contest has successfully completed its fifth year.

During the 1999-00 academic year, the department applied for and received a $191,700 grant to offer a summer computer camp for local high school juniors and seniors. The summer camp was six weeks in length and covered the same material as the introductory general education college computer literacy course and the introductory CIS concepts course. Students also worked in teams, using the skills they learned in class, to conduct independent research on a technical topic of their choice with assistance from a CIS faculty member. The students developed a web-based presentation on the topic. The camp was funded by the Colorado Institute of Technology (CIT), a non-profit, statewide consortium of IT companies whose primary goal is to support IT education across the state and increase the number of IT-trained graduates available in the work force.

During the initial summer computer camp, student participants were provided with a scholarship for full tuition, fees and books, lunch, a six-week stipend of $1,260 and six-credits of college-level course work. The camp curriculum included lecture presentations, extensive hands-on laboratory work and the development of a team project using the application tools taught in the camp. Specific tools covered included Windows NT, MS Word, MS Excel, MS PowerPoint, Netscape, HTML and Visual Basic. Students began the camp by participating in several team-building activities on the University Challenge Course, an outdoor team experience. In retrospect, the camp participants, CIS student assistants and faculty found this to be a valuable camp activity. It helped students and faculty to get to know one another in a more personal and informal atmosphere. It also helped build the "camp" theme for the intensive six-week educational program. A pre-test/post-test evaluation of the camp participants showed a marked increase in interest toward attending college and pursuing a computer-related career.

The camp was funded for a second summer in 2001, and the camp activities were redesigned to integrate lessons learned from the first camp. Changes to the summer camp included: no stipends for participants due to decreased grant funding and budget restraints, inclusion of intermediate-level computer applications for advanced students, the inclusion of engineering-related computer applications, and a pre-camp parent/student session to discuss the camp activities and career opportunities in the IT discipline. All students were required to participate in the Challenge Course at the start of camp and a post-camp picnic. The 2001 camp also did not include tuition and fee scholarship for students. Students were given the option of taking the courses for credit. The scholarships were eliminated as a cost-saving measure by the CIT. Students who selected the no-credit option were allowed to complete the courses for free. The total funding for the Summer 2001 camp was reduced to $74,000. The elimination of stipends and scholarships for camp participants significantly decreased interest in the program, evidenced by a drop in participants to 20 attendees in 2001 from 72 attendees in 2000. Planning for future summer camps will take this into consideration.

IT Industry and Working Professionals

The local IT industry and working professionals provide numerous opportunities for partnerships. The IT industry looks to local universities as a primary source of new workers. It is in their best interest to foster relationships to bring more students to them and to assist in directing the curriculum to meet their needs. Working professionals turn to local universities to provide retraining, additional degree opportunities, and outlets for community service delivering career-oriented lectures and serving on advisory boards. Partnerships between the CIS program and the IT industry and working professionals are fostered through the following activities: utilization of a CIS Industry Advisory Board for input related to curricular and partnering decisions, annual IT Guest Lecture Series bringing IT professionals into the university classroom for a two-day series, proposed Visiting IT Industry professorships to bring IT professionals into the classroom to teach courses in their area of expertise, and a proposed Web-based IT curriculum (BS and MSIS) to meet the needs of working professionals ready to upgrade IT skill levels and/or obtain IT degrees.

The CIS Industry Advisory Board was formed in 1977, one year prior to the formation of the CIS department. The CIS Industry Advisory Board has served a major role developing and restructuring the departmental curriculum for over two decades. Membership on the board has varied across the years from eight to fifteen working IT professionals. Members are selected from throughout Colorado with an emphasis on companies that have traditionally hired USC CIS graduates. The average length of membership on the board is three-to-five years. As a rule individuals serve on the board until they move to another company.

The board meets annually during the Spring semester. Meetings are typically one-half day, but have been scheduled for a full day when major curriculum changes and other issues are being considered. Due to the rapid changes that have taken place in the IT industry since the program's inception, the board members have been kept busy considering the appropriate direction for the departmental curriculum. The three primary questions that are addressed annually are: What changes need to be made to existing courses? Which (if any) new courses should be considered? Which (if any) courses should be dropped from the curriculum? Since answers to these questions are not cut and dried, board meetings usually include a considerable amount of lively discussion. Board members from different segments of the industry will often have radically different opinions regarding specific courses. One item that is discussed every year is which programming languages are appropriate for the curriculum. For example, the discussion over the role of COBOL and whether or not to continue requiring it, offering it as an elective or eliminating it from the curriculum entirely, continued for more than five years.

The board also considers questions of a broader scale. In recent years the question of how and to what extent to integrate the object-oriented paradigm into the curriculum occupied several meetings. By far the largest issue considered by the board since the creation of the initial curriculum was how to structure the new CIS program (1994) after eliminating the three original program options. The board provided guidance and legitimacy to the new curriculum. With the continued help of the CIS Industry Advisory Board, the curriculum continues to evolve and grow to meet the needs of the region.

In addition to providing curricular guidance, the CIS Industry Advisory Board has also provided input regarding issues such as enrollment enhancement, limited faculty resources, placement of graduates, development of internships and departmental funding opportunities. Recently, several members of the Board provided letters of support for the department to accompany a grant application to the Colorado Institute of Technology. The CIT strongly supports the concept of industry and academic partnerships, and believes that any program receiving grant funding should have such partnerships in place.

The CIS Guest Lecture Series was initiated in 1997 to bring together CIS students and IT professionals from across the region. The series has been extremely successful and is lauded by students and IT professionals alike. For two days, each CIS class hosts a guest lecturer. The lectures are open to all USC students and members of the local community. Lecture topics are related to the topics of the class hosting the lecture. Lecture topics from the Fall 2000 series included:

- Life After the University: Computer Job Opportunities in the New Millennium
- Real-World Unix: Problems and Solutions
- Computer Career Opportunities: Life in the Applications Development Fast Lane
- The Facts of Life in a Networked World
- C++ Programming: Building Objects for Tomorrow
- Web Development Tools
- Enterprise Java Programming
- Database Systems: Integrating Information in Large Corporations
- Software Project Development
- Visual Programming on the Web: Making Complexity Look Simple
- Computer System Design: Objects and UML in the Real World

Guest lecturers, who donate their time, are encouraged to focus the presentation on: how technology is used in their work environment, issues related to transitioning from university to the work force, how course work completed in college assists on the job, career opportunities in specific segments of the discipline/market and strategies for obtaining work after graduation. The lecturers appreciate the opportunity to share their experiences with students, and the students benefit by getting information from a new perspective. Student comments after the series reveal that not only do the students have a better idea about what they will be doing after graduation, but they have renewed motivation for completing the degree and doing well in the classroom. In addition, the lecture series provides an opportunity for faculty to renew connections with past graduates and other IT professionals in the region. Many of these contacts lead to internships and full-time job opportunities for CIS students.

Each year, one faculty member is selected to coordinate the series. The coordinator sees to it that each class has a guest lecturer; sets up coffee, breakfast and lunch for the lecturers and faculty; sends out thank you letters to lecturers after the series; sends news releases to the local newspaper and other media; sets up advertising in the local school paper; and develops the lecture series brochure that is distributed in all CIS classes and across the campus. The most recent IT Guest Lecture Series included 14 IT professionals and was attended by over 300 students and community members.

Two additional proposed partnering activities with the local IT industry will be discussed in more detail in the future directions section of the chapter. These proposed activities include: Visiting IT Industry professorships to bring IT professionals into the classroom to teach courses in their area of expertise, and a proposed Web-based IT curriculum (BS and MSIS) to meet the needs of working professionals ready to upgrade IT skill levels and/or obtain IT degrees.

Regional Small Business Partnerships

Partnering with regional small business is currently provided through two activities: student teams designing and implementing working computer systems in regional business and non-profit organizations as part of a senior design project course, and providing an informal placement service of CIS students into part-time computer-related jobs in local businesses.

The senior professional project course has been part of the curriculum for over a decade. It was recently formatted as a six-credit course, with three hours of lecture/discussion and six hours of lab. Lab credits require the students to meet two hours per week for each credit. The lab time allows students to have six hours per week in which they are scheduled to work together on the project. This has solved one of the biggest problems with team-based projects, finding a time when all team members can meet. During the Fall semester the class is scheduled Tuesday and Thursday afternoons from 12:30 to 5:00pm. During the Spring semester the class is scheduled Tuesday and Thursday evenings from 5:30 to 9:00pm plus Saturdays from 9:00 to 12:00pm. The Spring schedule is designed to accommodate students in the evening/weekend CIS program. Since making this change, the course has increased the project success rate to an average of 85%. A successful project is defined as one in which the company implements all or part of the system as designed by the students, and the students meet all the requirements for course deliverables.

Projects are located in several ways: local businesses and nonprofit organizations call the CIS department looking for assistance with IT projects; CIS Industry Advisory Board members suggest projects in their organization; CIS faculty, graduates or current students hear of possible projects in general conversations; or companies that have had successful projects completed in the past ask for additional student teams to complete new projects.

When the semester begins, the instructor compiles a list of possible projects. Students complete a survey that describes the type of work they would like to do after graduation and the type of project they would like to work on. The instructor then matches the student interests with the projects and assigns each student to a team of three-to-four students. Although many projects overlap skill areas, they may generally be classified as database development, network design and implementation, software application development or web application development. Most projects require a team to be involved to some degree in all of these areas.

The senior professional project course is structured along the same lines as a live project in any corporate business. Once the students are assigned to project teams and team leaders are selected, they are given a general list of deadlines, deliverables and presentation times. Students must then construct, implement and complete a detailed project plan. Project deliverables include: an initial charter agreement between the team and the company, a requirements definition, a detailed design, an installation and implementation plan, technical documentation, user documentation and a disk with the completed system. Two presentations are required. The first is at mid-term. Students present an overview of the system design, areas of concern and future directions. The second presentation is completed during finals week. Students show a demo of the system, describe system problems and successes, and discuss lessons learned.

As a result of the quality of the completed projects, the department has developed a strong reputation across the region as a good source of technical assistance in completing small- to mid-scale IT projects. During 2000-01, 17 projects were completed, with several on the waiting list. Since more projects are available each year than student teams to complete them, the scope and type of project assigned to students can be selectively determined. Preference is frequently given to non-profit organizations and small businesses that could not otherwise afford to have the projects completed. In this way, the university is making a contribution to the local community as well as providing a great learning opportunity for students.

During the past two decades, the CIS department has become a resource for local businesses to find students to work on small projects or to work as part-time employees for the company. Providing this informal placement service has proved beneficial to both the students and the companies needing assistance. There are two issues that must be addressed by any academic department choosing to provide this type of service to the local community. The first is the question of pay rate. Some organizations call expecting to get students to work for free. They assume that the students benefit from the experience of an internship and do not need to be paid. While students do indeed benefit from the practical experience, the majority of our students work to support themselves and cannot afford to work for free. In addition, the faculty firmly believes that if a company receives benefit from student work, they should pay for it. If an organization is a non-profit or too small to realistically pay for IT development, and the work can be completed in 10-15 weeks by a four-student team, we refer the organization to the senior professional project course or to one of our other courses. The database or web development courses often have students complete small projects that can be either book-based case studies or real-world scenarios.

The second issue that must be addressed in placing students in local part-time jobs is how to notify students and match the right student with the right job. Several methods of notifying students of job opportunities have been tested. The most effective was using a listserv to notify all CIS majors and minors of job and other opportunities that are available. This worked well until students decided not to use the university mail system. Students moved their primary accounts to Yahoo, Hotmail or other readily accessible e-mail systems. Since the university address listing could no longer be used to obtain student account identifiers, it became more and more difficult to update the listserv. Currently, jobs are posted on a job web site and on a bulletin board near CIS faculty offices. Faculty also announce job openings in classes.

Employers often request that the university refer one right student for the job. This can lead to issues related to fairness in selecting the students. As a result the CIS department faculty no longer screen student applicants. Skill requirements and courses that would provide the skills are posted for the students. It is then left to the employer to screen and interview all candidates who apply. This is a very satisfactory method that avoids legal issues surrounding how students are notified of and selected for part-time jobs.

The CIS department has also partnered with regional businesses, non-profit organizations and government agencies to set up formal internships. The internships are typically funded by the organizations for a period of six months to three years. Several of the companies have employed two-to-three students continuously for multiple years. Although these formalized internships are difficult to identify and establish, a key departmental goal is to cultivate more of these opportunities in the future.

Currently, over 50% of junior and senior CIS students are working in computer-related jobs outside of school. Most of these students were placed through the informal job placement service, formal internships, or by word-of-mouth when a current student who was placed in the job graduated or moved on to another position. In addition, as a result of our senior professional project course, graduating students can list real-world IT project experience on their resume.

Two additional proposed activities for partnering with regional small businesses will be discussed in the Future Directions section of the chapter. These include a student IT consulting center and a student-faculty-industry research program.

FUTURE DIRECTIONS

The activities proposed in this section require additional funding and resources not readily available within most small regional universities. To expand the CIS Partners in Excellence program to include these proposed activities, funding from external sources must be secured. A variety of public and private grant programs are being explored to this end.

USC was designated a Hispanic Serving Institution (HSI) in 2000. This designation is provided for universities whose Hispanic student population exceeds 25% of the enrolled full-time students. The designation opens several opportunities for grant funding available only to HSI and other minority serving institutions. In addition, several funding agencies, such as NSF, give a priority to HSI and other minority serving institutions. The CIS faculty are currently researching the additional funding opportunities that may now be available to extend our Partners in Excellence program.

The CIS department faculty hopes to expand their funding search into the private sector. The primary objective of this activity is to obtain funding from regional IT industries to fund various departmental projects. These projects will vary depending on the on-going needs of the program. Many activities will fit into the department's current Partners in Excellence program; others will be more internally focused.

The Computer Information Systems program at the University of Southern Colorado has been nominated three consecutive years for recognition of excellence in a statewide award program funded by the Colorado Commission on Higher Education (CCHE). The CIS program has proposed that the CCHE fund an expansion of the "Partners in Excellence" program to include: Visiting IT Industry Professorships to bring IT professionals into the classroom to teach courses in their area of expertise, a student IT consulting center to provide IT assistance to regional small businesses, and a student-faculty-industry research program. A second grant proposal has been presented to the Colorado Institute of Technology to fund a proposed Web-based IT curriculum (BS and MSIS) to meet the needs of working professionals ready to upgrade (or obtain) IT skill levels and/or degrees. These proposed activities are discussed below.

The proposed Visiting IT Industry Professorship program is a unique concept developed by the CIS faculty to partner with regional IT industry to meet the shortage of qualified IT faculty in the classroom. The Visiting IT Industry Professorship (VIIP) program will provide funding to pay a per-semester honorarium to IT professionals to teach full time at the university in their area of expertise. For the program to work effectively, companies in the region must buy in to the concept and be willing to allow their employees a 16-week leave to teach classes at the University. The program parameters allow companies to choose to either continue to pay employees full time, half time or only maintain the employees' benefits. The VIIP professors would teach two or three classes (a maximum of two preparations). The VIIP professorships could be extended to a second semester with the agreement of the VIIP professor and the sponsoring company. Funding for the program has been requested for five years.

Five years of funding for a student IT consulting center has also been requested. The consulting center will provide short-term technical assistance and training to regional businesses for expanding or developing their IT operations. The center would also provide part-time employment and valuable real-world experience to CIS students. The grant proposal includes: funding for two students to manage the consulting office; funding to provide the first eight hours of free consulting to organizations; funding for one-half release time for a CIS faculty member to supervise the center; and funding for basic office supplies, telephone service, a computer and printer. The consulting center rates would vary depending on the task. After five years, when the grant funding is ended, the center will be self-supporting.

A student-faculty-industry research program has also been proposed. The purpose of the program is to provide a research center for regional IT businesses. The center will pair faculty with teams of students to collect and analyze data related to the IT needs of individual businesses and the various communities within the region. The grant proposal provides funding for faculty release-time, travel and supplies to collect and analyze data. The center will provide invaluable information to local industries and communities regarding IT needs and future development. Students will learn basic research skills and make contacts in the community that may help them in finding a job after graduation. Faculty will have the opportunity to utilize their statistical analysis skills to assist the community and collect data that can be used in their own research and publication.

The proposed Web-based IT curriculum (BS and MSIS) would meet the ever-expanding need of working professionals to upgrade (or obtain) IT skill levels and/or degrees. The grant proposal requests funding for two CIS faculty positions to develop an on-line curriculum. Although students could complete the majority of their course work on-line, each course would include a weekend on-campus component for examinations and presentations. Students would be required to travel to campus twice each semester on Saturday to take examinations and make presentations demonstrating the quality of work they had performed while completing the courses off-campus. The student curriculum would also include the completion of at least one IT-related project in their local community. The two faculty positions would be fully funded for the first two years of the program, then the funding would decrease each of the next three years as the University takes over funding of the program.

GUIDELINES FOR DEVELOPING PARTNERSHIP PROGRAMS

Drawing on 23 years of experience in developing partnerships between the USC Computer Information Systems program and the community, this section presents the key lessons learned. The lessons are summarized in Table 2 and discussed below. Ideally, academic IT departments will find this information useful in developing and implementing their own partnership plan.

Within a small regional university, there are very few resources and built-in structures to support the faculty in developing a partnership program. At the same time, the small size of the local community provides easy access to a variety of partnering entities. The first and arguably highest hurdle to overcome is deciding as a faculty to take the initiative to develop partnerships. Once a commitment is made in this direction, the faculty can map out a partnership strategy.

The CIS Partners in Excellence program at USC did not start with a plan to develop community partnerships. The program evolved as part of an effort

Table 2: Key Lessons Learned Developing IT/Community Partnerships

- Program faculty must decide to take the initiative to develop IT/community partnerships and map out a partnership strategy.
- Partnership strategy and partnering programs should leverage the strengths of the existing program and faculty, and exploit existing opportunities.
- To succeed, a partnering program must be flexible enough to meet the on-going/changing demands of various partnering constituencies.
- Focus initial partnering activities on low-cost alternatives, and seek grant funding to proceed beyond the basic program.
- Avoid taking on too many partnering activities.
- Maintaining the quality of partnering activities should be a priority.

to increase departmental enrollments. It soon became obvious to the faculty that the best way to increase enrollments was through the establishment of community partnerships.

One of the most important lessons learned is that for a partnering program to succeed, it must be continuously redesigned and recreated to meet the ongoing and changing needs of the various partnering constituencies. Due to limited financial resources, CIS Partners in Excellence initially relied on low-cost partnering activities. Grant opportunities beyond the two funded proposals are now being explored to expand USC CIS partnering programs beyond the initial basic activities.

Another important lesson learned from the CIS department partnering experience is that a departmental partnering strategy must consider existing strengths and opportunities, and that it is an evolutionary process. The initial partnering activities can be relatively painless and inexpensive. Setting up an Industry Advisory Board is a natural fit for IT programs. Local IT professionals consider it an honor to be invited to work with an academic IT department in this capacity. Once the Industry Advisory Board is in place, the department should look to the curriculum for opportunities to integrate real-world activities into specific courses. Once courses are identified, faculty must make contacts to find projects in local businesses that fit the courses. In a small community like Pueblo, the best source of such contacts is friends and neighbors of faculty, staff, students and members of local professional organizations. Larger communities and universities might find resources already established within the university infrastructure. The step into obtaining outside funding is an important one, opening previously unobtainable partnering opportunities. To be successful in this area, the department must have or develop a grant proposal writer. Opportunities for writing partnering proposals abound in state, federal and private funding venues. It is also important to consider local government and industry funding options.

Within the CIS department, the faculty is continually on the lookout for partnering opportunities. As the Partners in Excellence program has matured, the activities that tie into faculty strengths and areas of interest have improved. It is important not to take on too many partnering activities, necessitating the development of priorities in the types of partnerships that will be pursued. Maintaining the quality of partnering activities should be a priority.

CONCLUSION

While developing strong, enduring community partnerships is hard work, it becomes less of a challenge over time, and integrates smoothly into faculty responsibilities. Faculty soon realize that partnerships help pave the way to promotion and tenure by: enhancing teaching quality through the integration of real-world experiences in the classroom, contributing to scholarly activities through related research and grant writing, and providing an avenue for service to the community.

IT academic program partnerships with community organizations produce beneficial results for students, faculty, the university and all of the community constituents. Partnering with the high schools increases awareness of the program and the boundless job opportunities available after graduation. Partnering with the IT industry leads to a stronger curriculum, job opportunities for students, technically current adjunct faculty to teach classes and opportunities to pursue private sources of funding. Partnering with local small business provides student internships, live-case study opportunities, and a side-benefit of enhancing the perception of the quality of the program and the university across the region. Finally, partnering with working professionals leads to increased enrollments and the opportunity to meet a community and industry need for upgraded technical skills in the work force.

REFERENCES

Alexander, M. (1990). College means business with IS. *Computerworld,* 24(2), 55, 62-63.

Bertin, C. K. (1998). *Critical Skills & Knowledge Requirements of Information Systems Professionals: A Survey of Industry and Academic Viewpoints.* Unpublished doctoral dissertation, The University of the West Indies, St. Augustine, Trinidad.

Kass, R. (1992). Academic questions. *Bank Systems & Technology,* 29(9), 62-70.

Lee, D. M. S., Trauth, E. M. and Farwell, D. W. (1995). Critical skills and knowledge requirements of IS professionals: A joint academic/industry investigation. *MIS Quarterly,* 19(3), 313-340.

Lemos, R. S. (1985). The MIS education crisis: 10 steps for industry. *Journal of Information Systems Management,* 2(2), 24-30.

Matkin, H. N. (2000). *Consensus of Academic and Industry Experts and Practitioners on Essential Information Systems Curriculum Elements: A Delphi Study.* Unpublished doctoral dissertation, Texas A&M University.

Quarstein, V. A., Ramakrishna, H. V. and Vijayaraman, B. S. (1994). Meeting the IT challenge of business. *Information Systems Management,* 11(2), 62-70.

Rifkin, G. (1987). Top students shunning MIS (Part 1). *Computerworld.* 21(24), 120-121.

Tobias, Z. (2001). Making the grade. *Computerworld.* 35(12), 42.

Trauth, E. M., Farwell, D. W. and Lee, D. M. S. (1993). The IS expectation gap: Industry expectations versus academic preparation. *MIS Quarterly,* 17(3), 293-307.

Wells, S. J. (1999). Novices fill technology gaps. Technology retraining internship program in Virginia. *HRMagazine,* 44(12), 74-78.

Wells, T. D. and Sevilla, C. (2001). Forming a dialogue with academia: Industry requirements versus academic programs. *Information Systems Management,* 18(1), 80-83.

Yaffe, J. (1989). MIS education: A 20th century disaster. *Journal of Systems Management,* 40(4), 10-13.

Chapter IX

Theoretical Foundations for Enterprise Systems Technology Collaborations: An Adaptive Structuration Framework

Cindy LeRouge and Harold W. Webb
University of South Florida, USA

Industry/academic collaboration, involving the utilization of advanced information technologies (AITs), is an expanding phenomenon involving a substantial commitment of resources. This chapter presents a comprehensive framework for studying this phenomenon by extending adaptive structurization theory at the inter-institutional level. We suggest propositions, derived from the framework, to advance further research and to inform decision-making by stakeholders in industry/academic collaborations.

THE EMERGENCE OF TECHNOLOGY COLLABORATIONS

Alfred P. Sloan, Jr., former chairperson of General Motors once stated:
When the annals of our time are recorded, it will most likely be found that the two greatest contributions of our time have been the U.S. University and the U.S. Corporation: both mighty

forces, both uniquely American. If these two forces can go forward together in understanding and cooperation, there is perhaps no problem beyond their joint power for resolution. If, however, they choose to go their separate ways, there is no solution of any problem affecting either that is likely to be long lasting (Slaughter, 1990, p.9).

Consistent with Sloan, many educators and industry leaders believe industry/academic collaboration can initiate transformations by providing opportunities and resources not otherwise attainable (AAA Changing Environment Committee,1998; Beckman et al., 1997a; Mead et al., 1999a; Powell et al., 1997; Sikkel et al., 1999; Wohlin & Regnell, 1999). Whether one agrees with these sentiments or supports the position of complete academic independence from industry, the existence of industry-academic collaborations is a true and existing social structure with cultural roots that has taken on a new dimension in a technological age. Our purpose is neither to advocate nor reject these alliances, but to acknowledge the technological dimensions of this phenomenon for purposes of study and provide perspectives for decision-making and action for those who lead these relationships and whose lives they may affect.

Collaboration can be defined as "a joint effort wherein each party provides specific products and services toward a common goal" (Beckman et al., 1997b, p.50). Collaborations may be in the form of strategic alliances, collaborations or joint ventures. Industry/academic collaborations present complex challenges as institutions with diverse missions, goals and cultures join together in various levels of formality. The range of formality in industry/academic collaborations may extend from informal guest speakers to formal joint venture graduate programs (Mead et al., 1999) to product development research. The scope of this chapter considers industry/academic collaborations involving any exchange of advanced information technology (AIT) resources between academia and industry for the purpose of deriving joint outcomes. In these instances, the AIT may be viewed as a participating "entity" in shaping the nature and direction of the collaboration.

In exploring collaborations, curriculum studies provide indications that industry needs, as well as student needs, are actualized in various components of higher education programs. Examples of industrial involvement in the development or emergence of programs and curricula can be found in the fields of accounting and management information systems as indicated below:

- The Report of the Changing Environment Committee of the American Accounting Association mentions both industry partnerships/

alliances and market-driven education as opportunities for business programs. These opportunities have arisen from developments in the environment such as the increased prominence of both "for-profit" universities and "corporate" universities (AAA Changing Environment Committee, 1998).

- The endorsement of professional organizations, as well as industry participation in curricula development, is exemplified in the Master of Science in Information Systems (MSIS) 2000 Model Curriculum. The collaborative effort of the Association for Computing Machinery and the Association for Information Systems is intended to serve both academia and industry. The curriculum guide includes objectives from an employer's point of view to: 1) provide academia with validating feedback regarding relationships among course sets that enhance the marketability of graduates; and 2) aid in alleviating the projected shortage of workers possessing information technology and systems development skills (Gorgone et al., 2000).

Practical and Philosophical Roots

Both philosophical and practical points of view provide justification for the current influence of technology in collaborative relationships. Academic recognition of business community needs is philosophically rooted in the industrial paradigm of education prevalent in Western culture. This paradigm "emerged as advocates of strong nation-state and a capitalist economy discovered that workers at all levels must be increasingly equipped with scientific and technical know-how in order to sustain social innovation and economic expansion" and looked to educational institutions to facilitate this purpose (Rascheke, 1999 p.2). Application of the industrial paradigm in education has been influenced by significant changes observed in the economy over the past few decades including: globalization, declining profit margins, the rise of service industries as a dynamic profit sector and the growth of high technology. High technology, in particular, is perceived as a means to achieving increased economic expansion and attaining positions of leadership in global markets (Slaughter, 1990).

Recognizing the needs of the business community is practically rooted in academic efforts to attract students, provide career preparation for "in-demand" fields, and open avenues for field and practice-oriented research. Though industry/academic relationships may wax and wane over time, reports of a significant shortage of qualified information technology professionals have fueled collaborations geared toward technology and high-tech industries (Fitter, 1998; Gantz, 1999; Maglitta, 1997). Accordingly, this demand may be seen as an influential force in the evolution of industry/academic collaboration impacting college curricula and resource requirements.

Through technology collaborations, industry participants hope to achieve two major objectives. The first is to address the demand for skilled high-technology workers who are prepared for lifelong learning. The second is to explore realistic solutions to the real-world business problems industry faces (Sikkel et al., 1999). The desired skill profile of an advanced information system professional is a function of the organizational environment, assigned tasks and technologies used (Chaudhury, 1997).

University Mission and AIT Appropriation

Universities must balance their three fundamental missions, namely teaching, research and service. In the course of pursuing these traditional missions, universities interact and collaborate to varying degrees with industry to serve basic educational and self-sustaining objectives and to serve social ends. Though we acknowledge technological collaborations can be associated with all missions, we choose to focus our exposition on technological collaborations involved in teaching and research processes, specifically the appropriation of AITs.

Some academics see appropriation of AITs for educational use as a potential means to enhance conceptual knowledge with real experience and to diversify educational methods (Watson & Schneider, 1999; Becerra-Fernandez et al., 2000). In deploying in-demand technologies in the educational process, collaborative relationships simultaneously affect the progress of the technology, credentials of a future workforce and educational transformation. As such, the presence of large-scale software systems in colleges is both a manifestation of the technology demands of the business community as well as an artifact of industry/educational institution collaboration.

There are many AITs currently appropriated in university settings such as computer-aided software engineering tools, enterprise systems and database tools. The appropriation of AITs may be found in business, computer science and engineering curricula among others. Industry/academic collaboration involving AITs (hereafter referred to as AIT Educational Collaborations) consume valuable academic and IT industry resources to establish technical infrastructure, deployment methods and support systems. The presence of these systems places substantial demands on the collaborative parties. The distribution of effort and ultimate outcomes of the AIT deployment depends on the course participants choose to take in adopting technology and developing collaborative relationships.

There are a multitude of directions AIT deployment may take and hence a number of questions are associated with this phenomenon including:

- How does the deployment of AITs within the educational curriculum facilitate the educational process?
- To what degree should these resources be utilized in education?
- What tools and methods should be used to deploy these resources?
- What should be the role of the AIT vendor or consultant?
- Can academic independence be maintained within a strong industry collaborative relationship?

Need for a Framework

A framework "is helpful in organizing a complex subject, identifying the relationships between the parts and revealing the areas in which further developments will be required" (Sprague, 1980). Without a framework that identifies relevant variables affecting AIT deployment in academic settings, it is challenging at best to begin to assess the impact of varying degrees of adoption, identify effective processes of deployment, and move towards assessing costs and benefits. Though we have noted frameworks for industry/academic collaboration (Mead et al., 1999), none have considered the implications of AITs on the evolution of such collaborative relationships.

To address this need, we propose a framework with the goals to:

- provide a theoretical model to guide stakeholders in their decisions and actions;
- develop a set of research propositions that will support a stream of research to better understand and explain the phenomenon of AIT Educational Collaborations, particularly the critical success factors, costs and benefits.

It is our hope that this framework will stimulate discussion, cogent decision-making, exploration and advancement.

To attend to the goals of this exposition, we begin by setting AIT Educational Collaborations within the framework of Adaptive Structuration Theory (DeSanctis & Poole, 1994). Next, we set forth propositions to guide future research and explicate supporting interrelated constructs within the matrix of social and technical dependencies comprising industry/academic collaborations. We introduce our constructs through example by using enterprise systems within the context of colleges of business and focus on evolution within the educational environment as a result of AIT collaborations. We exemplify using enterprise systems and provide supporting comments from two academic electronic mailing lists related to the appropriation of such systems since evidence indicates that these systems have current and future presence in higher education systems. The level of commitment required for adoption of these high-demand systems also suggests the potential for a considerable effect size.

THEORETICAL FRAMEWORK – ADAPTIVE STRUCTURATION

Metaphorical Introduction to Adaptive Structuration Theory (AST)

Collaborative practices are not fixed in time, but follow an evolutionary course of "production and reproduction across time and space," known as structuration (Giddens, 1982). Structuration theory provides a basis for theorizing about the relationships between technological change, beliefs, action and structures (Kling, 1994). According to Giddens (1979), the application of institutional resources in the course of daily life shape and mold the long-term development of institutions. Correspondingly, the application of industry and academic resources in the process of appropriating the AIT shape and mold the long-term development of the collaboration between the institutions.

As an extension of structuration theory, adaptive structuration theory (AST) has been used as a framework to study organizational change that occurs as advanced technologies are utilized. Adaptive structuration is a socio-technical perspective that introduces human actors and organizational context as moderators of the impacts of technology (Gopal, Bostrom & Chin, 1993; Poole & DeSanctis, 1992). This perspective posits that the adoption of an advanced technology is a process of organizational change that results from the mutual influence of the technology and social processes.

Structuration theory is considered by many to be complex and difficult to understand because of its dynamic nature. To demonstrate the application of this theory, we first introduce a metaphor to show how the dynamics of adaptive structuration could work in a relatively simple environment and set a foundation for further explanation in the complex environment of AITs. The array of issues, choices and outcomes of collaborative efforts (appropriation moves) in deploying AITs for educational purposes can be likened to a theatrical production, with the script representing the AIT. In relation to the deployment of AITs, the outcomes of performances and the historical evolution of appropriating the script are determined more often by the collaboration of individuals involved in delivering the performances to the audience than by the original script.

The extent of ambiguity in the script creates interpretive latitude that may result in a gap in spirit between the performance and the original script. Even beyond this natural gap, various versions of the play emerge as each production company translates the script into its given context. Ultimately, these cascading interpretations impact performance outcomes and future refinement. However, though performances and interpretations may greatly differ, the presence of a script does provide structural boundaries, which sets a scripted play apart from unguided improvisation. Thus, a myriad of deliberate choices are made within script guidelines.

There is no ideal set of algorithms the playwright, producers, director, actors, set designers and other stakeholders can follow as they proceed with decisions and actions. Instead, a series of situationally negotiated actions set the course. Stakeholders recognize that each decision and action is a recursive process of transformation affecting both the outcomes of performances as well as the structure of the collaborative relationship among stakeholders.

The purpose of a play is to entertain and sometimes to evoke awareness or make a transforming statement. Effort is no guarantee for success for all or even one of these goals. Each production has its own outcomes and each outcome is subject to the individual critiques of the players, reviewers, and patrons who compare their perceptions of actual performance with their version of participation goals. However, theatrical success is not purely random. Knowing the controllable and non-controllable variables involved in a production, and the relationship of those variables to the collaborative process and the ultimate performance (i.e., a framework), affords stakeholders the advantage of recognizing the issues, making informed choices and visualizing expected outcomes.

AIT Collaborations and AST

Within adaptive structuration theory, the outcome of action is both structure and structuring (product and process) that can set the condition for its own continuation (Shotter, 1983). It is our premise that human actors and organizational context are moderators of the dynamic impacts of AITs appropriated in academic settings where each collaborative entity strives to fulfill its own needs. Such dynamics have an effect not only on the outcome of the appropriation, but also on the evolution of the relationship between industry and academia. Educational methods adopted, such as participation in real-world projects (Wohlin & Regnell, 1999), provide indications of an iterative development process.

Structuration has at its core motivated and practical actions. Those interacting in the structuration process possess both the capability to follow another course of action as well as general knowledge of the relevant system and related structural properties (Giddens, 1982). There are no rigid rules followed. Instead rules and resources embodied in social institutions are appropriated by participants and enter into the production and reproduction of the social system (Poole & DeSanctis, 1992). Industry/academic collaborative interaction is embodied in the appropriation of the AIT and the educational process.

Figure 1: Adaptive Structuration Theory Applied to Industry/Academic Collaborations involving AITs (adapted from DeSanctis and Poole, 1994)

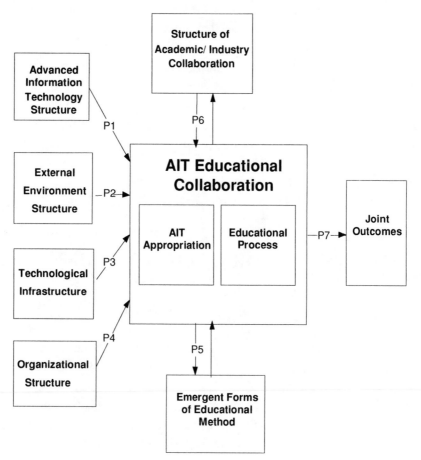

The interaction among industry, academia and the AIT leads to choices regarding educational process strategy including the selection of learning model(s) and supporting technologies. Educators determine the strategy and degree of appropriation for these mammoth enterprise systems in designing course content and process. The degree of appropriation has been addressed by academic institutions in a variety of ways and range from adding exemplary material within existing courses to adding new courses to adding new degree programs. For example, recent case study research describing the integration of enterprise systems in business schools discusses the development of specialized enterprise modules or program tracks that provide student options in areas of study (Becerra-Fernandez et al., 2000; Watson & Schneider, 1999).

Within the framework of adaptive structuration, we suggest it is the implicit structures underlying the collaboration system in conjunction with the technology and educational activities that affect the joint outcomes related to the purpose and the evolution of the collaborative relationship. Outside sources of structure including external environmental structure, technological infrastructure and organizational structure are forces that affect appropriation of the AIT, the educational process, and ultimately the joint outcomes and structure of the collaborative relationship. As the number of academic institutions adopting AITs increases, we believe AIT outcomes will vary according to the structures in place and deployment decisions.

Our model of the constructs and relationships is represented in Figure 1. The model presented provides propositions for study and the potential for future research. Additionally, the model provides a framework for decision making in an academic AIT appropriation context. Model constructs and attributes are summarized in Tables 1a and 1b.

ADVANCED INFORMATION TECHNOLOGY – SPIRIT AND STRUCTURE

One of the premises of Adaptive Structuration Theory (DeSanctis & Poole, 1994) is the interplay between a given information technology and the social process of technology use, which may result in the technology being used in many different ways (Orlikowski & Robey, 1991). One reason for this is that information technologies have been demonstrated to have different meanings for various users within an organization. This is because norms and interpretive schemes within the organizational context inform an individual's social construction of that technology, leading to variations among users in the meaning of a given technology (Orlikowski 1992).

Table 1a: Constructs of Interest

Construct	Attributes
Advanced Information Technology Structure (Enterprise Systems)	◆ Structural features (*Restrictiveness; Level of sophistication; Comprehensiveness [suite of applications supporting diverse functions]; Learning curve*) ◆ Spirit (*Enterprise-wide strategy; Daily operations; Management support system; Strategic planning tool; Convergence with educational goals*)
External Environment Structure	◆ Accreditation standards & Curriculum studies ◆ Technology vendor market position and status ◆ Industry standards & Technology trends ◆ Technology market competition & End user demands ◆ Technology-enabled labor supply
Technology Infrastructure	◆ Software & Hardware ◆ Internal maintenance & Software support ◆ Database creation and maintenance ◆ Computer lab facility & Student remote access ◆ Industry donation or grants to support technology infrastructure
Educational Organization Structure	◆ Departmental structure ◆ Major program requirements ◆ Course objectives ◆ Instructor preferences
AIT Appropriation	◆ Appropriation moves (*Direct use, relate to other structures, interpretation of structures or judgment of features*) ◆ Faithfulness ◆ Instrumental uses ◆ Attitude

Table 1b: Constructs of Interest (cont.)

Construct	Attributes
Education Process	◆ Learning models *(Collaborative learning; Hands-on experience; Simulations; Conceptual presentations; Programmed instruction; Real-world exposure; Case studies)* ◆ Supporting technologies *(Textbooks on technology; Presentation tools; Asynchronous communication tools; Synchronous communication tools; Computer-based training modules)*
Modified Forms of Educational Method	◆ Educators enrolling in corporate training programs ◆ Project/task specific internships ◆ Industry experts participating in classroom presentation ◆ Students/educators participating in AIT-specific electronic mailing list ◆ Credit and/or increased access to technology training programs for students ◆ Industry development of targeted educational tools, databases and exercises
Joint Outcomes	◆ Student learning/education in technology arena ◆ Increased work pool & Employable students ◆ AIT market exposure ◆ Contribution to industrial research and development effort & academic research ◆ Continued/enhanced program attractiveness
Structure of Academic/ Industry Collaborations	◆ Rules *(Curriculum development studies; Curriculum development research; Industry development; Corporate training programs)* ◆ Resources *(Technology alliance programs; Field research)*

Two ways have been suggested within Adaptive Structuration Theory to describe the contributing social structures offered by an AIT. The first, "spirit," can be thought of as the intended purpose and utilization of the system. The second, "structural features," refers to the types of rules and resources offered by the system (DeSanctis & Poole, 1994).

With respect to technology "spirit," there is a natural gap in appropriation between business use and academic use of enterprise systems. The spirit of enterprise systems can be described as information technology structures designed to integrate operational-level transaction processing, multi-level decision support and strategic management of major corporations. However, the goals of enterprise systems used in colleges of business are primarily educational and exploratory in nature. The utilization of an enterprise system in the educational process involves the instantiation of a variety of business scenarios occurring in a curriculum track, enterprise system specific courses or topics in a selected course. This gap in system goals and values may have implications for the appropriation of the AIT and the direction of the collaboration. Educators recognize this natural gap as expressed by the following academic electronic mailing list comment:

> *"I would love to turn out bachelor's graduates who can command jobs as implementation consultants. That is unrealistic. I'll have to settle for turning out graduate accountants who have an understanding of the impact of ERP systems on both local and global management environments"* (Accounting Education using Computers and Multimedia List Serve, 1999).

Beyond the natural "business versus educational use" gap described, individual academic institutions, departments, course leaders and industry participants may each interpret the role of the AIT as an educational tool in a different way and assume assorted courses of action. These choices in spirit deal with "how real" and to what extent the AIT is introduced into the learning experience. Alternate interpretations, regarding the most appropriate and useful degree of spirit integrity, shape the AIT appropriation.

To address our second item, enterprise systems have "structural features," which guide functionality and introduce constraints. Enterprise systems are a comprehensive suite of modules that support diverse organizational functions and processes. Though the software code and functional capabilities form some boundaries, the navigation options within those boundaries are vast. Software magnitude and complexity contribute to the educational challenge of bringing these systems into business colleges and may have implications for the negotiated process of industry/academic collaborations.

The suites developed by major enterprise vendors commonly contain more than 15 modules, each is geared toward a different industry process and requiring a significant training investment (Baan Software Products, 2000; JD Edwards Product Modules, 2000; Oracle Applications Web Page, 2000; SAP Education Online, 2000). For example, SAP offers some certification programs requiring over 40 days of classroom training. As indicated by the following educator comment, enterprise systems challenge colleges with a level of sophistication that affords flexibility in feature set and appropriation but requires a substantial training investment to achieve minimum acceptable performance.

"The main problem with the ERP concept is that it is very complicated – lots of information scattered over different software modules which interact with each other in complex ways. Without a 'divide and conquer' learning strategy, the student can easily get lost in the multiple screens of the software. The curriculum breaks those theoretical concepts which are tightly integrated in the software" (IS WORLD List Serve- ERP Remarks, 1999).

It is up to educators to determine which course or courses are the appropriate forums for introduction and appropriation of these systems, and which parts of these complex systems to utilize.

In recognizing that AIT structure and spirit have an effect on the relationship between industry and academic actors and the appropriation of AITs in colleges of business, we propose:

P1 - To the extent that AITs vary in their structural and spirit feature sets, the depth and breadth of appropriation in academia will affect the nature of AIT Educational Collaborations.

EXTERNAL SOURCES OF STRUCTURE

A report of the American Accounting Association determined that "the markets for accounting students will drive the 'models' of education, including delivery, content and pedagogy" (AAA Changing Environment Committee, 1998). Likewise, the market for information systems professionals who can understand, develop and utilize enterprise systems is strong and growing (Watson & Schneider, 1999). Initially the growth in enterprise systems was uncertain due to saturation of Fortune 500 companies and the complexities of implementation. However, enterprise systems have found new avenues of opportunity through such channels as e-commerce, customer resource management and modules orientated towards the service industry (Stedman, 2000; Wilson, 2000). As such, the enterprise market seems strong with a corresponding demand for educated graduates (Watson & Schneider, 1999).

Indications of outside sources of structure, namely market structure, are suggested by the following comments provided by academics:

- *"Installed SAP R/3 v4.0b a few weeks ago, so our experience is minimal." "Benefits have begun already—for example, one of my students got a great internship at E&Y where she will be working in their SAP practice, by only mentioning that we had begun to work with SAP the previous night's class!"* (Accounting Education using Computers and Multimedia List Serve, 1999).

- *"It looks like the companies that hire our students will be demanding that our students know something about ERP technology in the future. As a practical matter, it's probably good to be able to respond to that demand"* (Accounting Education using Computers and Multimedia List Serve, 1999).

In recognizing that external structures have an effect on the relationship between industry and academic actors and the appropriation of AITs in colleges of business, we propose:

P2 - The nature of AIT Educational Collaborations depends on external sources of structure such as technology-enabled labor supply, AIT market competition and academic accreditation standards.

TECHNOLOGY INFRASTRUCTURE

A practical component in any study of the appropriation of AITs is a basic cost/benefit analysis. Are the total system costs incurred rewarded with an enriched educational experience and employable graduates? Technology infrastructure can be a major cost consideration. Industry may facilitate appropriation through donated services; however, colleges may face additional costs. Enterprise systems are large-scale AITs requiring a significant commitment of academic resources (Becerra-Fernandez et al., 2000; Watson & Schneider, 1999), as expressed by the following list serve comments.

- *"Also watch out! It is a big sink of time and can take you away from other endeavors in your life"* (IS WORLD List Serve- ERP Remarks, 1999).

- Software: *"All the suppliers offered to provide it for free or almost free, including the installation, BUT with minimal support commitment. They wanted to charge for the support"* (IS WORLD List Serve- ERP Remarks, 1999).
- Hardware: *"You need a strong computer host-server, which can support (via networking) a class of computers. You need a lot of memory, disk space and an unloaded computer network"* (IS WORLD List Serve- ERP Remarks, 1999).
- Operations: *"You can provide a faculty person release time to take care of technology"* (IS WORLD List Serve- ERP Remarks, 1999).
- Training: *"You also need to provide 'release time' for faculty to go through the training and develop courses"* (IS WORLD List Serve- ERP Remarks, 1999).
- Leadership/Management: *"Make sure that you have a core group that include accounting & production faculty that can steer the program"* (IS WORLD List Serve- ERP Remarks, 1999).

These systems typically cannot be deployed without support from enterprise vendors or consultants. One academic stated, *"The very nature of the work has forced us to work closely with the whole SAP community, the company, the partners and customers to establish educational needs and modes of delivery"* (Accounting Education using Computers and Multimedia List Serve, 1999). Hence, some form of collaborative relationship seems a precursor for the existence of these systems in academic settings.

In recognizing that technological infrastructure has an effect on AIT Educational Collaborations, we propose:

P3 - The nature of AIT Educational Collaborations depends upon the technological infrastructure required to deploy AITs in academic settings.

EDUCATIONAL ORGANIZATION STRUCTURE

The philosophies of appropriating enterprise systems among educational entities vary widely and influence AIT appropriation moves. The educational organization's structure influences AIT collaboration according to: its perspective on industry involvement, the potential employment of the technology as a marketing tool to attract students, and industry market demands for the technology and for students. Several issues may arise from these influences:

- If resource constraints mandate the implementation of a single enterprise system, could the college be transmitting a product endorsement message that in turn constrains the scope of the curriculum?
- Are there positive or negative connotations, from a student or industry perspective, for a college of business known as an Oracle, SAP or Sybase "shop"?
- Do companies place any implicit or direct pressure on colleges to exclusively employ their software?

Additionally, the balance between conceptual technology education and the development of technology skills is a pervasive philosophic quandary. Colleges of business innately want students to matriculate successfully into the business world. Peak performance and continued growth in the business environment are enhanced by a foundation of abilities and knowledge consisting of appropriate skills, rules, concepts and attitudes. All learning manifests the goals of enabling cognitive, behavioral or affective change that last beyond the educational environment regarding some combination of skills, rules, concepts, and attitudes. Yet, learning may occur in various forms from self-education to experience, to training, to formal college education. Therein emerges the college of business quandary of pedagogical responsibility, capability and propriety. To what degree should colleges of business be the vehicle for learning skills, rules, concepts and attitudes that promote success in the business environment? Conversely stated, what aspect of core knowledge and ability acquisition should be left to other forms of learning such as training or self-study? The myriad of choices involving the degree of focus and amalgamation of skill-based and conceptual knowledge in the deployment of enterprise systems surface issues related to this quandary.

One educator position is that, *"Faculty evaluating the implementation of an ERP system such as SAP, PeopleSoft, Oracle or Baan must first look at their school's mission and current pedagogy. To really take full advantage of the enterprise resource planning concept, significant curriculum changes would probably be necessary"* (Accounting Education using Computers and Multimedia List Serve, 1999).

Conceptual knowledge may be presented in terms of rules or attributes, examples and non-examples (Gibbons & Fairweather, 1998). For example, enterprise system exposure may be used to present conceptual illustration of various topics, rather than dwelling on the operation of the technology as indicated by the following comment, *"We base all of our AIS curriculum on a database approach (although I would prefer to call it an enterprise information architecture approach). I believe strongly that the enterprise modeling orientation that permeates most of our other classes is the conceptual basis on which to understand both currently available and future implementation platforms anyway"* (Accounting Education using Computers and Multimedia List Serve, 1999).

The educational process and appropriation of the system in this circumstance may differ from the appropriation and process geared towards skill acquisition. One academic aptly states the dilemma associate with a "skills" approach: *"It looks like some schools are training students to be very knowledgeable SAP consultants – in effect doing what SAP does in their corporate training. You will have to decide if that is a proper way to approach this"* (Accounting Education using Computers and Multimedia List Serve, 1999).

In recognizing that the technological infrastructure has an effect on the relationship between industry and academic actors and the appropriation of AITs in colleges of business, we propose:

P4 - The nature of AIT Educational Collaborations depends on organizational structures, such as academic departments, major program requirements and course objectives.

MODIFIED FORMS OF EDUCATIONAL METHOD

Enterprise systems are adaptable to many models of learning and may be used to support a number of educator objectives. The model of learning chosen may affect the instructor's approach and utilization of these tools. Is conceptual presentation and demonstration adequate or do students require an experiential learning model (Leidner & Jarvenpaa, 1995)? For example, with respect to experiential learning, enterprise systems can be used to create the necessary learning environment. This approach requires students to work through business problems by presenting an operational system with data that represents the business scenario.

In making these choices, modified forms of educational method and variations in pedagogy arise as demonstrated in the following electronic mailing list comments:

- *"I have a case study (Wizard confectionary) which I use as a basis for parts of the course. It needs enriching and I would be happy to consider sharing this globally with people who will add to it...We are developing, in the next few months, some two-hour practical sessions, which are aimed at getting business students to play with SAP under controlled conditions. We will probably make this available on the Web server*" (IS WORLD List Serve- ERP Remarks, 1999).

- "*We had a three-week hands-on period, including using some CBT courses on SAP as well as SAP itself, in our ACELAB*" (Accounting Education using Computers and Multimedia List Serve, 1999).

- "*I divided the class into functional teams, and set them loose with JDE. I literally told them to do research on how their functional area should be run, then try to discover if they could make JDE fit the bill...I've also added the design of an executive interface for the functional area, and the students are going to attempt to create it using the JDE tool kit that enables their 'Idea to Action' concept*" (Accounting Education using Computers and Multimedia List Serve, 1999).

Emergent forms of educational method may include introducing new participants into the collaboration. To illustrate, consider the following electronic mailing list statement:

"We rely on input from consultants on the content side...We found that the consulting firms were VERY keen to deliver guest lectures, and we used this to the hilt, which raised the perceived status of the course appreciably" (IS WORLD List Serve- ERP Remarks, 1999).

Emergent educational methods may involve restructuring programs and curricula. The KnowDule approach to presenting ERP systems used by Louisiana State University is a demonstration of an emergent curriculum method. The 10 KnowDules are intended to be adaptable to different instructors, pedagogies, student levels and academic programs (Watson & Schneider, 1999). The University of Arizona proposed an integrated case development project resulting in multiple SAP modules in four to five courses (AAA Changing Environment Committee, 1998). Florida International University's College of Business Administration offers a capstone integrated ERP course that includes aspects of operations management, managerial accounting and marketing management (AICPA/AAA Information Technology Visioning Conference Task Force, 1998).

Modifications in educational method evident in software engineering research on industry/academic collaborations suggest additional appropriation moves that can influence collaborative relationships involving AITs, including:

- Accelerated internship programs (Powell et al., 1997; Wohlin & Regnell, 1999).
- Independent study support.
- Industrially experienced teachers (Wohlin & Regnell, 1999).

- Vendor-sponsored training programs (Beckman et al., 1997a).
- Jointly developed courses (Wohlin & Regnell, 1999).
- Participation in maintenance efforts.
- Research within industry (Wohlin & Regnell, 1999).

In recognition of the existence of the potential of emergent forms of educational method resultant from the appropriations of AIT in education and the educational process, we propose:

P5 - Modified educational methods emerge as the technology and educational processes are utilized and facilitated by AIT Educational Collaborations.

STRUCTURE OF ACADEMIC/INDUSTRY COLLABORATION

The collaborative system is not a recognized organization, but a structured social practice of interdependence that has broad spatial and temporal extension (Giddens, 1982). There are no global, formalized standards for the appropriation of enterprise systems in educational settings or specifications for industry's participatory role in this phenomenon.

Though some industry alliance programs may require agreements regarding the donation or support of AITs (SAP Education Online, 2000), educational methods and processes are guided by practice and choice. Participation and selection of an alliance program is guided by choice and alliance programs themselves are subject to an evolutionary process as evidenced by the following insights:

- Participant in SAP Tertiary Education Program (TEP) – *"We had quite a lot of support from SAP itself." "After some coyness, SAP has really come to the table." "Happily, we were able to provide substantial input into the formulation of the TEP, which is being rolled out globally"* (IS WORLD List Serve- ERP Remarks, 1999).
- *"SAP's Sapient College division in Australia was really helpful." "We are still in the middle of this and will be forever. We will need to build much closer links with industry and have had great support from the whole SAP community in course development and delivery"* (Accounting Education using Computers and Multimedia List Serve, 1999).

There exist, however, certain practices, or implied dynamic rules, embodied in the implementation of AITs in business colleges and the collaborative system created between industry and academia. The existence of enterprise alliance programs may be considered a representation of social practices affecting the structure of academic/industry collaboration. Representations of the implied social practice may also be found in such documents as curriculum guides that indicate industry participation and the study of enterprise system concepts (Mulder, 1999; Gorgone et al., 2000). To illustrate:

- The Information Systems Centric Curriculum '99 (ISCC, a collaborative academic/industry task force supported in part by National Science Foundation Grants) includes a requirement for knowledge and skills pertaining to enterprise systems within a profile that graduates should satisfy. This is in addition to a requirement to prepare students for life-long learning (Lidtke & Stokes, 1999).
- MSIS 2000 mentions ERP as a component of one of its representative career tracks and frequently alludes to enterprise systems in addressing curriculum content (Gorgone, et al., 2000).

Structures suggested for a successful collaboration based upon case study experience (Powell et al., 1997) include:

- Central coordination point
- Right mix of knowledge and experience
- Cooperative planning and scheduling
- Flexibility to change curriculum
- Communication to build teamwork
- Balance to maintain objectivity

Additional work is needed to investigate the practices and resources that comprise the structure of academic/industry collaboration, as there are indications of emerging structures and "best practices" for colleges of business. Accordingly, we propose:

P6 - New forms of industry/academic collaboration emerge as AITs facilitated by collaboration are deployed in academic settings.

JOINT OUTCOMES

AIT appropriations in academic settings possess innate outcome challenges and ambiguities.

The purpose of the enterprise appropriation and industry/academic collaboration is to achieve mutually beneficial joint outcomes for both academia and industry. Desired outcomes may include facilitating the educational mission, gaining competitive advantage, accessing educational resources, enhancing reputation, increasing revenue and providing a staffing source (Mead et al., 1999). The college, industry or both may desire each of these goals.

Just as success is not guaranteed in implementing these systems in an industry setting, desired joint outcomes from academic appropriation are not guaranteed, as can be discerned by the subsequent variations in commentary on AIT appropriation:

- *"All groups were able to produce very high-quality reports that provided both functional and JDE overviews of their area. I was thrilled." "The initial benefits that I have seen are that the students become both frustrated with the complexity of an ERP package, yet manage to learn how to navigate it. I truly believe many of them will face similar challenges in their working environments, and the second time they're thrown in will be much easier than the first"* (Accounting Education using Computers and Multimedia List Serve, 1999).

- *"The benefit of adopting an ERP package as a teaching platform is that you get to teach information systems the way they write about it in the books: unified chart of accounts, unified database, management reporting that is timely, has the correct content ad form and timeliness, and so on. It's hard to over-estimate the benefit of squaring your practice with your theory"* (Accounting Education using Computers and Multimedia List Serve, 1999).

There are potential outcome risks an educational entity may experience regarding close industrial collaboration even if "desired" outcomes are achieved. An example is a myopic focus on short-term educational tasks (Wohlin & Regnell, 1999) rather than on fundamental concepts and principles.

- *"In my opinion, the primary benefit of using SAP is the ability to introduce students to 'real-world' applications and the complexities that go along with that. The benefit, as it turns out, is also a significant drawback as well." "Students tend to get bogged down in the complexities of navigating through the menu paths to find information. The result that I've found most common is that students are able to execute menu path instructions and find information, but possess limited ability to interpret that information and integrate it with other knowledge. I believe this is due primarily to the fact that traditional students have extremely limited knowledge of how businesses function"* (Accounting Education using Computers and Multimedia List Serve, 1999).

- *"The faculty involved in the project are evaluating the students' level of performance and we are getting some conflicting results. Some believe the project is working very well, others are debating the pedagogical issues related to using ERP.*" "*I personally believe that students will benefit from possessing a fundamental knowledge of ERP systems and business processes. However, I am not yet convinced that SAP R/3 is necessarily the best route to accomplish that objective*" (Accounting Education using Computers and Multimedia List Serve, 1999).

Further research is needed regarding the joint outcomes of the appropriation of AITs as a component in the academic/industry collaboration process and the effects of underlying structures. Hence, we propose:

P7 – The joint outcomes of introducing AITs in academic institutions are dependent on the:

- **AIT**
- **External structure**
- **Technological infrastructure**
- **Organizational structure**
- **Appropriation process**
- **Educational process.**

FUTURE RESEARCH

AIT appropriation and associated collaboration decisions may affect the educational foundation and career prospects of the technological work force, calling for further research to investigate this phenomenon. Appropriate methodological approaches should be considered in examining theoretical constructs. Survey, case studies and quasi-experimental studies seem appropriate. One avenue is to formulate hypotheses based upon the propositions presented and directly test the model. For example, researchers may investigate the implications of various alliance programs or appropriation methods at different colleges.

CONCLUSION

Adaptive structuration recognizes that technology appropriation may be a key factor in the evolution of affected social structures. Adaptive structuration theory gains predictive and descriptive power by addressing social complexities and actions as factors closely integrated with advanced information technologies. An extension of adaptive structuration theory as a research framework for industry/academic collaboration and as a means to elucidate the factors in decision making for appropriation moves is the major contribution of this exposition.

From a practical perspective, industry and consumers of academic education often desire practical training and education from academic institutions to prepare students for present-day opportunities. The appropriation of AITs in colleges of business is a modern phenomenon that aspires to bridge the industry-academic gap while fulfilling educational goals. However, the costs of appropriation may be high and the impact of appropriation on educational processes and collaborative relationships may be either minor or dramatic. Thus, the joint outcomes of AIT appropriations and collaboration are uncertain. Stakeholders should recognize the potential influence of structure and social context on desired outcomes when embarking on the process of industry/academic collaboration.

REFERENCES

AAA Changing Environment Committee. (1998). *The Future Viability of AAA Members' Programs: American Accounting Association.* Retrieved February 3, 2001, from the World Wide Web: http://accounting.rutgers.edu/raw/aaa/about/reports/chngenv_1.htm.

AICPA/AAA Information Technology Visioning Conference Task Force (1998). Training business students for the next information revolution. Paper presented at the *AICPA/AAA Information Technology Visioning Conference*, November 19-21, Dallas, Texas.

Baan Software Products. Baan Company. (2000). Retrieved April 2, 2000 from the World Wide Web: http://www2.baan.com/cgi-bin/bvisapi.dll.

Becerra-Fernandez, I., Murphy, K., & Simon, S. J. (2000). Integrating ERP in the business school curriculum. *Communications of the ACM*, April, 1-4.

Beckman, K., Coulter, N., Khajenoori, S. and Mead, N. R. (1997). Collaborations: Closing the industry-academia gap. *IEEE Software*, November/December, 49-57.

Chaudhury, A. (1997). Introducing client/server technologies in information systems curricula. *The DATA BASE for Advances in Information Systems*, 28(4), 20-32.

DeSanctis, G., & Poole, M. S. (1994). Capturing the complexity in advanced technology use: Adaptive structuration theory. *Organizational Science*, 5(2), 121-147.

Enterprise Resource Planning Education Modules (1999). Messages posted on Accounting Education using Computers and Multimedia electronic mailing list. Retrieved from the World Wide Web: http://www.trinity.edu/rjensen/245glosap.htm.

ERP Remarks. (1999). Messages posted to IS World electronic mailing list. Retrieved from the World Wide Web: http://www.uark.edu/depts/cisqinfo/hardgrave/erp.htm.

Fitter, F. (1998). Annual training survey: Personal trainers. *ComputerWorld*, March 30.

Gantz, J. (1999). How you gonna keep your IT staff down on the farm. *ComputerWorld*, August 30.

Gibbons, A. S., & Fairweather, P. G. (1998). *Computer-Based Instruction*. Englewood Cliffs: Educational Technology Publications.

Giddens, A. (1979). *Central Problems in Social Theory*. Berkeley: University of California Press.

Giddens, A. (1982). *Profiles and Critiques in Social Theory*. Berkeley: University of California Press.

Gorgone, J. T., Gray, P., Feinstein, D. L., Kasper, G. M., Luffman, J. N., Stohr, E. A., Valacich, J. S. and Wigand, R. T. (2000). MSIS 2000 model curriculum and guidelines for graduate degree programs in information systems. *The DATA BASE for Advances in Information Systems*, 31(1), 3-48.

Gopal, A., Bostrom, R., & Chin, W. W. (1993). Applying adaptive structuration theory to investigate the process of group support system Use. *Journal of Managment Information Systems*, 9(3), 45-63.

IS World List Serve. (1999). ERP Remarks, [List Serve]. IS World. Available: http://www.uark.edu/depts/cisqinfo/hardgrave/erp.htm [03/07/00].

JD Edwards Product Modules. (2000). *JD Edwards*. Retrieved April 2, 2000 from the World Wide Web: http://www.jdedwards.com/products/promodules.asp.

Kling, R. (1994). Technology, ideology and social transformation: The case of computerization and work organization. *Revue' International de Sociologie*, 2(3), 28-56.

Leidner, D. E., & Jarvenpaa, S. L. (1995). The use of information technology to enhance management school education: A theoretical view. *MIS Quarterly*, 19(3), 265-296

Lidtke, D., & Stokes, G. (1999). An information systems-centric curriculum, ISCC '99. *The Journal of Systems and Software*, 49, 171-175.

Maglitta, J. (1997). Train in vain. *ComputerWorld*, August.

Mead, N., Bechman, K., Lawrence, J., O'Mary, G., Parish, C., Unpingco, P., & Walker, H. (1999). Industry/university collaborations: Different perspectives heighten mutual opportunities. *The Journal of Systems and Software*, 49, 155-162.

Oracle Applications Web Page. (2000). *Oracle Corporation*. Retrieved April 2, 2000, from the World Wide Web: http://www.oracle.com/ applications/content.html.

Orlikowski, W. J. (1992). The duality of technology: Rethinking the concept of technology in organizations. *Organization Science*, 3(3), 398-427.

Orlikowski, W. J., & Robey, D (1991). Information technology and the structuring of organizations. *Information Systems Research*, 2(2), 143-169.

Poole, M. S. and DeSanctis, G. (1992). Microlevel structuration in computer-supported group decision making. *Human Communication Research*, 19(1), 5-49.

Powell, G. M., Diaz-Herrera, J. L., & Turner, D. J. (1997). Achieving synergy in collaborative education. *IEEE Software*, November-December, 58-65.

Rascheke, C. (1999). Beyond education: The age of transaction and the "scene" of digital learning. *Syllabus Magazine*, 13(4), 2.

SAP Education Online. SAP America, Inc. – Education. (2000). Retrieved April 2, 2000, from the World Wide Web: http://wwwest03.sap.com/ usa/education.

Shotter, J. (1983) "Duality of structure" and "intentionality" in an ecological psychology. *Journal for the Theory of Social Behavior*, 13, 19-43.

Sikkel, K., Spil, T. A. M., & Weg, R. L. W. v. d. (1999). A real-world case study in information technology for undergraduate students. *The Journal of Systems and Software*, 49, 117-123.

Slaughter, S. (1990). *The Higher Learning and High Technology*, 19. Albany, NY: State University of New York Press.

Sprague, R. H. J. (1980). A framework for the development of decision support systems, *MIS Quarterly*, 4(4), 1-26.

Stedman, C. (2000). Expand ERP beyond the back office. *Computerworld*, 34 (January 3), 13-16.

Watson, E. E., & Schneider, H. (1999). Using ERP systems in education. *Communications of the Association for Information Systems*, 1(9), 1-48.

Wilson, T. (2000). Handing off the burden: Customers gain outsourcing options for J. D. Edwards ERP packages. *Internetweek*, January 17, 13.

Wohlin, C., & Regnell, B. (1999). Strategies for industrial relevance in software engineering education. *The Journal of Systems and Software*, 49, 124-134.

Chapter X

Success Factors for Industry-University Collaboration Through IS Industry Boards: A University Case in a Developing Country

Carlos Navarrete
California State Polytechnic University–Pomona, USA

James Pick
University of Redlands, USA

This chapter examines the success factors for industry-university collaboration through IS industry boards. Based on an in-depth case of industry-academic collaboration in Mexico, the chapter addresses the following research questions: What are the critical success factors for achieving good outcomes from an IS industry board? What factors impede the achievement of good outcomes from such a board in a developing nation? What factors are distinctive and serve to differentiate IS industry boards of developing nations from those of advanced ones? In the case study, the IS industry board enhanced the IS academic program's curriculum, the university's computer labs, the student internship program, and faculty training. This case demonstrates that the critical success factors for the IS industry board were top management support, the department chair's interpersonal skills, board member selection, proper board management, and appropriate university policies regarding industry-university collaboration. The experiences of developing and advanced nations for such boards are mostly similar, but differ due to lack of tenure track careers for IS faculty in the developing nation under study.

INTRODUCTION

Since universities started offering academic programs in IS, they have been facing the challenge that information technology change triggers: new industry demands, academic programs updates, faculty training, lab enhancements, and development of didactic materials. Without knowing the ultimate direction and future impacts of several technologies, IS faculty have had to update and many times modify their academic programs faster than what is recommended for the programs' evaluation and quality. It is critical for this quality and even viability of IS programs that they keep up to date with current technology and industry practices. IS programs, for instance, that fail to recognize today the dynamic changes in the Internet and e-business run the risk of becoming albatrosses that do not have credibility in industry. This chapter examines the role of the IS industry board in industry-academic interactions in information systems (IS) programs.

There are many forms of interactions between academia and industry, including corporate boards, student internships, faculty internships, corporate grants, speaker series, partnership courses, and curriculum revision committees (Schenk and Pick, 1998), website corporate partnerships (Kock et al., 2000), work contracts for IS students in industry (McGowan and Cornwell, 2000), and others. This chapter focuses solely on industry advisory boards to IS programs. The industry advisory board is widely utilized by IS programs. It is defined as a group of IS faculty, industry representatives, and others, with the goals of improving academic programs and industry knowledge and performance. It meets regularly to discuss issues in curriculum, research funding, internship opportunities, industry trends, job markets for program graduates, and other relevant topics at the interface between the IS academic program and IS industry practitioners. Although many benefits have been reported from such IS industry boards, problems and concerns have also occurred. The chapter will explore pluses and minuses of the IS industry boards in practice, and suggest ways to foster more successful boards.

The chapter is based on an in-depth case study of industry-academic collaboration located in a developing nation, Mexico. All of the prior literature of case studies on collaboration of IS programs and industry were from advanced nations (Kock et al., 2000; Schenk and Pick, 1999), although one research project presented several case studies on more generic, non-IS collaborations between industry and academic in developing nations (Oblinger, 1993). However, it is a fundamental purpose of this chapter to provide more balance in the research literature by analyzing in depth a case study of an IS-discipline-based industry board from a developing nation. Then the findings for a developing nation can be compared with the large body of findings existing in the literature for advanced nations, mostly in the U.S. Distinctive features, operational parameters, and success factors of IS industry boards for a developing nation can be identified and explained.

We discuss the following research questions:

1. What are the critical success factors for achieving good outcomes from an IS industry board in a developing nation? What factors impede the achievement of good outcomes from such a board in a developing nation?

2. Based on the results for the previous question. and on literature studies for advanced nations, what factors are distinctive and serve to differentiate IS industry boards of developing nations from those of advanced nations?

The methodology is case study (Yin, 1994). Case study analysis is commonly utilized in IS research, including in-depth cases as in the present research. The present case was documented through detailed record keeping and tracking for a period of five years by one of the present authors.

This research is exploratory, since there is only one in-depth case that is examined. The chapter calls at its end for additional case studies in order to test the results with a robust sample of cases. Nevertheless, the chapter contributes to understanding for the first time, in a developing nation, the IS industry board as a key factor for the success of IS academic programs.

BACKGROUND

The need for industry-academic ties stems from the locus in industry of research, products, technologies, real-world advice, and ideas that are valuable to universities. At the same time, universities can provide to industry basic and applied R&D, academic ideas and knowledge, new workforce, i.e., student graduates, and faculty consulting advice.

The recent changes in the focus of the academy points towards universities with more market and customer orientation, greater flexibility of delivery, and more emphasis on performance (Oblinger, 1993). Although these changes have made inroads only at certain institutions, the general trend is in this direction. As universities come to resemble somewhat more industry, greater ties may be possible. This resemblance is because the cycle of developing degree programs and offerings in universities has often come to resemble more marketing, product development, and strategic planning in industry. In other words, universities are doing market analysis to decide in which program areas they will compete and are studying in advance the professional profile its prospective students will have. The program development steps follow many of those of industrial product development, including prototyping, testing, competitor benchmarking, pricing, and market feedbacks. There is strategic planning, including how markets, programs, and core competencies intersect.

There is a limited body of prior case studies on industry-academic linkages. Rather than review the literature exhaustively, several studies are referred to. Parker (1993) presented a broad study of industry-academic partnerships in both advanced and developing nations, but ones not involving the IS discipline. Parker sees the underlying driver leading to growth in these partnerships as universities' need for revenue enhancement. However, Parker cautions that some of the most financially successful cases of industry-academic linkages had the focus on collaboration, not on revenue generation. When the focus was centered on revenue generation, often results were poor.

The Parker study looked at four different models of industry-academic partnering in Turkey, the UK, Slovenia, and South Korea. In the cases of Turkey and the UK, a displaced emphasis on revenue led to disappointments, while in Slovenia and South Korea, the collaboration was built first and the overall outcomes were highly successful, without impeding academic freedom or educational quality. Parker points to the following factors as encouraging success in ties: collaboration incentives, work on partnership building, care in project selection, institutional factors, and the positive role of proximity.

Among the barriers to success are lack of translation into application and the research deficits of developing nations. There are many instances when linkages or ties are established, only to falter before being translated into positive applications. Parker ascribes the reason for this to lack of correct skills and foresight by both academics and corporate participants. The second barrier relates to differences in industry R&D in developing nations. For instance, Parker mentions that Mexico predominantly has industries, for which little native R&D is being conducted. Instead, the industries depend on the import of technology and innovations, often relying on the parent companies based abroad. This points to the need to understand the differences in the exchange model for developing nations.

Several studies delineate models and cases of university-IS academic partnerships (Schenk and Pick, 1998; Maehl, 2000; Kock, Auspitz, and King,

2000). One research framework for these partnerships consists of a two-dimensional grid of exchange, with one dimension being the amount of resources available for the exchange and the second the comprehensiveness of activities (Schenk and Pick, 1998). Arrayed along this grid are exchanges that vary between one small advisory committee and very little resources up to elaborate set-ups with an IT research center, industry workshops, extensive research internships, and large-scale industry grant funding. The paper points to the need to match the comprehensiveness of activities with the appropriate size of resources. The paper includes four case studies of university-industry exchanges, located at different points on the grid. The most common form of exchange for all the cases was industry-IT program board or advisory group. One of the cases involving success with industry boards was University of Redlands (Schenk and Pick, 1998; Maehl, 2000). Among the success factors for this case were clear mission given to the industry board, careful choice of members, and clear objectives for meetings and follow-through for action items. For the large-sized case of UCLA, the industry board was the original locus of exchange, out of which much more was developed over time.

Industry-IT program partnerships today can be based on the evolving Internet/Web technologies. For instance, at Temple University a course was designed for industry experts to interact with students. The locus of exchange was a website with rich course materials and student products (Kock, Auspitz, and King, 2000). This was highly successful partly because of the convenience factor for busy industry personnel and because it appealed to technologically savvy IS majors.

In summary, today's more complex industry and university environments give ample opportunity for many types of positive exchanges. At the same time, barriers and obstacles may prevent successful outcomes. The relatively scarce literature on developing nations (and none for their IS programs) indicates that the model may change in certain ways for exchanges in the context of those countries. The wide variety of types of exchange set-ups for IS programs in the U.S. can be understood better by considering exchange along a two-dimensional grid of comprehensiveness and resource amount. Finally, the industry board has been a mainstay exchange mechanism for a variety of universities and regions.

IS Industry Board Definition

An industry board is a committee composed commonly of 10 to 12 members, having strong IS experience and relevant industry participation. The committee members in some way are interested in the IS/IT university programs, university development, and university-community enhancement relationships. Several reasons explain why it is not recommended to have more than 12, nor less than 10 members on the board. Among the reasons we can cite are: group efficiency and effectiveness, number of board proposals, member participation and recognition, and reasonable balance in the number of industrial sector or entities represented in the board. In particular, the offsetting reasons include the following: (1) Since member participation is honorific, the board should not be too big. Being part of the board represents an academic and professional recognition; a reduced number adds distinction to the board membership. On the other end of things, managing meetings with more than 12 participants becomes inefficient. (2) The faculty consulting opportunities grow with the number of board members, so you may want to have as many board members as you can properly involve in advisory board's agenda. (3) A smaller number of members reduces board effectiveness, if the members cannot attend or keep working on the board. (4) It is recommended to have as many constituencies represented on the board as possible.

Based on the prevailing situation for IS/IT program(s) and the objective of attaining future industry-university relationships, the university (chair and dean) should select the industry sector they want emphasized on the board, and then set a list of candidates from that sector. Then the IS program proposes and invites those candidates with strong experience and relevant industry participation. It is important that the honorary invitation to become a member of the board is given to the individual in a personal capacity, not to him/her acting as president or director of a given organization. In this way the invitation to become part of the board translates into a professional recognition of the candidate, and at the same time avoid problems or work interruption when a board member changes position or company.

Once the board is constituted, a two-fold evaluation should be designed. First, the evaluation of the board should be focused on board activities, its projects, and advising follow up. And second, the university should prepare the evaluation of the impact of the board on the academic programs, the department, and the university. Measurement of the board's impact should reflect the purposes of the board and its agenda.

A CASE OF AN IS PROGRAM AND ITS IS INDUSTRY BOARD

Universidad Iberoamericana (UIA) is a private university in Mexico City. The University has 10,000 undergraduate students, and 1,000 graduate students. The UIA lost its campus to an earthquake in 1979. Building a new campus in another location in Mexico City unfortunately hurt the academic development plans of the university. The IS Department and its academic programs (undergraduate, graduate, and departmental service) struggled during the early 1980s. By 1987 the IS Department situation was characterized by: lack of proper IS laboratories, few faculty members, faculty without strong academic or industry careers, stagnant student enrollments, and lack of IS and computing leadership within the university.

In 1987 the university's authorities decided to promote an IS industry board to enhance IS programs. The President of UIA personally invited the future board members (see Table 1).

The IS industry board met two times a year, with monthly updates. That is to say, the chair of the department wrote and distributed a progress report on the department's projects among the board members once a month. The chair also met separately with one or two members if a given project asked for such close oversight/cooperation. After every board meeting, the board had lunch or dinners with the university's Principal and top management members, during which a summary of the meeting and future actions were outlined to the university top management.

The term of membership service was set for three years. However, after four years of operation, five members were rotated mainly because of residence changes.

Table 1: IS/IT Industry Board Members (1988)

Board Member	Affiliation	Industry Sector
Alfredo Capote	IBM of Mexico (Marketing Director)	Hardware and software vendor
Manuel Diaz	HP of Mexico and Latinamerica (President)	Hardware vendor
Arturo de la Torre	Ministry of Planning and Control (Director)	Mexican federal government
Fernando Espinosa	Transport Ministry	Mexican federal government
Antonio Fajer	Informatica Timon (President)	IS/IT consulting
Sergio Ferraguth	Cullinet Mexico (President)	Software vendor
Carlos Gonzalez	NCR de Mexico (President)	Hardware and software vendor
Luis Gutierrez	DEC of Mexico (President)	Hardware and software vendor
Antonio Galaz	Grupo Cifra (CIO)	Retail
Gillermo Levine	Universidad Autonoma Metropolitana (Research Director)	Education

The role of the IS/IT university board went far beyond everyone's expectations. In fact, the IS department could not take advantage of all the opportunities that the board brought to the department and its programs. Every year, the results were more encouraging, and positive results led to more challenging projects.

The Impact of the IS/IT Board at Universidad Iberoamericana

Among the positive impacts of the IS industry board on IS Department performance were to help in enhancing the programs' curricula, the university computer labs, the students' internship programs, and the faculty training and consulting-like project participation (see Table 2).

The IS students benefited from the new undergraduate and graduate curricula, for which the IS board sanctioned the content and curricular orientation. In the instance of UIA's new graduate program in IS, after approval by the board, it was further presented to CONACYT—the premier federal science and technology government funding agency. CONACYT evaluated the UIA graduate program and granted its accreditation. All accredited programs constitute CONACYT's excellence roster. The impact of becoming part of this roster is twofold. First, it gives recognition to the university, the department, and the program. The second advantage is

Table 2: IS/IT Board Impact on IS Department and its Academic Programs

PARAMETER	With IS Board (1988-1992)	Without IS Board (1992-1996)
Undergraduate student population	Grew from 260 in 1987 to 610 by 1992	Lowered from 610 to 310
Graduate student population	Grew from 40 in 1987 to 82 by 1992	Lowered from 82 in 1992 to 12 in 1996
Graduate program quality	Certified by CONACyT, and part of the excellence roster	Dropped from CONACyT's excellence roster
University Service	1,700 student-courses, 200 part-time professors IS Department in charge of the academic computing service	800 student-courses 60 part-time professors
Computer labs	Grew from 40 screens to 450 screens	Grew from 450 to 1,200 screens, but IS Department controlled only 400 screens
IS faculty	Grew from 6 to 13	Reduced 13 to 8
IS faculty salary	40% above the university's regular salary	At the norm of university's regular salary
Projects with industry	Several (see Table 3)	None
Students' Internships	Regular program with 60 positions per year	No longer a regular program, no more than 10 positions yearly

Table 3: Examples of IS/IT Projects Promoted by the IS/IT Industry Board

Project	Description
Computer Literacy Program	Course design and training program for 800 Hewlett Packard Personnel.
IS Security Executive Program	Executive program for IS banking personnel.
IS Network Security Program	IS network security procedures and policy design and implementation for an international bank.
Telmex Quality Suppliers Control Information System	Information system to control, register, and monitor suppliers.
Systems Audit	Audit of information systems of INCOREC.
Assets Control Information System	Information system that allowed Procter and Gamble to monitor and quantify companies' assets.

financial. Any new student accepted into a program belonging to the roster automatically receives a CONACYT scholarship that covers tuition and personal expenses. Consequently, programs in the roster attract better students and better faculty. Thanks to the IS board, also, the undergraduate and graduate students had access to up to 60 internship positions annually. Some of the students (20 in a good year) took part in industry projects that were led by IS faculty members.

With respect to the faculty, they benefited from the IS/IT board through software training programs such as in C language, Unix, DB2, operation systems, etc., and through taking part in industry consulting projects (see Table 3). Based on this training and participation, the IS faculty increased their income 40% on average. Lastly, the impact of the board at the university level was important. First, the board allowed the university to increase the competitiveness of its academic programs. Secondly, thanks to the board's support, the university enhanced its computer labs, investing only about 30% of the market value of the labs. Third, the university increased its own revenue without financial cost. The board did not directly fund the operational projects in the IS department. However, it did indirectly help the department and its programs through hardware donations, hardware/software discounts, free faculty training, and payments to the university for consulting and internship projects realized by IS faculty and students.

The IS/IT Board Collapse

Subsequently, however, the lack of industry-university collaboration slowed down the IS Department performance in the period from 1992 to 1996

(Table 2). The reasons why the IS Department stopped performing were: (1) organizational change, and (2) mismanagement of the board. Organizationally, a new university rector and a new IS chair took over. The new rector wanted to enhance collaboration with industry, and he promoted a project to start operating a university-wide Research Center. Faculty were given a choice to remain at the Department with mainly teaching load, or to join the Research Center, which mainly focused on industry collaboration and applied research.

In the Systems Department, the new chair lost the best faculty to the Research Center, and instead focused on operating the academic programs. Along the way, the IS Industry Board ceased operating with it, leading to the board disappearance.

By 1996 the undergraduate IS curricula was not being updated and was losing its appeal for new students. The demand for the program declined to 310 students. In the case of the IS graduate program, an early '90s new curriculum failed to receive CONACYT accreditation, and by 1994 the program was excluded from CONACYT's excellence roster. By late 1996 a new academic curriculum was developed for both programs. Without any feedback from industry experts or the former best faculty now at the Research Center, the suitability of the programs faltered. The new programs failed to attract new students, and by 1997 the university closed the graduate program, which had only 12 students.

Regarding the Research Center side, in 1995 the university's top management closed it. The university union did not allow the Center operation. According to the union, allowing the Center to work would have promoted stratification of the faculty into first-class and second-class.

Slowly, the IS Department lost IS/IT leadership within the university. Lastly, the IS Department faculty body declined to eight full-time professors, and they stopped taking part in any industry-related projects. By 1998, with less than 200 students in its undergraduate programs and 40 of them in the new graduate programs, the IS Department disappeared. Since then, the Engineering Department of the University has overseen both IS programs.

FINDINGS AND RECOMMENDATIONS

There are several concerns regarding industry-university collaboration. These concerns inhibit university attempts to take part in or promote industry programs, while others restrict companies' willingness to partner with universities. For the former, we can cite the following concerns: the university may lose academic control of its programs. If you invite software or hardware vendors to take part on university committees, you end up having to buy their products. High-caliber industry members do not want to, or cannot participate in university-related activities. It is costly to have an industry board. On the other hand, when a faculty takes part in industry projects, he/she ends up either quitting his or her faculty position or behaving as a part-time professor with an office at the university. You only can have industry-related programs if you have a huge faculty body. Professors do not want to take part in industry projects. The university needs a bigger budget to support projects recommended by the IS/IT board. And if a project fails, the university social recognition or reputation is destroyed.

However, the IS programs' experience at UIA shows that properly managed all these concerns can be avoided or minimized. For example, in particular, during the period the board was extant, the IS Department never lost the control of its academic programs. On the contrary, the Department curricula became quite competitive, enlightened by the advice of the IS industry board. The graduate program was certified by CONACYT, while the undergraduate program reached its maximum demand in new students. Having several hardware and software vendors on the IS industry board allowed the UIA to have huge discounts vis-à-vis the hardware and software market costs. Furthermore none of the board members promoted his company products in the board meetings or at the university. On the contrary, they submitted proposals to enhance the computing infrastructure with donations, or with discounts of up to 80% for software and 52% for hardware. This helped a lot, since the university's computing infrastructure was the main concern together with curricula updating, when the board was constituted for the first time in late 1987. The lesson is that high-caliber IS executives are usually willing to participate and contribute to a university's development. None of the IS executives invited to the IS board rejected the invitation to join, and all of them closely worked with the Department Chair without any economic compensation.

As for the faculty part, it is true that when faculty take part in industry projects, they can be invited to become part of the company, and possibly leave the university. Even though that happened several times, it should not be seen as a failure in the industry-university relationship. On the contrary, it involved a regard by industry of the high-quality of the university team, and it also contributed to the university prestige, social recognition, and professional fitness.

The other concern regarding faculty that they become more and more involved in industry projects, while diminishing other academic activities, is also true. The way UIA managed to avoid this undesirable output was to limit faculty participation to one or two projects per year depending on the duration and time demand of them. We find out that some professors were not enthusiastic toward taking part in industry projects. However, little by little they accepted the possibility, given the broad range of opportunities available to faculty.

From the industry standpoint, the main identifiable limitations to taking part in projects with universities are the following: confidentiality problems, assessing the project costs, and unfairness to universities in competition with consultancy firms. Companies consider that partnering with universities exposes their strategies, processes, IT infrastructure, and IT development plans. Another problem is the amount to be paid for the projects to the university. Since the university is using faculty and students, several companies want to pay much less for a university project than what they would have to pay to a consultant firm. On the other hand, universities accepting this condition are strongly criticized by consulting firms. These firms consider that universities unfairly compete with them for industry projects. First, they argue, universities do not have to allocate overhead for this kind of projects. Buildings, hardware, software, and staff are usually covered by the student tuition income. Especially in the case of hardware and software, universities get better prices than private companies, because they are oriented to train students in teaching activities. Furthermore, faculty usually get training without cost or with a very affordable cost.

The experience at the Iberoamericana shows that these concerns are pertinent. In Mexico there is a positive attitude toward industry-university collaboration. However, examples of this collaboration are scarce. Specifically, the instance of industry projects developed by faculty and students had a mixed outcome. On the one hand, industry was willing to contract the university's service, but at a lower price than what they would pay for the same project to a consulting firm. The solution to the perceptions of university cost is to explicate to industry the university policy toward industry-university projects. The policy establishes the hourly wage for faculty, including the project leader; the hourly wage by students according to their categories if there are such categories; and the overhead paid to the Department and the university. This policy was presented to the IS board. Since the board considered it a sound policy, when the university was recommended for a consulting project by a member of the board, the costing part and the revenue distribution were known up front.

IS BOARDS' SUCCESS FACTORS

The Iberoamericana experience with IS industry boards demonstrates several critical success factors, including:

- Top management support
- Chair's interpersonal skills
- Board member selection
- Proper board management
- University policies regarding industry-university collaboration

The President and the university's top management should be aware of the fast-moving aspects of technology. It is critical for the quality and even viability of IS programs to keep up to date with current technology and industry practices. If the IS board strategy is focused to foster industry-university collaboration, the university President should take charge of the board protocol, and the university's top management should set academic-industry IS project policy. This policy should address project costing, faculty and student participation, project overhead, and income distribution. Lastly, university's top management should be aware that some projects will fail, and that faculty departures to industry will occur, due often to successful projects.

In order to succeed in productively working with an IS board, the IS Department chair should have outstanding interpersonal skills. Under the IS board strategy to promote industry-university collaboration, the IS chair became the link between the board and its members and the university top management, the department faculty, the students, and the IS programs. To succeed in properly linking different goals and visions, the chair has to play several roles and to interact with different groups in different settings.

Another critical condition to succeed in industry-university collaboration through IS boards is the board member selection. First, the board candidates should be invited after a careful assessment of the IS programs' situation and programs' goals and objectives. Then, the university can seek high-caliber IS executives to invite. This invitation should be linked with the program evaluation and desired goals, so future IS board members can weigh their potential contributions.

The IS board should be managed. That is to say, the number of meetings per year, the agenda of the meetings, the protocol before and after the meetings, and the board communications call for scrupulous control. A high-caliber IS executive cannot be expected to attend more than three meetings a year. The meetings should be arranged in an executive fashion. Board members should have all the materials and the agenda in advance, with clear meeting objectives. The board should be notified of the progress and task fulfillment of the IS programs.

Lastly, a university policy toward industry-university collaboration is fundamental for the success of the relationship between the IS programs and different companies. The policy should address limits on participation, costing procedures, revenue distribution, conditions for student involvement, and the authority of the university to monitor the IS Department to comply with university policy, whether arranged by time periods or by projects.

There are some differences in these success factors for a developing country versus an advanced one. The faculty differences are the most important ones. To start out with, a faculty member in Mexico does not have access to a tenure track academic career. Few universities require graduate studies to become an undergraduate professor. Consequently, academic careers in IS are not positively regarded compared with IS industry careers. This places a double challenge to university management: (1) to hire young faculty and (2) to train and to retain excellent professors.

On the other hand, there is no difference between a developing country and a developed one on the salary gap between IS faculty and IS industry positions. In both types of countries, salaries of IS faculty are lower than salaries of IS professionals in industry. IS industry boards, promoting industry-university collaboration, can help in closing the salary gap, orienting curricula updates, and achieving the academic goals of the academic unit and the university. The IS industry board can contribute to the quality of IS programs, the availability of computers labs, the size and quality of internships for students, and the research productivity of professors.

CONCLUSIONS

Because of IS academic programs' concern for fast-moving aspects of the technology, it is critical for the quality and even viability of these programs that they keep up to date with current technology and industry practices. There are many forms of interaction between academia and industry: faculty and student internships, partnership courses, and curriculum revision committees, among others. The chapter focused on the industry advisory board for IS programs: a committee composed of 10 to 12 members, with strong IS experience and relevant industry participation. Analyzing a case in a university on a developing country, the chapter addressed critical success factors for achieving good outcomes with an IS industry board, and what factors are distinctive and serve to differentiate IS industry boards in developing nations from those in advanced ones.

The IS industry success factors are: top management support, IS chair's interpersonal skills, board member selection, proper board management, and an university policy toward industry-university collaboration. Based on these factors, the IS advisory board of the IS programs at Universidad Iberoamericana encouraged: enrollment growth, program quality increase, computing lab enhancement, and IS faculty salary increase. On the other hand, the case analyzed shows that without top management support and proper industry feedback, the academic programs shrink, the IS Department loses the control of academic labs, and the quality of the programs lowers. All these factors led up to the university closing the IS Department.

Finally, there are some differences between developing countries and advanced ones. The faculty differences are the most important ones. In many developing countries, for example, there is not access to tenure track careers. However, there are some similarities regarding the faculty and industry gap, industry involvements encouraging IT innovation and development, and strong demand for human resources trained in the latest technologies.

These similarities certainly emphasize a common purpose in attempts to link IS programs to industry. More cases of formal relationships in this field should allow more research directed to enhance IS programs thanks to industry-university partnerships.

REFERENCES

Kock, N., Auspitz, C. and King, B. (2000). Closing the industry-university gap through Web-supported course partnerships. In Chung, H. M. (Ed.), *Proceedings of AMCIS 2000 Conference*, 3, 1774-1779. Atlanta, GA: Association for Information Systems.

McGowan, M. K. and Cornwell, L. W. (2000). A university and corporation partnership for student employees. *Journal of Computer Information Systems*, 40(4), 106-111.

Maehl, W. (2000). Collaborating with corporate clients to create new programs: Bachelor of Science in Information Systems, University of Redlands. *Section in Lifelong Learning at its Best*, 225-231. San Francisco, CA: Jossey-Bass.

Oblinger, D. (1993). *Transforming the Academy to Improve Delivery of Services: Redesign for Reallocation*. Norwalk, CT: IBM.

Parker, L. (1993). Industry-university research collaboration: An option for generating revenue. In Altbach, P. G. and Johnstone, D. B. (Eds.), *The Funding of Higher Education*, 101-122. New York: Garland Publishing Inc.

Schenk, K. D. and Pick, J. B. (1998). A framework for successful partnerships between industry and academia. *Journal of Computer Information Systems*, 39(1), 65-71.

Yin, R., K. (1994). *Case Study Research: Design and Methods*. (2nd Ed.). Thousand Oaks, CA: Sage Publications.

Section IV

Digital Divide Issues

Chapter XI

The Camfield Estates – MIT Creating Community Connections Project: High Technology in a Low-to-Moderate Income Community

Randal Pinkett
MIT Media Laboratory, USA

This chapter is a case study of a community-university partnership that is investigating strategies to bridge the "digital divide" by examining the role of community technology for the purpose of community building in a low- to moderate-income housing development. Since January 2000, the Camfield Estates-MIT Creating Community Connections Project, a partnership between the Camfield Tenants Association and Massachusetts Institute of Technology, has taken place at Camfield Estates, a 102-unit, low- to moderate-income housing development in Roxbury, Massachusetts, and its surrounding environs. This chapter includes the history and background of the project, the theoretical frameworks guiding the initiative, the project methodology that has been employed to integrate community technology and community building, early results, and a set of recommendations and lessons learned for other initiatives.

INTRODUCTION

The digital divide (NTIA 1995, 1997, 1999, 2000), the gap between those who benefit from new technologies and those who do not, has received considerable attention in the new millennium as organizations from the public, private, and nonprofit sectors have partnered with communities to address this critical issue (Robinson, 2000). In urban and rural neighborhoods across the country, there are examples of successful initiatives to provide economical access and promote meaningful use of technology, as a means toward achieving tangible and sustainable outcomes in areas such as education, employment, health care, and more (Benton, 1998; Chow, Ellis, Mark, & Wise, 1998; Lazarus & Mora, 2000; Mark, Cornebise, & Wahl, 1997; Schon, Sanyal & Mitchel, 1999). Not surprisingly, universities have (Bishop et al., 1999; Chapman & Rhodes, 1997; Cohill & Kavanaugh, 1997; Hampton & Wellman, 1999; Resnick, Rusk, & Cooke, 1998; Turner & Pinkett, 2000) and will continue to play an important role in these initiatives, given the intellectual and technological resources they bring to bear on the problem.

Historically, one of the major challenges associated with community collaborations is the "inside-outside tension" resulting from the delineation between internal and external actors, which is perhaps best characterized as the distinction between "us" and "them" (Aspen Institute, 1999). This tension manifests itself in a variety of ways. From the "inside" perspective, neighborhood residents and governing boards, seeking to leverage the resources and expertise of researchers, funders, and technical assistance providers, must do so in a way that advances, and does not compromise their own goals and objectives. From the "outside" perspective, non-residents, seeking to support and learn from community members and organizations, must do so in a way that fosters ownership and empowerment, as opposed to reliance and dependence. As universities expand the scope of their work to include high technology in low- to moderate-income and underserved communities, the inside-outside tension will undoubtedly arise as it has in the past. However, the need for a greater awareness of and sensitivity to these issues is only heightened by the challenges associated with the ongoing use of technology, such as installing new systems, and maintaining and upgrading existing systems. Without careful attention to this dilemma, community-based organizations could easily be saddled with a prohibitively higher total cost of ownership than experienced before.

The ideal scenario for communities and universities to truly work together as partners is one where the needs of both parties are met and the community's capacity is strengthened as a result of the partnership. These goals are most likely to be met (and the inside-outside tension is most likely to be resolved) in projects that engage community residents as active participants in the process, ensuring that they have a strong voice in determining outcomes for their community, while still leveraging the contributions from the university. As Kingsley, McNeely, and Gibson (1999, p. 7) explain:

> *"Community participation" is not enough. The community must play the central role in devising and implementing strategies for its own improvement. This does not mean that outside facilitators cannot help show them the way, or that they cannot accept outside help or accomplish goals by partnering with outside agencies, but neighborhood residents must feel that they "own" the improvement process.*

The Camfield Estates-MIT Creating Community Connections Project, a community-university partnership between the Camfield Tenants Association (CTA) and the Massachusetts Institute of Technology (MIT), has endeavored to exemplify this notion.

Started in January 2000, the Camfield Estates-MIT project has the goal of establishing Camfield Estates as a model for other housing developments as to how individuals, families, and a community can make use of information and communications technology to support their interests and needs. To achieve this goal, CTA and MIT have formed a unique partnership with support from various organizations in the public, private, and nonprofit sectors. This multi-sector collaboration (Robinson, 2000) has joined to create an infrastructure at Camfield Estates that combines the three primary models for *community technology* (Morino, 1994; Beamish, 1999): a *community network* where state-of-the-art desktop computers, software, and high-speed Internet connectivity have been offered to every family; a *community technology center (CTC)*, located on the premises in the community center; and *community content* delivered through a community-based web system, the Creating Community Connections (C3) system, along with a *community building* agenda (Aspen Institute, 1997; Kingsley, McNeely & Gibson, 1999; Mattesich & Monsey, 1997). Note that there is a parallel and related initiative being conducted at Camfield to build empowerment and self-sufficiency among residents that is beyond the scope of this chapter.

This chapter is a case study of the Camfield Estates-MIT project to date, including the history and background of the project, the theoretical frameworks guiding the initiative, the methodology that has been employed, early results, as well as a set of recommendations for future community-university partnerships involving technology.

HISTORY OF THE CAMFIELD ESTATES-MIT PROJECT

Camfield Estates, formerly Camfield Gardens, is a predominantly African-American, low- to moderate-income housing development in the Roxbury section of Boston, Massachusetts. Camfield is a participant in the U.S. Department of Housing and Urban Development's (HUD) demonstration-disposition or "demo-dispo" program. Demo-dispo was implemented by HUD in 1993, as a strategy to deal with its growing inventory of foreclosed multi-family housing, much of which was in poor physical and financial condition (MHFA, 2001). Through this national demonstration program, approved only in the City of Boston, the Massachusetts Housing Finance Agency (MHFA) was designated to oversee the renovation and sale of HUD properties to resident-owned organizations. As a result, the 136 low- to medium-rise apartments of Camfield Gardens were demolished in 1997 and residents were relocated throughout the greater Boston area. Reconstruction of the property was completed in 2000 as residents returned to Camfield Estates, 102 units of newly built townhouses. The renovated property also includes the Camfield Community Center which houses meeting space, management offices, and the Neighborhood Technology Center (NTC), a CTC and HUD Neighborhood Networks site, managed by Williams Consulting Services, and supported by MHFA. Finally, in 2001, HUD disposed (transferred ownership) of the property to the non-profit Camfield Tenants Association, Inc. (CTA), making Camfield the first of several participants in the demo-dispo program to successfully complete the process.

The Camfield Estates-MIT Creating Community Connections project was initiated in January 2000, by graduate students and faculty from the MIT Media Laboratory, MIT Department of Urban Studies and Planning, MIT Center for Reflective Community Practice, and MIT Laboratory for Computer Science. These researchers shared an interest in the role of technology for the purpose of building community, empowerment, and self-sufficiency in a low-income community. Camfield was identified as an excellent site to examine these issues and conduct a longitudinal study for numerous reasons, including the strong leadership exemplified by CTA, the cable-modem Internet capabilities in each unit, and the presence of NTC, along with its associated course offering and ongoing technical support. However, what made Camfield particularly attractive were the prospects to sustain the initiative as a result of their leading role in the demo-dispo program and impending ownership of the property.

The W.K. Kellogg Foundation provided primary support for the project in the form of a monetary grant, followed by in-kind donations from Hewlett-Packard Company (computers), RCN Telecom Services (cable-modem Internet service), Microsoft Corporation (software), and ArsDigita Corporation (software and technical support), with additional support from MHFA, Williams Consulting Services, Lucent Technologies, HUD, the Institute for African-American eCulture (iAAEC), YouthBuild of Boston, and the William Monroe Trotter Institute at the University of Massachusetts at Boston.

Exploratory meetings between CTA, MIT, Kellogg, and Williams Consulting took place during the winter of 2000, culminating in final approval of the project by CTA. Under CTA's leadership, in the spring of 2000, a nine-person committee was established to oversee the project's implementation, which consisted of three Camfield residents, two representatives of CTA, two members of Williams Consulting staff, and two researchers at MIT. The project officially began in June 2000.

BACKGROUND: COMMUNITY TECHNOLOGY AND COMMUNITY BUILDING

One of the project's goals is to explore the synergy between *community technology* (Morino, 1994; Beamish, 1999) and *community building* (Aspen Institute, 1997; Kingsley, McNeely, & Gibson, 1999; Mattesich & Monsey, 1997). *Community technology* has been referred to as "a process to serve the local geographic community – to respond to the needs of that community and build solutions to its problems" (Morino, 1994, p. 1), and defined as "using the technology to support and meet the goals of a community" (Beamish, 1999, p. 366). *Community building* is an approach to community revitalization that is focused on "strengthening the capacity of residents, associations, and organizations to work, individually and collectively, to foster and sustain positive neighborhood change" (Aspen Institute, 1997, p. 10).

To date, three primary models have emerged for community technology, *community networks, community technology centers (CTCs),* and *community content*, all of which have been deployed at Camfield and combined with a *community building* agenda:

- *Community networks* are community-based electronic network services, provided at little or no cost to users. Every family at Camfield has been offered a state-of-the-art computer, software, and high-speed Internet connectivity via cable-modem.

- *Community technology centers (CTCs),* or community computing centers, are publicly accessible facilities that provide computer access for people who can't afford a computer, as well as technical instruction and support. As mentioned earlier, the Camfield Estates Neighborhood Technology Center (NTC) has been established in the Camfield Community Center where comprehensive courses as well as technical support are provided.

- *Community content* refers to the availability of material that is relevant and interesting to a specific target audience (e.g., low-income residents) to encourage and motivate the use of technology (Lazarus & Mora, 2000). The Creating Community Connections (C3) System, a community-based Web system, has been co-designed between MIT students and Camfield residents using the application service provider (ASP) model; Camfield residents create and maintain the content, while MIT administers and maintains the associated hardware and software.

To promote *community building,* Camfield residents and MIT researchers have been actively involved in "mapping" and "mobilizing" community assets and resources to create connections among residents, local organizations and institutions (e.g., libraries, schools, etc.), and neighborhood businesses.

THEORETICAL FRAMEWORK: SOCIOCULTURAL CONSTRUCTIONISM AND AN ASSET-BASED APPROACH TO COMMUNITY TECHNOLOGY AND COMMUNITY BUILDING

Since the project's inception, a heavy emphasis has been placed on engaging the residents at Camfield as active agents of change, as well as active producers of community information and content. This theoretical framework is grounded in theories of sociocultural constructionism (Pinkett, 2000) and asset-based community development (ABCD) (Kretzmann & McKnight, 1993). These theoretical frameworks have proven extremely useful for conceptualizing how a community-university partnership involving technology can foster community empowerment, rather than dependency.

Sociocultural Constructionism

Sociocultural constructionism, here applied to community technology, is a synthesis of the theories of *social constructionism* (Shaw, 1995) and *cultural constructionism* (Hooper, 1998), both extensions of the theory of *constructionism* (Papert, 1993). *Constructionism* is a design-based approach to learning, drawing on research showing that people learn best when they are active participants in design activities (Papert, 1993), and that these activities give them a greater sense of control over (and personal involvement in) the learning process (Resnick, Bruckman & Martin, 1996). There are two extensions to constructionism that demonstrate its relevance to the social and cultural context that surrounds engagement with technology, as well as the role of community technology for the purpose of community building:

- *Cultural constructionism* argues that individuals learn particularly well through creating objects in the world that express their cultural identity and have shared meaning within their home cultures (Hooper, 1998). A cultural construction could be a personal website, electronic community newsletter, or any other project that is an expression of cultural identity, and at the same time facilitates an engagement with new knowledge. Cultural constructionism is a useful framework for identifying ways technology can advance the interests and needs of an individual learner.

- *Social constructionism* states that individual developmental cycles are enhanced by shared constructive activity in the social setting, and the social setting is also enhanced by the developmental activity of the individual (Shaw, 1995). Shared constructive activity refers to the creation of "social constructions," of which there are five types: 1) social relationships, 2) social events, 3) shared physical artifacts, 4) shared social goals and projects, and 5) shared cultural norms and traditions. Social constructionism is a useful framework for identifying ways in which technology can advance the interests and needs of a community of learners.

Sociocultural constructionism argues that "individual and community development are reciprocally enhanced by independent and shared constructive activity that is resonant with both the social setting that encompasses a community of learners, as well as the culture identity of the learners themselves" (Pinkett, 2000, pp. 4-5). Sociocultural constructionism yields an approach to community technology that regards community members as the active producers of community information and content, rather than passive consumers or recipients.

Asset-Based Community Development

Asset-based community development (ABCD), a particular model, or technique, for community building, assumes that social and economic revitalization starts with what is already present in the community, not only the capacities of residents as individuals, but also the existing commercial, associational, and institutional foundation (Turner & Pinkett, 2000). Asset-based community development seeks to leverage the resources within a community by "mapping" these assets and then "mobilizing" them to facilitate productive and meaningful connections.

Kretzmann and McKnight (1993) have identified three characteristics of asset-based community development:

- *Asset-based*: Asset-based community development begins with what is present in the community, as opposed to what is absent or problematic in the community. It is focused on indigenous assets as opposed to perceived needs. An asset-based approach involves community residents, organizations, institutions (e.g., libraries, schools, etc.), and businesses.

- *Internally focused*: Asset-based community development calls upon community members to identify their interests and build upon their capacity to solve problems. One of the distinguishing characteristics of the ABCD approach is its heavy emphasis on leveraging that which is in the community first, before looking to (but not excluding) outside entities and/or resources.

- *Relationship driven*: Community building has also been defined as "any identifiable set of activities pursued by a community in order to increase the social capacity of its members" (Mattesich & Monsey, 1997, pp. 8-9). Consequently, asset-based community development encourages the ongoing establishment of productive relationships among community members, as well as the associated trust and norms necessary to maintain and strengthen these relationships.

Asset-based community development is an approach to community building that sees community members as active agents of change, rather than passive beneficiaries or clients.

Community Social Capital and Community Cultural Capital

In theory, the sociocultural constructionist and asset-based community development frameworks foster positive changes in *community social capital* and *community cultural capital*, as a result of promoting residents as active, rather than passive participants in the process.

I define *community social capital* as the extent to which members of a community can work and learn together effectively. Community social capital is based on the concept of *social capital* first introduced by Coleman (1988) and extended by Putnam (1993, 1995). This definition of community social capital is similar to Mattesich and Monsey's (1997) definition of social capacity. I define *community cultural capital* as various forms of knowledge, skills, abilities, and interests, which have particular relevance or value within a community. Community cultural capital is based on the concept of *cultural capital* first introduced by Bourdieu (1977) and extended by Lamont and Lareau (1988). This definition of community cultural capital is similar to Zweigenhaft's (1993) definition of cultural capital.

In practice, the sociocultural constructionist and asset-based community development frameworks help operationalize a methodology for integrating community technology and community building.

CAMFIELD ESTATES-MIT PROJECT METHODOLOGY

In June 2000, the project committee outlined a methodology to integrate community technology and community building, consisting of five interrelated, and at times parallel phases, as shown in Figure 1: I. Pre-Assessment and Awareness, II. Community Technology: Introductory/Specialized Courses and C3, III. Community Building: General and Specific Asset-Mapping, IV. Online and Offline Asset-Mobilization, and V. Post-Assessment and Evaluation.

Figure 1: Camfield Estates-MIT Project Methodology

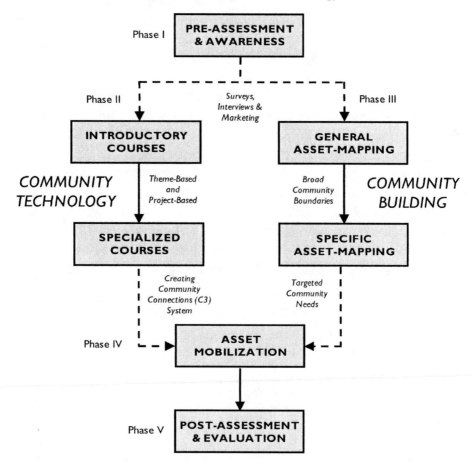

Phase I: Pre-Assessment and Awareness

During the summer of 2000, we developed a pre-assessment survey instrument to collect data in the following areas: *community interests and satisfaction, social networks (strong and weak ties), neighboring, awareness of community resources, community satisfaction, community involvement, empowerment, self-sufficiency, computer experience, hobbies, interests and information needs, assets and income, and demographics.* The survey was designed for two purposes. First, to provide strategic direction for the community building and community technology initiative by identifying the interests and needs of residents. This information would shape the nature of online and offline activities to be planned in the future. Second, to provide baseline and formative data for the research study. This information would be used to perform a comparative analysis of a similar data set to be gathered approximately one year later.

During this same period, an awareness campaign was conducted to inform residents about the initiative. A series of mailings were distributed describing the project's goals and objectives, and offering a new computer, high-speed Internet connection, and comprehensive courses at NTC, for adults 18 years and older that completed the courses, completed the preliminary interview, and signed an informed consent form granting permission to track the web-traffic at Camfield through a proxy server (aggregate patterns of use only, and not individually attributable). An open forum was also held in the community center for questions and answers. While families were encouraged to attend the training, at least one adult from each household had to fulfill these requirements in order to receive the computer and Internet access. Given the fact that NTC was primarily used by youth at this time (O'Bryant, 2001), it was the decision of the committee to restrict participation to adults only, as we believed it would motivate parents to attend the training for the benefit of their children.

August 2000 marked the deadline to sign-up for the project, and 33 of the 66 families at Camfield elected to participate in Round I. Subsequently, and just prior to the introductory courses, three committee members administered the preliminary survey via one-on-one interviews with each of these participants (lasting between approximately one and four hours).

Phase II: Community Technology – Introductory/ Specialized Courses and the Creating Community Connections (C3) System

From September to October 2000, introductory courses were offered at NTC to Round I participants. The activity-based curriculum lasted eight weeks (two sessions per week, two hours per session) and covered various aspects of computer and Internet use. In November 2000, specialized courses were offered on how to use the Creating Community Connections (C3) System, available through the Camfield Estates website (http://www.camfieldestates.net), as shown in Figure 2. Whereas the introductory curriculum was designed solely by Williams Consulting Services, with input from MIT, the C3 curriculum was co-designed by both parties.

C3 is a database-backed web system designed to establish and strengthen relationships between community residents, local businesses, and neighborhood institutions (e.g., libraries, schools, etc.) and organizations. Designed at the MIT Media Laboratory, and based on the principles of sociocultural constructionism, C3 serves two primary functions:

- As a *community intranet,* C3 facilitates community communication and information exchange with the following features: resident profiles (cataloging formal and informal skills and interests obtained during specific asset-mapping, described in greater detail below), community calendar of events, community discussion forums, community e-mail lists (listservs), community chat rooms, community news and announcements, surveying, and more.

- As a *community extranet,* C3 facilitates asset-mapping and asset mobilization among residents, organizations, and businesses with the following features: organization and business database (visualized using a geographic information system (GIS) that represents this data in the form of a map with hyperlinked symbols for various resources), job and volunteer opportunity postings, online résumés, personal home pages, personalized web portals, electronic commerce, and more.

Figure 2: Creating Community Connections (C3) Systems

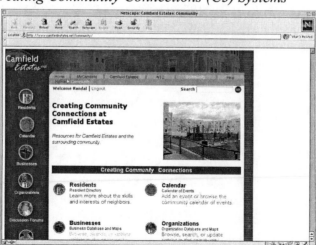

C3 is built using the ArsDigita Community System (ACS), an open-source software platform. C3 is delivered using an application service provider (ASP) model; Camfield residents create and maintain the content, while MIT administers and maintains the associated hardware and software.

C3 was first prototyped in December 1999, as a collaborative effort between students in MIT Course 6.916: Software Engineering of Innovative Web Applications, researchers at the Asset-Based Community Development (ABCD) Institute at Northwestern University, and residents at Northwest Tower, a federally assisted affordable housing development in Chicago, Illinois (Turner & Pinkett, 2000). A modified and improved version of the system was co-designed and implemented by MIT students and Camfield residents one year later.

In November 2000, 31 families received computers, software, and subsequent high-speed Internet access, having fulfilled the aforementioned requirements. In January 2001, a second awareness campaign was conducted and aimed at the 47 families still eligible for the project (the number of occupied units had increased from 66 to 80), including another round of mailings and meetings. After the second deadline passed, only eight additional families elected to participate in the project, the majority of whom were Spanish-speaking, as we were late distributing the flyers in their native-language during Round I.

Unwilling to accept these numbers as being representative of residents' interest, we embarked on a grassroots, door-to-door, outreach campaign to make sure people were fully aware of this unique opportunity. As a result, we were able to increase Round II numbers from eight to twenty-seven families, raising the total number of families participating in the project to 60 out of 80 eligible units. Interestingly, for those residents that did not participate in Round I, but decided to participate in Round II, the most commonly cited reasons were:

1)   miscommunication/misunderstanding ("I never received any of the flyers"),
2)   skepticism ("It sounded too good to be true"), and
3)   they already owned a computer and weren't as quick as others to move on the opportunity.

For those residents that did not participate in either Round I or Round II, the most commonly cited reasons were:

1)   lack of relevance ("I just don't want to be involved"),
2)   too many responsibilities, including a few single mothers juggling multiple obligations, and
3)   a health-related condition preventing involvement.

A third awareness campaign will be conducted at the end of Round II, along with a flexible training program (e.g., one-on-one instruction), which will hopefully enable the participation of residents who were interested, but unable to participate in Rounds I and II.

Phase III: Community Building – General and Specific Asset-Mapping

Per the asset-based community development approach, a resident-led general asset-mapping took place during the summer of 2000, with technical assistance from researchers at MIT. It consisted of mapping all the organizations, institutions (e.g., libraries, schools, etc.), and businesses within an approximately 1.5-mile radius of Camfield, as shown in Figure 3. This broad attempt to identify community resources was done to obtain local information of potential benefit to residents that would eventually be made available through C3, and as a preparatory step for more specific asset-mapping to be conducted after analyzing the results of the pre-assessment. Not surprisingly, the mere process of gathering this information served to heighten residents' awareness of assets in their own neighborhood. For example, the first-pass general asset-map was conducted within a few square blocks of the property. Residents soon discovered there were very few organizations and institutions in this catchment area, and only a small cluster of businesses. The decision was then made to expand the radius of the asset-map to 1.5 miles, which captured approximately 757 businesses, 178 organizations, 67 churches, and 29 schools.

Specific asset-mapping began in November 2000, and consisted of mapping the formal and informal skills of residents, as well as a more detailed mapping of a targeted sample of the organizations, institutions, and businesses previously identified during general asset-mapping. The former activity took place during the final two weeks of the introductory and specialized courses. Using C3, residents entered their formal and informal skills and interests, by selecting from an inventory of more than 150 items. Given this information, residents could now

Figure 3: Camfield Estates Asset-Map

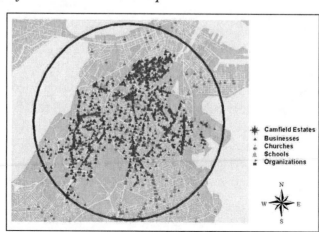

Table 1: Please rank the following issues in terms of their importance to you.

Issue	Rank
Safety/environment	1
Employment	2
Housing	2
Education	4
Health care	5
Child care	6
Parenting	7
Community activism	8
Political involvement	9

use C3 to identify neighbors who could perform plumbing, babysitting, web design, etc., or neighbors who were interested in learning these skills. Again, residents were often pleasantly surprised to learn about the talents and abilities of their neighbors. The latter activity is presently underway, and is being informed by the results of the pre-assessment. For example, Table 1 lists the issues deemed important according to residents.

This information also gives insight to the community assets and resources that can be brought to bear in addressing these issues. During general asset-mapping, only basic information was obtained for community organizations, institutions, and businesses (e.g., name, address, contact information, products/services for businesses, programs/services for organizations and institutions, etc.). During specific asset-mapping, to begin addressing top-ranked issues such as employment, housing, child care, and health care, we can obtain more detailed data (e.g., hours of operation, eligibility, fees, etc.) on this focused subset of the community resources deemed important to residents, who can then publish this information online using C3. We can also involve the resident social services coordinator in connecting residents to these programs/services.

Phase IV: Online and Offline Asset-Mobilization

Asset-mobilization involves devising strategies to create community connections between residents, organizations, institutions, and businesses, which previously did not exist, toward achieving specific outcomes. Asset-mobilization will be heavily informed by the pre-assessment, and will likely involve outreach and the formation of new community partnerships. For example, Table 2 identifies items residents would like to see made available on the Camfield website.

Several of these items are now available through the C3 system, such as the resident profiles module. However, based on these results we will continue to add

Table 2: What would you like to see made available on the Camfield website?

Item	Rank
Employment opportunities	1
Camfield resident's information	2
Education	3
Local news	4
Safety	5
Government information	6
Health care	7
Community calendar of activities and events	7
Business information	9
Volunteer opportunities	10
Organization information	11
Weather	12
Sports	13
Regional and national news	14
Classifieds (want ads)	14
Electronic commerce	14
Online forums and discussion groups	17
Arts and entertainment	18

Table 3: What topics would you like to see addressed through training?

Topic	% Requested
Creating my own website	83%
Accessing government information online	78%
Accessing community information online	74%
Protecting my children from certain online content	68%
Finding jobs online	68%
Helping my children in school	65%
Starting a business	65%
Managing my finances	64%
Shopping for groceries online	36%

new modules including a job posting board, and education- and safety-related features, by partnering with relevant community entities. Table 3 ranks the topics residents would like to see addressed through follow-up training.

We have already started to offer theme-based workshops at NTC to Round I participants in many of these areas. Tables 1 and 2 also reveal that employment is an important issue among residents. Given this information and the infrastructure now in place at Camfield, we can enact a number of online and offline strategies to address this issue. First, during specific asset-mapping we can obtain detailed information on the job training programs and employment agencies already identified during general asset-mapping, and again, residents can publish this content to C3, while the resident social services coordinator can play a role in leveraging these resources. Furthermore, we can partner with these organizations to design a follow-up training curriculum that meets the demands of the job market, filter job opportunity postings through C3, and even match these postings against the skill and interest profiles of residents.

With respect to community social capital, we anticipate residents connecting with other residents (e.g., leveraging neighbors skills, interests, etc.), local organizations and institutions (e.g., utilizing services, programs, etc.), and neighborhood businesses (e.g., identifying products, services, etc.). In fact, even in the project's relative infancy, a few stories have already begun to emerge. For example:

CTA is always looking to provide opportunities for youth to get involved in the community. Ms. Johnson, a CTA board member, attends a local church that would like to create a website, yet lacks the expertise to build one; she is looking for assistance. Meanwhile, several people at the development have completed the web design course at NTC and are looking for opportunities to apply their skills in a new and meaningful context. Using the C3 system, these residents were able to publicize their skills to the church, while the church was able to easily identify someone with these skills, and notify them via e-mail of this worthwhile opportunity.

We envision similar scenarios such as parents exchanging their child-rearing practices via e-mail, NTC classmates relying on one another to solve technical problems in a chat room, residents identifying volunteer opportunities from a discussion forum, or adults obtaining a new job from employment postings available online.

With respect to community cultural capital, we anticipate residents producing information and content on the Internet that reflects their interests and needs, and explicates knowledge indigenous to the community. This will be done by creating personal websites, configuring e-mail lists, posting messages to the discussion forums, and contributing activities to the community calendar of events. Again, we have already observed promising activity in this area thus far. For example:

Since completing the introductory courses on basic computer and Internet use, Mr. Williams has started his own home-based business on the web that involves direct sales of health-care products. He is interested in developing better marketing materials, in hopes of advertising his business to other residents in the development.

Using the C3 "Help" discussion forum, he solicited advice regarding good books on word processing and layout/design. Furthermore, he anticipates using the C3 calendar of events, e-mail lists, and news and announcements discussion forum to publicize his business to neighbors, and announce a reception in the community center where he will showcase his products.

We envision similar scenarios such as a group of single mothers creating an e-mail list to discuss their experiences, a senior creating a website containing her favorite recipes, the tenants' association publishing their newsletter electronically, and the social service coordinator advertising activities on the community calendar of events.

CTA and MIT will continue to work closely with residents and the broader community to leverage the established infrastructure and demonstrate the possibilities resulting from a sociocultural constructionist and asset-based approach to community technology and community building.

Phase V: Post-Assessment and Evaluation

In the summer of 2001, a post-assessment and evaluation was to be conducted. At that time, a comparative analysis was to be performed against the pre-assessment interviews and other sources of data (proxy server logs, C3 server logs, direct observation) to quantify and qualify our progress to date.

Recommendations for Community-University Partnerships

The following six recommendations are offered for communities and universities entering partnerships, particularly those involving information and communications technology. They are not presented as strict rules to follow, but rather lessons learned as a result of our experience with the Camfield Estates-MIT project thus far.

1) *Conduct ongoing assessment to establish a baseline and guide implementation.* Good survey instruments are designed with outcomes in mind, and if done properly, the information gleaned can be very useful. The Camfield Estates-MIT preliminary survey data has been invaluable. It has provided tremendous insight into how technology can be made relevant to people's lives. It is important to note that the survey was designed for two related, yet distinctly different purposes. First, to obtain baseline data for later comparative analysis, and second, to obtain formative data that would guide the project's implementation. With community building identified as an agreed-upon goal (among others) at the project's inception, both Camfield residents and MIT researchers were able to provide specific input to the survey's design in this regard.

This ensured the results not only benchmarked certain outcomes, but also advanced the initiative toward achieving these outcomes.

2)   *Recognize that "process" is just as important as "product."* In this context, process refers to maintaining a "commitment to community building, capacity building, empowerment, [and] participation" (Aspen Institute, 1999, p. 14). Product refers to more concrete outcomes such as a training curriculum, software product, or a research report. The distinction between product and process has also been characterized as the difference between short-term, "intermediate outcomes," such as collective goal setting and relationship building, that are building blocks for longer-term, "final outcomes," such as an increase in the number of students engaged in community projects, or markers of neighborhood improvement (Dewar, 1997). In community-university partnerships, trust, clarification of roles, responsibilities and expectations, and mutual understanding must all be developed and cannot be taken for granted. Despite the fact that process-related activities are often time and resource consuming, they should be valued as being supportive of, rather than subordinated to, product-related outcomes.

3)   *Demonstrate relevance clearly.* At times, it has required nothing short of going door-to-door to demonstrate the relevance of technology, as evidenced by the grassroots mobilization required to solicit Round II participants. We have endeavored to demonstrate relevance in two particular ways. First, by providing a curriculum that is activity-based and combines a variety of learning objectives, rather than focusing on narrow skill development such as how to use a mouse or a keyboard. For example, to teach participants how to use a browser and the printer, they are instructed to use a search engine to locate information on a topic of interest to them, print out each of their results, and summarize which search terms and associated results they found to be useful. Second, by emphasizing outcomes instead of access. For example, an elderly woman at Camfield was one of the project's staunchest opponents. Upon initial contact, she flatly refused being involved. Rather than focusing on the computer and Internet service (access) as a selling point, one of the instructors introduced her to the information she could obtain online and the people with whom she could communicate to improve her quality-of-life (outcomes). A few weeks later, she commented, "This computer is better than all of my medication combined!" Other initiatives have expressed a similar observation (Cohill & Kavanaugh, 1997).

4)   *Link curriculum to outcomes.* One of the areas we improved upon between the Round I courses and the Round II courses was linking the curriculum to

our desired outcomes. The Round I curriculum was more generic when compared to the Round II curriculum, which achieved greater depth with respect to how technology could support community building. We dedicated more time to learning the C3 modules, and exploring how these modules could improve communication at the development. Furthermore, once the results of the pre-assessment were compiled, we were able to follow-up the activity-based curriculum, and couple it with a theme-based curriculum. These thematic workshops (e.g., using online educational resources) were designed around the areas deemed important by residents, as articulated during the preliminary interviews.

5) *Establish multi-sector collaborations to build capacity and promote sustainability.* CTA has established relationships with universities, government agencies, corporations, foundations, nonprofit organizations, and neighboring tenants' associations. HUD and MHFA have played a critical role with respect to the demo-dispo program, which will ensure NTC remains operational. Support from Kellogg, Hewlett-Packard, Microsoft, and others has been instrumental in establishing a state-of-the-art technological infrastructure. MIT's strength in areas such as research, education, and technology positioned the institute to provide useful technical assistance, evaluation, software development, and more. Similarly, each of the remaining entities, which span the public, private, and nonprofit sectors, has contributed something different, yet valuable to sustaining this initiative. However, it is CTA's demonstrated commitment to internal capacity-building, which is strengthened by their ability to cultivate and leverage these relationships, that ultimately bodes well for these efforts to be sustained.

6) *Engage residents as active participants in the process.* Although the Camfield Estates-MIT project was initially proposed by MIT to CTA, MIT researchers did not approach this initiative as if we had all the answers. Instead, we have worked hard to create an atmosphere of trust and mutual respect with CTA and the broader community at Camfield. The process has not been easy; rather, it has required relationship building, commitment, patience, and empathic listening on both sides. From the beginning, CTA and MIT recognized that these foundational elements were fundamental to the project's success. Collectively, we acknowledged that for residents to feel a sense of ownership and empowerment, they must be actively involved in the process.

CONCLUSION

The digital divide is a modern-day reflection of historical social divides that have plagued our society for years. Over the past decade, the community technology movement has gathered momentum toward closing the gap. Meanwhile, the community building movement has wrestled with directly related issues, such as the war on poverty, for more than a century. The intersection between these domains holds tremendous possibilities, as both efforts seek to empower individuals and families, and improve their overall environment. Ironically, approaches that combine these areas have received very little attention. In fact, community technology efforts are often completely decoupled from community building initiatives. While community residents and community-based organizations are pivotal to bringing these movements together, universities have a responsibility too. Participatory research, evaluation, technical assistance, fundraising, program design and implementation, curriculum design, and the like, represent only a modicum of their potential contribution.

Looking forward into the 21st century, colleges and universities must engage communities in long-term, institutional partnerships, which transcend the involvement of students, faculty, and administration. These partnerships must move beyond traditional departmental boundaries, and rethink the ways in which campus resources are leveraged. In this spirit, I offer three roles for universities in community-university partnerships:

- *University as Intermediary.* Many have argued that the successes of community development corporations (CDCs) are largely attributable to the support of capacity-building, intermediary organizations such as the Local Initiatives Support Corporation (LISC) and the Enterprise Foundation (Lynn, 1993; Peirce & Steinbach, 1987). Similarly, the community technology and community building movement is in need of reliable, stable institutions to simply mediate connections between organizations, both locally and regionally (Sandor & Scheuerer, 2000). For the past two years, with support from the Lucent Foundation and the National Conference for Community and Justice (NCCJ), the MIT Media Laboratory and Department of Urban Studies and Planning have played this role for five community-based organizations in greater Boston through the Boston Youth and Community Connections (BYCC) program. BYCC has brought these organizations together to collaborate around the themes of youth development, diversity, and technology.
- *University as Center of Excellence.* Studies have also pointed to the need for independent organizations to provide capacity-building support to community-based organizations, as well as their regional and national intermediaries (Melchior, Thorstensen, & Shurkin, 1998). This includes

activities such as "workshops and training programs on basic, practical issues associated with the introduction and use of technology," "assessing technology needs," "technology planning," "using technology in creating learning-rich activities," and more (Melchior, Thorstensen, & Shurkin, 1998, p. 33). As established centers of teaching and learning, it seems only natural that universities assume this responsibility, particularly in the communities where they are situated. Since 1993, the MIT Media Laboratory has provided similar support to the Computer Clubhouse Network, a national network of CTCs where youth become fluent with technology (Resnick, Rusk, & Cooke, 1998). Clubhouse mentors and staff visit the lab regularly for onsite training and development.

- *University as Application Service Provider (ASP) and Developer.* An application service provider (ASP) is a third party that offers individuals or organizations access to applications (such as software) and related services via the Internet. ASPs can almost eliminate the need for full-time technical staff and lower the total cost of ownership for technology. The relatively low marginal cost to provide Internet hosting and maintenance makes IT-related departments at universities an attractive community partner as an ASP. In 1995, Multi-User Sessions in Community (MUSIC), a community networking system, was developed at the MIT Media Laboratory and deployed in Dorchester, Massachusetts, and a low-income housing development in Newark, New Jersey, as part of the "Making Health MUSIC" project (Shaw & Shaw, 1998; Shaw, 1995). Similarly, the Creating Community Connections (C3) System is being delivered to Camfield Estates by MIT as an ASP. We are now investigating ways to provide C3 for other communities in a similar fashion.

At MIT, the Center for Reflective Community Practice (CRCP) is one example of these three roles in action within the university. CRCP is housed in the Department of Urban Studies and Planning, a department with expertise in teaching, learning, research, and training of professionals in the field of urban planning and development. Through a range of long-term relationships, CRCP offers the opportunity to link students and faculty at MIT with community partners for mutual benefit, and to help develop the resource and leadership capacity of low-income communities and communities of color. It also allows community- and university-based partners to engage in community practice and in strategies for change in more thoughtful and deliberative ways, leading to a new and shared knowledge base of resources and approaches that include the best practices of both community-based and academic teaching and learning. CRCP has identified Camfield as one of a few communities it will work with over the next five years. As part of this effort, a resident of Camfield was selected as a Reflective Practitioner Fellow for the 2000-2001 academic year. With this commitment in place, Camfield and MIT will continue to explore the mutual benefits associated with a long-term, institutional, community-wide partnership.

We are only beginning to witness the wonderful stories that will emerge from the Camfield Estates-MIT Creating Community Connections project. Our goal to establish Camfield as a model for other communities manifests itself in two ways. First, as a methodology that can be replicated in other communities seeking to strengthen relationships between residents, organizations, and businesses in their neighborhood. Second, as an example that demonstrates the limitless possibilities when community members are engaged as active agents of change and active producers of information and content. Years from now we expect to see new areas within cyberspace that belong not only to residents at Camfield Estates, but other low- to moderate-income communities across the globe.

ACKNOWLEDGEMENTS

The Camfield Estates-MIT Creating Community Connections project has been a true team effort. Leadership at Camfield Estates consists of Paulette Ford, CTA President, and Nakia Keizer, Project Leader and MIT Reflective Community Practitioner, along with the following board members and advisors: Constance Terrell, Malissa Evans, Luon Williams, Edward Harding, Susan Terrell, Marzella Hightower-Hunt, Cora Scott, Alberta Willis, Minnie Clark, and Daniel Violi. At MIT, Randal Pinkett, PhD candidate, MIT Media Laboratory, and Richard O'Bryant, PhD candidate, MIT Department of Urban Studies and Planning (DUSP), are the co-principal investigators, under the supervision of Professor Mitchel Resnick, MIT Media Laboratory; Professor Joseph Ferreira, Jr., DUSP; Professor Ceasar McDowell, DUSP; and Director of the Center for Reflective Community Practice (CRCP); Professor Brian Smith, MIT Media Laboratory; and Professor David Gifford, MIT Laboratory for Computer Science (LCS), with assistance from undergraduate students Megan Henry and Wei-An Yu, and the members of the Epistemology and Learning Group at the MIT Media Laboratory. Without support from the following individuals and organizations, as well as countless others, the project would not have been possible: Dr. Gail McClure and Caroline Carpenter, Kellogg Foundation, Thaddeus Miles, Massachusetts Housing Finance Agency (MHFA); Wayne Williams, Jackie Williams, Garfield Williams, and Luis Herrera, Williams Consulting Services; Donna Fisher, Cornu Management; Bess Stephens, Catherine Gowen, Camilla Nelson and Robert Bouzon, Hewlett-Packard Company; Dave Mitchell, Microsoft Corporation; John McGeough and Ken Rahaman, RCN Telecom Services; and Philip

Greenspun, ArsDigita Corporation. I would particularly like to thank Mitchel Resnick, Richard O'Bryant, and Ceasar McDowell for their assistance with this chapter and overall support. Above all, I would like to thank all of the residents at Camfield Estates for the wonderful opportunity to work together with them. For more information about the Camfield Estates-MIT project, visit http://www.camfieldestates.net.

REFERENCES

The Aspen Institute. (1997). *Voices from the Field: Learning from the Early Work of Comprehensive Community Initiatives.* Washington, DC: The Aspen Institute. Retrieved from the World Wide Web: http://www.aspenroundtable.org/voices/index.htm.

Beamish, A. (1999). Approaches to community computing: Bringing technology to low-income groups. In Schön, D., Sanyal, B. and Mitchell, W. J. (Eds.), *High Technology in Low-Income Communities: Prospects for the Positive Use of Information Technology*, 349-368. Cambridge, MA: MIT Press.

Benton Foundation. (1998). *Losing Ground Bit by Bit: Low-Income Communities in the Information Age.* Washington, DC: Benton Foundation. Retrieved from the World Wide Web: http://www.benton.org/Library/Low-Income/home.html.

Bishop, A. P., Tidline, T. J., Shoemaker, S. and Salela, P. (1999). *Public Libraries and Networked Information Services in Low-Income Communities.* Urbana-Champaign, IL: Graduate School of Library and Information Science, University of Illinois at Urbana-Champaign.

Bourdieu, P. and Passeron, J. C. (1977). *Reproduction in Education, Society and Culture.* Translated by Richard Nice. Beverly Hills, CA: Sage.

Chapman, G. and Rhodes L. (1997). Nurturing neighborhood nets. *Technology Review,* October.

Chow, C., Ellis, J., Mark, J. and Wise, B. (1998). *Impact of CTCNet Affiliates: Findings from a National Survey of Users of Community Technology Centers.* Newton, MA: Education Development Center, Inc. Retrieved from the World Wide Web: http://www.ctcnetorg/impact98.html.

Cohill, A. M. and Kavanaugh, A. L. (1997). *Community Networks: Lessons from Blacksburg, Virginia.* Blacksburg, VA: Artech House Telecommunications Library.

Coleman, J. S. (1988). Social capital in the creation of human capital. *American Journal of Sociology*, 94, S95-S120.

Dewar, T. (1997). *A Guide to Evaluating Asset-Based Community Development: Lessons, Challenges and Opportunities.* Chicago, IL: ACTA Publications.

Hampton, K. and Wellman, B. (1999). Examining community in the digital neighborhood: Early results from Canada's wired suburb. In Ishida, T. and Isbister, K. (Eds.), *Digital Cities: Technologies, Experiences, and Future Perspectives*, 194-208. Heidelberg, Germany: Springer-Verlag Berlin/ Heidelberg.

Hooper, P. (1998). *They Have Their Own Thoughts: Children's Learning of Computational Ideas from a Cultural Constructionist Perspective.* Unpublished PhD Dissertation. Cambridge, MA: MIT Media Laboratory.

Kingsley, G. T., McNeely, J. B. and Gibson, J. O. (1999). *Community Building Coming of Age.* The Urban Institute. Retrieved from the World Wide Web: http://www.urban.org/comminity/combuild.htm.

Kretzmann, J. P. and McKnight, J. L. (1993). *Building Communities from the Inside Out: A Path Toward Finding and Mobilizing a Community's Assets.* Chicago, IL: ACTA Publications.

Lamont, M. and Lareau, A. (1988). Cultural capital: Allusions, gaps and glissandos in recent theoretical developments. *Sociological Theory,* 6(2): 153-168.

Lazarus, W. and Mora, F. (2000). *Online Content for Low-Income and Underserved Americans: The Digital Divide's New Frontier.* Santa Monica, CA: The Children's Partnership. Retrieved from the World Wide Web: http://www.childrenspartnership.org.

Lynn, L. A. (1993). *Report in Commemoration of the Twenty-Fifth Anniversary of the National Advisory Commission on Civil Disorders.* Washington, DC: Milton S. Eisenhower Foundation.

Mark, J., Cornebise, J. and Wahl, E. (1997). *Community Technology Centers: Impact on Individual Participants and Their Communities.* Newton, MA: Educational Development Center, Inc. Retrieved from the World Wide Web: http://www.ctcnetorg/eval.html.

Massachusetts Housing Finance Agency. (2001). *MHFA's Demonstration Disposition (DemoDispo) Program History.* Retrieved from the World Wide Web: http://www.mhfa.com/dev/dp_ddhistory.htm.

Mattessich, P. and Monsey, B. (1997). *Community Building: What Makes It Work: A Review of Factors Influencing Successful Community Building.* Saint Paul, MN: Amherst H. Wilder Foundation.

Melchior, A., Thorstensen, B. and Shurkin, M. (1998). *The Uses of Technology in Youth-Serving Organizations: An Initial Scan of the Field.* Waltham, MA: The Center for Human Resources, Bandeis University.

Morino, M. (1994). *Assessment and Evolution of Community Networking.* Paper presented at Ties That Bind, at Apple Computer, Cupertino, CA.

National Telecommunication and Information Administration. (1995). *Falling Through the Net Full Report*. Retrieved from the World Wide Web: http://www.ntia.doc.gov/ntiahome/fallingthru.html.

National Telecommunication and Information Administration. (1997). *Falling Through the Net II: New Data on the Digital Divide*. Full Report. Retrieved from the World Wide Web: http://www.ntia.doc.gov/ntiahome/net2/falling.html.

National Telecommunication and Information Administration. (1999). *Falling Through the Net III: Defining the Digital Divide*. Full Report. Retrieved from the World Wide Web: http://www.ntia.doc.gov/ntiahome/fttn99/contents.html.

National Telecommunication and Information Administration. (1999). *Falling Through the Net IV: Toward Digital Inclusion*. Full Report. Retrieved from the World Wide Web: http://www.ntia.doc.gov/ntiahome/fttn00/contents00.html.

O'Bryant, R. (2001). Establishing neighborhood technology centers in low-income communities: A crossroads for social science and computer information technology. Forthcoming in *Projections: The MIT Student Journal of Planning–Making Places Through Information Technology*, (2)2.

Papert, S. A. (1993). Instructionism vs. constructionism. In Papert, S. (Ed), *The Children's Machine*. New York, NY: Basic Books.

Peirce, N. R. and Steinbach C. F. (1987). *Corrective Capitalism: The Rise of America's Community Development Corporations*. New York: Ford Foundation.

Pinkett, R. D. (2000). Bridging the digital divide: Sociocultural constructionism and an asset-based approach to community technology and community building. Paper presented at the *81st Annual Meeting of the American Educational Research Association (AERA)*, New Orleans, LA, April 24-28. Retrieved from the World Wide Web: http://www.media.mit.edu/~rpinkett/papers/aera2000.pdf.

Putnam, R. (1993). The prosperous community: Social, capital, and public life. *The American Prospect*, 26, 18-21.

Putnam, R. (1995). Tuning in, tuning out: The strange disappearance of social capital in America. *PS: Political Science & Politics,* December.

Resnick, M., Rusk, N. and Cooke, S. (1998). The computer clubhouse: Technological fluency in the inner city. In Schön, D., Sanyal, B. and Mitchell, W. J. (Eds.), *High Technology in Low-Income Communities: Prospects for the Positive Use of Information Technology*, 263-286.

Cambridge, MA: MIT Press.

Resnick, M., Bruckman, A. and Martin, F. (1996). Pianos not stereos: Creating computational construction kits. *Interactions*, September-October, (3)6. Retrieved from the World Wide Web: http://el.www.media.mit.edu/el/Papers/mres/chi-98/digital-manip.html.

Robinson, R. (2000). The role of information technology in economic development of the inner city. In *Proceedings of the 2000 Inner City Business Leadership Conference*. Boston, MA: Initiative for a Competitive Inner City (ICIC), November.

Sandor, L. and Scheuerer K. (2000). *Surely Someone Knows How To Do This: Organizing Information Flows of Community Technology Centers*. Ann Arbor, MI: School of Information, University of Michigan. Retrieved from the World Wide Web: http://www.si.umich.edu/community/connections/findingsreport.html.

Schön, D. A., Sanyal, B. and Mitchell, W. J. (Eds.). (1999). *High Technology and Low-Income Communities: Prospects for the Positive Use of Advanced Information Technology*. Cambridge, MA: MIT Press.

Shaw, A. and Shaw, M. (1998). Social empowerment through community networks. In Schön, D., Sanyal, B. and Mitchell, W. J. (Eds.), *High Technology in Low-Income Communities: Prospects for the Positive Use of Information Technology*, 316-335. Cambridge, MA: MIT Press.

Shaw, A. C. (1995). *Social Constructionism and the Inner City: Designing Environments for Social Development and Urban Renewal*. Unpublished PhD Dissertation. Cambridge, MA: MIT Media Laboratory.

Turner, N. E. and Pinkett, R. D. (2000). An asset-based approach to community technology and community building. *Proceedings of Shaping the Network Society: The Future of the Public Sphere in Cyberspace, Directions and Implications of Advanced Computing Symposium 2000 (DIAC-2000)*, May 20-23, Seattle, WA. Retrieved from the World Wide Web: http://www.media.mit.edu/~rpinkett/papers/diac2000.pdf.

Zweigenhaft, R. (1993). Prep school and public school graduates of Harvard: A longitudinal study of the accumulation of social and cultural capital. *Journal of Higher Education*, 64(2), 211-225.

Chapter XII

Research Partnerships to Support Rural Communities in Malaysia with Information and Communication Technologies

Roger Harris
Central Queensland University, Australia

Governments and aid agencies now recognize the potential for sustainable economic development from the deployment of information and communication technologies (ICTs) among marginalized and poor populations. Yet such populations have little or no access to such technologies. Deriving sustainable development from the provision of such access requires more than mere technology. The emerging discipline of Community Informatics addresses community-based approaches to development with ICTs. New knowledge is required to understand how development activities can be merged with Community Informatics in a way that is capable of providing sustainable benefits to communities in developing countries. This chapter describes a university-based research initiative that builds on community partnerships that have been fostered in an action research project aimed at deriving tangible benefits for a remote rural community from the use of ICTs.

INTRODUCTION

This chapter introduces a university-based initiative for bringing the benefits of information and communication technologies (ICTs) to the marginalized rural populations of the Malaysian state of Sarawak, on the Southeast Asian island of Borneo. Firstly, we will situate contemporary ICTs within the development arena, discussing the potential for sustainable development and significant improvements in well-being that seem to exist from the provision of access to Internet-based information to rural populations in developing countries. This will be followed by a description of an emerging discipline of practice and academic endeavour, known as Community Informatics, that seeks to address the challenges and opportunities that exist for communities to realize their development aspirations through the use of Internet-based resources. We will then proceed to examine the application of Community Informatics to the special case of rural and remote communities in developing countries, arguing that in terms of the digital divide, such communities stand to benefit the most relatively from further diffusion of ICTs throughout the developing world. The discussion is then situated within the particular context of Sarawak, Malaysia. This is followed by a description of the proposal by researchers in a university in Sarawak to focus attention on the pursuit of workable and sustainable solutions to the problems associated with the provision of access to ICTs to remote rural communities through the establishment of a university-community partnership in the form of a research centre. This is based on practical experiences with a research project that has introduced ICTs to a remote rural community. The objectives of the chapter are to describe the formation of a set of partnerships between a university with growing research capacity and relevant experience, with a range of agencies that can synergize with and mobilize that capacity towards the solving of a topical problem. In the example described, the university in Sarawak partners with a development research agency, local private concerns and a government organization to address the problems and opportunities concerned with the application of ICTs to rural development in the Malaysian State of Sarawak.

RURAL ICT FOR DEVELOPMENT

Governments and aid agencies worldwide are beginning to recognize the potential for sustainable human development from the deployment of ICTs among marginalized and poor populations. However, huge disparities in access exclude the majority of the world's population, those living in the developing countries, from the benefits that ICTs can bring. South Asia and Sub-Saharan Africa, for instance, have only 1.5 telephone lines for every 100 people, compared to 64 per 100 in the USA. Over five billion people do not have access to a telephone line.

The inequalities in access to ICTs do not stop at the regional or national level. Rural communities are generally less well served than their urban compatriots in terms of access to both computing and telecommunications. In parts of Asia and Africa, rural telephone density is less than one-fifth of that in the largest cities. The ratio of urban to rural telephones in South Asia is 7:1 (World Bank, 1998/99). According to the United Nations Development Program (UNDP), strengthening rural telecommunications must be treated as a central parameter for any sustainable human development strategy aimed at poverty alleviation and reduction (UNDP, 1999). The UNDP suggests that one of the most promising approaches might be the provision of rural telecommunications services on a community basis organized in the form of a public utility. UNDP recommends comprehensive pilot/demonstration projects so that the full potential of the telecommunications and various multimedia technologies could converge into the creation, operation and funding of a (digital) system for public use at the rural level (UNDP, 1999).

Many believe that a huge potential for widespread ICT-induced development exists, offering hope for some of the most impoverished and remotest communities in the poorest countries of the developing world. In the least-developed nations, around half of the population survives on incomes of less than US$1 per day. Clearly, such people have no hope whatsoever of owning their own computer, and any access to ICTs that they might be provided with would have to move away from the personal nature of the PC and more towards perceiving it as a communal resource.

The goal of one telephone line for every household appears to be unrealistic in low-income countries, as does any hope of PC diffusion to the extent found in the developed world. Alternative approaches to the delivery of ICT services based on treating them as shared community resources mean that many people who would otherwise never have the opportunity of using a computer or the Internet will be able to do so.

The International Labor Organization suggests, "It is vital that (community ICT) prototypes be carefully scrutinised with a view to identifying effective models of exploiting ICT fully for poverty alleviation and emancipatory purposes" (ILO, 2001). No single ideal solution has emerged as a standard approach, which is hardly surprising given the novelty and rapidly changing nature of the technology, the diversity of development problems and the range of settings in which they can be found. The search for suitable mechanisms for delivering ICTs to rural communities is being undertaken by a variety of organizations, aid agencies, research centres, academic groupings, non-government organizations and social activists worldwide. Of relevance here is the emergence of the new discipline of Community Informatics, as a blend of the fields of Communications, Media Studies, Development Studies and Information Systems. Community Informatics pays attention to the physical communities and the design and implementation of technologies and applications which enhance and promote their objectives. Community Informatics begins with ICTs, as providing resources and tools that communities and their members can use for local economic, cultural and civic development, and community health and environmental issues among others (Gurstein, 2000).

In the following sections we will describe how the study of Community Informatics relates to rural development. We will then proceed to describe how a consideration of both the problems of rural development and the solutions potentially available from an understanding of Community Informatics led to a pioneering research project in Sarawak, Malaysia, and how the experiences with this project led to the proposal for a research centre based on a university-community partnership.

COMMUNITY INFORMATICS

Community Informatics is an approach to ICTs that includes concern for access to the hardware, the software, the connectivity and the information. It is also concerned with the use to which the technology is being applied and with the user who is using it, particularly within the context of the users' physical community. Incorporating the user and his/her community into the system design process introduces new elements and new stakeholders into an extended approach to ICT design, development and implementation (Dienes, 1999). Community Informatics extends the socio-technical approach to information systems design beyond organizations into the realm of communities. In many cases this includes virtual communities, groups of individuals that are geographically dispersed but which share some common professional, recreational or other interest (Preece, 2000). Our concern, though, is with physical communities, where shared communal use of ICTs presents opportunities for social economic and cultural development at the level of the community. Table 1 models the evolving Information Systems discipline. It maps the historical trajectory of Information Systems as a discipline against the development of the technological trajectory of ICTs. The community approach to ICTs offers one of the most viable means of achieving better lives for the vast majority of the world's population and for those who are currently the least served, rural communities in developing countries.

A number of technologies are of interest to Community Informatics, and

Table 1: Information Systems as an Evolving Discipline

Dominant Technology	Information Systems Locus	Work Group Focus	Dominant Referent Discipline	Scope
1960-70 Mainframe Computers	Electronic Data Processing	Clerical Staff	Computer Science	The Organisation
1970-80 Mini Computers	Management Information Systems	Managers	Management	
1980-90 Personal Computers	End-User Computing	Knowledge Workers	Organisational Behaviour	
1990-2000 Networks	Strategic Information Systems	Shareholders	Economics Marketing	
2000- The Internet	Community Informatics	Citizens	Social Science	Society

these can merge to offer opportunities for overcoming the isolation which many communities in rural environments experience. Such ICTs are being seen as a potential "leveller," allowing those previously made marginal to participate more actively and effectively (Gurstein, 2000). They are summarized in Table 2.

Community Informatics applications cover a wide range, summarized in Table 3.

Community Informatics, then, provide a framework for understanding the issues, opportunities and challenges embodied in the delivery of benefits to rural communities in the developing world through the deployment of ICTs. However, in applying the precepts of Community Informatics to such communities, it is useful to understand that:

- Rural communities that are distant from services that are readily available to urban communities have particular needs for information which require specific channels of delivery, e.g., market prices, agricultural support.
- Information that is provided to remote communities is of greater intrinsic value than that provided to urban communities, where it is easier to obtain

Table 2: Technologies of Interest to Community Informatics

Technology	Issues
Hardware	Costs of acquisition and maintenance. Increasing specifications and rapidly changing functionality leading to a short cycle of apparent obsolescence. Under-utilisation of PCs, shared access.
Software	Cost, continuous and unnecessary upgrades, changing formats, open source software.
Connectivity	Cost of increasing requirements for bandwidth, new technologies: fibre optics, coaxial cable, satellite, cellular.
Bulletin Boards	Dial-up, store and forward at low-cost Bulletin Board Service (BBS).
Community Networks	Dial-up internet access, evolving from BBS to Internet Service Provider (ISP).
UseNet, News, E-Lists	Discussion lists as asynchronous communication.
World Wide Web	Community web sites, portals, chat groups.
Broad Band	Video, videoconferencing, graphics, animation.
Geographic Information Systems	Integrated databases linked to maps, graphical displays.

information from a variety of alternative sources.

- Providing access to ICTs in rural settings is generally perceived as unprofitable, and therefore requires innovative forms of business operation, public-private partnership and local management that acknowledges the higher relative value of information in rural societies as compared to urban.

- Rural information networks do not only require "spoke-and-hub" models in which information flows are concentrated between peripheral and central locations. Experience suggests that farmer-to-farmer networks are significant contributors to rural development. Consequently, planning needs to take account of information provision and sharing capabilities among rural communities, as well as information demands from central

Table 3: Community Informatics Applications (Gurstein, 2000)

Community Internet Access	Public access to ICTs.
Community Information	Local interests, listings, directories, events, entitlements, public health, e-genealogy.
Civic/Community Participation Online	Electronic democracy, civic forms, public consultation, interaction with officials and politicians, electronic voting, polling.
Community Services	Registrations, certifications, counselling, licensing, employment information, small business support, mentoring.
Community E-Commerce	E-malls, local on-line commerce.
Education and Training	Lifelong learning, on-line distribution of course material, e-lists, chat, on-the-job training.
Community and Regional Planning	Community involvement in local land use and environmental planning, geographic information systems.
Telework	Remote on-line work.

sources.

• There are many experiments being undertaken into the use of ICTs by rural communities in developing countries. However, no commonly accepted approach has emerged as the most effective means for nurturing rural development with ICTs, partly because the conditions of deployment and public interaction with the technology differ greatly between each experiment and the socio-economic contexts are highly variable.

Effectively applying ICTs to rural development requires knowledge about and understanding of a range of technology, community and development issues. Much of this knowledge is location-specific, which requires development and technology practitioners to be able to apply appropriate methodologies and techniques necessary to elicit such knowledge in a variety of different situations. Community Informatics provides a forum for integrating these multiple perspectives, yet it is a young discipline with a small body of knowledge. The new knowledge that is required to adequately inform rural ICT-based development efforts is yet to be generated. Academic endeavors can contribute to the knowledge-forming processes that will be required to help practitioners and technology users achieve the full potential of rural ICTs. Academic efforts will be greatly enhanced through partnerships with community bodies and private organizations in which theories and techniques can be tested. Academic-community partnerships provide benefits to both the community agencies as well as to the academic partners who provide the assistance (Webb Collins, 2000).

In the following section we will situate the discussion of Community Informatics and academic support for rural ICTs within the specific context of Malaysia. Malaysia offers a suitable test bed for knowledge creation in this area because of the following factors:

- The government is aggressively pursuing an agenda for national development that is heavily based on ICTs.
- Although not yet fully developed, the economy is classified as "emerging," yet many of the distinguishing characteristics of the digital divide can be found there.
- A considerable proportion of the population lives in rural communities; in many cases, especially in the state of Sarawak, these are remote and isolated.

In the next section we will provide some background information on Malaysia and Sarawak in order to enable us to effectively situate research activities relating to rural ICTs into their context. This will help build the case for fostering the proposed university-community partnerships that can facilitate such research.

Malaysia and Sarawak

Malaysia lies just north of the equator in Southeast Asia. The nation is divided physically into two distinct regions, West, or Peninsular Malaysia, and East Malaysia. They are separated by 1,000 kilometers of the South China Sea. The capital, Kuala Lumpur, is situated in West Malaysia, with a population of around 1.5 million. The surrounding metropolitan areas of the Klang Valley have experienced rapid population growth in recent years as Malaysia's economy grew and rural populations migrated to the urban centres. Thailand borders West Malaysia to the north, and the island state of Singapore sits off its southern border. East Malaysia, comprising the states of Sarawak and Sabah, occupies the western and northern one-third of the island of

Borneo, bordering Indonesia and Brunei.

The Malaysian economy is a mixture of private enterprise and public management. It grew by an average of 9% annually between 1988 and 1996, and this growth resulted in a substantial reduction in poverty and a marked rise in real wages. By 1996, Malaysia had become the world's largest exporter of hard disc drives for personal computers. Malaysia is also the world's largest producer and exporter of edible oil (palm and palm kernel oil) and the world's largest producer and exporter of tropical hardwood logs and lumber. In 1999, foreign investors were continuing to commit large sums in the economy. In order to help position Malaysia economically and socially vis-à-vis its neighbors, competitors and more developed countries, some comparative data is provided in Table 4.

As part of its intentions for ICT-induced national development, the Malaysian Government has implemented a massive development project known as the Multimedia Super Corridor (MSC) (Harris, 2001). This is a 15 by 40 kilometer area encompassing Kuala Lumpur City Centre (the nation's capital) and the new international airport, as well as a new administrative centre, Putrajaya, and an "IT City," Cyberjaya, claimed as the world's first "intelligent city." ("Jaya" is a Malay word meaning "success".) The MSC is intended to "leapfrog Malaysia into the Information Age" and to help achieve the target for development that the government has set, that of achieving fully developed status by 2020 (Harris, 2001). Malaysia has used ICTs to build a national information infrastructure, and the government has developed a national vision for infusing ICTs into all sections of the nation's economic and social life. However, the rapid and vigorous adoption of ICTs in Malaysia is largely an urban phenomenon. Around 56% of the nation's telecommunications is

Table 4: Comparative Data

	Malaysia	USA	United Kingdom	Thailand	Indonesia	Singapore	South Korea	Hong Kong	Taiwan
Population (Millions)	20.5	270.1	57.6	59.5	209.8	3.4	46.4	6.7	21.9
Exports (US$ Billions)	$84.6	$625.1	$240.4	$57.3	$49.8	$144.8	$129.8	$180.7	$122.1
GDP Per Capita (US$)	$10,750	$30,200	$20,400	$7,700	$3,770	$21,200	$13,700	$26,800	$14,200
Telephones (Millions)	2.5	182.6	29.5	1.5	1.3	1.2	16.6	4.4	10.0
Televisions (Millions)	2	215	20	3.3	11.5	1.0	9.3	1.8	10.8
Source: CIA Factbook									

situated in the Klang Valley metropolitan area, centered on Kuala Lumpur.

Sarawak is Malaysia's largest state and its most sparsely populated. Of the total population of Malaysia of around 21 million, only about 1.7 million live in Sarawak. Slightly more than half of these live outside the urban centres. The population of Sarawak is ethnographically complex with more than 25 ethnolinguistic groups. The population is divided roughly equally between three main ethnic groups: the Chinese, the Malay and the indigenous groups. In Sarawak, the rural population is thinly scattered across Malaysia's largest state, and many have no access to a basic communications infrastructure such as roads and telephones. For many, rivers provide the principal means of transportation as well as information exchange. Nevertheless, such communities are not entirely cut off, far from it, and they are aware of the nation's development aspirations as well as the central role of ICTs in achieving them. However, for most, they consider their situation, within an agriculturally based economy and being outside the main urban centres, as being inappropriate for the useful application of computers.

More than half of Sarawak's population lives in rural communities. The last census in 1991 located 65% of Sarawak's people in rural locations. Many of these are isolated and unserved by roads. Sarawak's rural population is predominantly engaged in small-scale agricultural and fishing activities that support their subsistence. Small-scale trade in farm surpluses also takes place, and employment opportunities are available in plantation and logging operations. Family incomes are often below US$150 per month. Typical accommodation often consists of longhouse communities in which 20 or more families occupy a unit in a single dwelling. For many communities, the primary means of transportation is still by river.

Rural ICTs in Sarawak

The Government of Malaysia acknowledges that the nation's rural population has been left behind by the advances made with ICTs in the urban areas. The vast majority of the rural population in Sarawak has never come into contact with computers (Harris, 1999). Research carried out in Sarawak revealed that in one remote community where 140 households were surveyed, only one household contained a member who had heard of the Internet and 91% of the population had never used a computer (Songan et al., 2000).

Robert Chambers (1997) describes the term participatory action-reflection research as encompassing methods that combine action, reflection, participation and research. Participatory Action Research (PAR) seeks to actively involve people in generating knowledge about their own condition and how it can be changed. The techniques used in PAR include collective research through meetings, critical recovery of history, valuing and applying folk culture, and the production and diffusion of new knowledge through written, oral and visual forms. Chambers claims that PAR has contributed five normative ideas to development research:

- Professionals should reflect critically on their concepts, values, behaviors and methods.
- They should learn through engagement and committed action.
- They have roles as convenors, catalysts and facilitators.
- The weak and marginalized can and should be empowered.
- Poor people can and should do much of their own investigation, analysis and planning.

Gardner and Lewis (1996) characterize PAR as a loose group of methodologies whose main objective for development is the fulfilment of the human urge for engagement, rather than targeting poverty alleviation, basic needs or structural change. In this way, PAR seeks to avoid the dependency that results from many external interventions. Typically, catalytic initiatives are brought about by educated outsiders who encourage groups of people to get together and engage in their own social investigation. Eventually, as groups form links with other similar groups and encourage new ones, dependence on the internal-external stimulus falls away, though contact may be maintained. PAR provides constructive opportunities for the subjects of the research to tie the research agenda to their needs. Action research becomes a process in which research is combined with practical problem solving, with the participation of those who have identified and need to overcome a problem.

These descriptions of PAR resonate with the socio-technical perspective of information systems that Community Informatics advocates. PAR is considered highly appropriate for development research that seeks to demonstrate the value of information and ICTs to communities in developing countries. Davies (1994) underlines this observation by suggesting that the "revolution in information technology and communications has direct implications for the South and for development studies...in the emergence of participatory methods for data collection and analysis. Participatory techniques, just like changes in more conventional sources of information, are in part a result of, and dependent on, the international communications revolution." Within the PAR framework, the researchers in Sarawak have engaged community members to conduct surveys, perform interviews, adopt formal roles in the management of the research, participate in focus group meetings and hold community gatherings to perform decision making and to direct the conduct of the research. The techniques and principles of PAR were not created for the specific needs of designing and implementing ICT-based information systems within rural communities. A university-community partnership in Sarawak offers the opportunity to establish a research program capable of testing and developing theories that will contribute to the growing need for new knowledge to sustain rural ICTs. The next section proposes such a partnership.

AN ACADEMIC-COMMUNITY PARTNERSHIP FOR RURAL ICTS IN SARAWAK

Background: The Need for Research

In Malaysia, where the National Agenda for Information Technology (NITA) has placed IT at centre-stage in achieving developed status for the nation, rural populations continue to be sidelined by most IT initiatives. Realizing the benefits of linking rural communities to the information superhighway requires more than the mere provision of technology. If the special needs of remote and rural communities for information are not directly addressed, the effort to link them to existing information exchanges will not generate beneficial social returns. The Internet is populated for the most part by sophisticated urbanites. Having a research and education background, much of what is available on the Internet is useful for educators and learners who are engaged with the education system. Commercial organizations are fast catching up with their Internet strategies, but these are largely concerned with trade and economic activity that is not relevant to rural communities, least of all those in developing countries.

A program of information provision for rural and remote communities should start with an intimate understanding of the informational needs of those communities. Satisfying those needs appears to offer an opportunity for socially beneficial uses of ICTs, but solutions need to be tried and tested before the substantial resources that will be required to provide them on a widespread scale can be committed. In addition, understanding the information needs of communities is only the first step towards satisfying them. Consistent and reliable sources of the required information have to be identified and mechanisms set in motion that will ensure the information can be provided in a suitable fashion. This means working not only with the communities themselves, to identify the "pull" component of the information delivery requirement, but also it means working with the government agencies, NGOs, educational institutions and others, who will fulfill the "push" side of the information delivery process. Even when useful information exists, it may not be put to good use. The Malaysian Assistant Minister for Agriculture and Food Industries, Datuk

Ramsay Noel Jitam, was reported as saying that "although there has been a substantial increase in knowledge on crop production and protection, much of this knowledge remains at the level of researchers and has not filtered down to the farm level where it is of value" (Barui, 1998).

Telecommunications services can contribute to and sustain structural and economic development that will be capable of eliminating the disadvantages of rural life and to generally improve the quality of life in rural and remote areas. However, many of the most critical factors that enable rural areas to benefit from technology lie beyond the network and its elements. Sustainable business models, political will, skills training and education are just as critical, if not more so, than selecting the most appropriate technology from among a range of reasonable alternatives. Experience indicates that telecommunications-based applications are being designed and implemented by a wide variety of actors in addition to public telecommunications operators (PTOs). A significant portion of the expertise required to develop sustainable, communications-based applications for rural areas is located within the professional, academic, business and agricultural sectors, among others. The International Telecommunications Union library contains examples of applications introduced by physicians, educators, community organizations and governments. Furthermore, evidence suggests that the institutional and procedural profiles of traditional PTOs militate against the kind of organizational flexibility and adaptability that appears to be pre-requisite for implementing the small-scale power generation and telecommunications infrastructures that are typical of successful projects found in rural areas.

Accordingly, in an integrated program for rural development through the deployment of ICTs, there are likely to be provisions for organizational capacity building which go beyond the immediate identification of information requirements and technology installation. A scenario of complex and interacting forces emerges, involving the negotiation of multiple relationships within a diverse network of information providers and users. Engaging with ICTs for rural development therefore implies a commitment to all aspects of upstream and downstream development. A multi-disciplinary approach is essential in order to bring to bear the essential blend of technological, social and political skills that will ensure successful outcomes. Specialists in the human sciences will be required to augment the activities of technologists for the efforts of each to bear fruit.

International development agencies such as the United Nations and the World Bank are now convinced of the huge potential for opportunities for sustainable development that are available in modern ICTs. They recognize that many developing nations will need considerable assistance in deploying and diffusing IT among their citizens and especially in applying IT to the most pressing needs of their majority rural poor populations. However, in view of the alarming pace of development of IT and the rapidly widening gaps that are opening between rich and poor, the international agencies are scouring the world for solutions to the problems of applying IT to rural development. There are many examples in diverse regions around the world, and aid donors have been quick to recognize the potential for replicating such solutions on a wider scale.

The World Bank recognizes that narrowing the gaps in know-how that separate poor countries from rich, and poor people from non-poor, can increase economic growth in developing countries, raise incomes, reduce environmental degradation, and generally improve the quality of life, especially for the poor. They suggest that governments formulate a national strategy to narrow knowledge gaps, saying that the opportunities for countries to move to better practice are nothing short of stupendous. The bank recommends that governments promote domestic research and develop the capability to create knowledge locally that cannot be obtained from abroad. They suggest learning about the poor in order to involve them in projects that are designed for their benefit. They suggest giving voice to the poor, through better communications, in order to help them advocate policies which address their needs. The bank indicates that working through traditional channels and earning the trust of the poor is key to success. All these pre-requisites to solutions for reducing knowledge gaps in Malaysia imply original research aimed at developing local competencies within state institutions as well as among the affected communities themselves.

Many national aid agencies are willing to fund research into the delivery of IT to rural communities. They see a positive return on their aid investments among the examples of sustainable development that modern and rapidly developing ICTs are now capable of delivering. In times of economic hardships, such as those that have been prevailing in Malaysia, funding research presents a challenge as priorities are reassessed against intensified competition for scarce resources. The proposal for a university-community research partnership strengthens the ability of the institution to bid for international research funding for a diverse range of projects by demonstrating a prolonged commitment to research in the chosen field as well as an effective mechanism for managing that research.

A Rural Information Systems Perspective

The discipline of Information Systems (IS) is relatively new, and tidy definitions are elusive. Hitherto, we have been concerned with information handling activities in human organizations, which has usually implied business and government organizations, and occasionally, not-for-profit organizations. Until recently, such organizations were the principal users of ICTs. With the coming of the Internet, though, the data processing and informational needs of organizations no longer dominate the popular use of computers.

A university-community partnership for developing rural ICTs in Sarawak will apply the precepts of Community Informatics to rural communities by extending methodologies that have been deployed in organizational settings into community settings. The following perspectives will guide the research agenda:

- Information systems are more than technical artifacts, as they embrace the behaviors and aspirations of the people using them.
- Information systems are spreading beyond formal organizations and into society at large.
- Our interpretation of information systems, and the formulas that are applied to designing them, assume a structured context that is not in fact always present.
- A focus on the uses to which IT is actually put that is independent of the intentions or aspirations of the providers of the technology, rather than on the institutional interests that often accompany the deployment of technology.
- An interest in communities of users and the influence on the technology of the social dynamics of such communities, in conjunction with a recognition of the diversity of interests within such communities.
- A conviction that information and communication technologies have the potential to empower or liberate individuals, groups and communities, but that attention has so far been directed primarily to the goals of increased efficiency, control and effectiveness.
- A desire to promote creative and enabling applications of information and communication technologies that extend the scope of information systems in ways which empower and enfranchise presently excluded or marginalized individuals or groups.
- A preference for collaborative and participative modes of inquiry and system development (from Lynch, 1998).

The foregoing expresses a concern for the future direction of the IS discipline insofar as its earlier paradigms of intellectual pursuit have favored managerial and organizational perspectives to the detriment of social and human aspects. Rural communities in Sarawak provide an opportunity for revealing important new knowledge related to rural Community Informatics for development because of the following characteristics:

- In common with almost the whole of Asia, they include the majority proportion of the state's population.

- Malaysia's development aspirations promise an equitable distribution of benefit to all sections of society and they lean heavily on the promise of information and communication technologies.
- Rural communities will demand an even share in the fruits of development, yet it is unlikely that traditional infrastructures can be developed at the pace necessary to satisfy such demand.
- Rural isolation, arising from the under-developed nature of the state's infrastructure, has created a strong sense of community in rural locations.
- Arising also from the under-developed nature of the state's infrastructure, rural communities have been relatively starved of information so that unit improvements in information delivery can be expected to result in significant and measurable impacts.
- While technology is no longer a significant barrier to the delivery of improved informational services to rural locations, the institutional and organizational arrangements that are necessary to achieve such deployments are not yet in place.

Partnerships

Tthe researchers realized that the university should foster partnerships with the following bodies:

- the development community, for research funding and guidance;
- the Malaysian Government, for funding and as a potential promoter of widespread rural ICT facilities; and
- local providers of equipment and services.

Arising from the research in Sarawak, the following partnerships have been forged.

International Development Research Center (IDRC) Canadian Government

The IDRC was the initial funder of the research in Sarawak. This was provided as a result of an application to their Pan Asia Program that supports projects for ICT networking in Asia. The award was for CAD$75,000 and this enabled the university research team to implement the first telecenter in a rural location in Sarawak (Harris et al., 2001). A telecenter is a community centre that offers assisted access to various information technologies primarily for the purpose of community development (Gomez, 1999). The remote highland community of Bario in northern Sarawak was selected. It has a population of around 1,000 people. Baseline studies were conducted in order to understand the conditions of life in the chosen community and computers were progressively introduced, beginning with the school. A community telecenter was established with the intention of providing community access to computers and to the Internet. It is also intended to provide the school with access to the Internet.

During the early stages of the research in Bario, the IDRC initiated a collaborative association with several similar projects in Asia: two in India, one in the Philippines and one in Mongolia. Together with the Sarawak project, researchers from each were formed into a learning and evaluation group for the purpose of evaluating each other's projects and deriving lessons from the experiences. The group was named the Pan Asia Telecenter Learning and Evaluation Group (PANTLEG). Its aim is to meet yearly to conduct evaluation-cum-learning workshops at each other's projects. The first meeting took place in India in September 1999, the second in Sarawak, Malaysia in November 2000 and the third in Mongolia in June 2000. Group members will also participate in other workshops and conferences related to the topic of telecenter evaluation. The group members will contribute to the ongoing work at IDRC of formulating a framework for evaluation of projects related to information and communication technologies. Its main contribution is in the form of developing a methodology for telecenter evaluation based on the collection and analysis of stories relating to telecenter activities.

The PANTLEG partnership has been highly successful, as it has exposed the Sarawak research team to similar initiatives from which much has been learned about the application of ICTs to rural development. Key contributors to the group's successful activities include the enthusiasm of the individual group members and the facilitating environment established by the IDRC officers. Each visit has been documented in order to record the strengths and weaknesses of the project as well as to develop issues of concern to the group with regard to implementing rural ICTs. These include:

- standards for telecenter operation;
- policy environments for telecenter sustainability and propagation;
- cultural contexts of telecenter deployment; and
- extending capabilities to non-PANTLEG individuals and bodies, such as NGOs.

PANTLEG was funded by the IDRC with an initial grant of CAD$30,000. At its meeting in Mongolia, the members outlined a three-year mission to expand upon and to extend its activities beyond the initial funding period. PANTLEG has defined itself as "a network of telecenter practitioners and development organizations for learning and sharing strategies using ICT as a tool for social and human development in rural communities in Asia." It is to be a small IDRC-connected group with a virtual office. It will have a simple structure, composed of advisory and/or resource panels, and a coordinating body. Based on its mission, PANTLEG will:

- establish a telecenter Help Desk on the Internet;
- focus its internal activities on sharing of information through practical and learning exchanges, exposure visits between rural telecenters, workshops/seminars, and providing technical support;
- apply PANTLEG resources to rural development in Asia and beyond sharing resources for telecenter development;
- support and advise partners and other telecenter operations in Asia as well as the rest of the world; and
- secure sustainability by providing consultancy for donors and clients.

The Group will conduct research and develop research methodology by:

- promoting the PANTLEG approach to evaluation and learning through storytelling;
- writing the PANTLEG story, and in doing so, disseminating peer evaluation learning approaches that include community involvement and that are in support of socially oriented telecenters;
- conducting research, both individually and as a group, and presenting findings at conferences and publishing them in appropriate outlets;
- developing the stories methodology, which uses narratives as the basis of telecenter evaluation and associated learning, and defining and documenting the storytelling methodology for telecenter evaluation and development; and
- assisting individual and PANTLEG projects in obtaining funds.

As a virtual organization, the group will build a virtual office, consisting of:

- a server,
- a domain name;
- conferencing;
- chat;
- online help desk;
- mail list;
- bulletin board; and
- news, links and information for members and the public.

The Malaysian Government

Following the selection of Bario as the first research site, the nature of the research became known to government agencies involved with the infusion of

ICTs in Malaysian life. Specifically, the National Information Technology Council (NITC) under the chairmanship of the Prime Minister established a sub-committee, the Strategic Thrust Implementation Committee (STIC), under the Deputy Prime Minister. The STIC established five task forces to implement various initiatives throughout Malaysia that were concerned with engendering further use of ICTs. The research project in Bario was adopted as a joint project between two of these task forces, the E-Community Task Force, under the Minister of Energy, Telecommunications and Multimedia, and the E-Learning Task Force, under the Minister of Education. At this stage, the research project became known as e-Bario and it began to attract wider interest nationwide.

One consequence of this was that it effectively pre-determined the provider of telecommunications connectivity for Bario, in that the national carrier, Telekom Malaysia, which is part owned by the Ministry of Energy, Telecommunications and Multimedia, and which is a principal member and promoter of the E-Community Task Force, was directed to provide the telecommunications infrastructure for the e-Bario project. Another consequence was that additional funding became available to the project. Projects under STIC Task Forces were able to apply for government funds under a program named the Demonstrator Application Grants Scheme (DAGS), aimed at encouraging projects that would further infuse ICTs into national life. The project was encouraged to apply for such a grant, and was awarded one. Aligning its activities with a government program enabled the project to acquire funding as well as a strategic partnership with a supplier of technology critical to the aims of the research.

Comserv Multech Sarawak Limited, Sarawak, Malaysia

It became known to the researchers that a Malaysian company, Comserv Multech, had devised a program for providing computers to schools in Sarawak, along with a training program for IT literacy. The company heard about the university research and expressed an interest in working with the researchers in a rural school. They agreed to implement their program in the school in Bario, to provide computers and technical support, and to train a local resident as the trainer for the literacy program.

Comserv Multech took an active role in supporting the school computing facility. Their joint role combining technology provision with responsibility for learning outcomes ensured an active interest in the maintenance and upkeep of the computers, which was something new for the teaching staff. The training they provided for the locally recruited trainer enabled him to provide additional training to the adult members of the community, and the school principal allowed the school computers to be used for this purpose after normal school hours.

Cisco Systems (Malaysia)

Cisco Systems heard about the university research through the project's participation in the E-Community Task Force. They have offered to provide wireless networking technology for use at the project site in Bario in order to connect the community telecenter with other nearby locations, such as the clinic, in a local area network. Cisco Systems, Inc., is the worldwide leader in networking for the Internet. The company has been heavily involved with the development of the Internet in Malaysia through the provision of networking technology to the government. The partnership with Cisco came about as a result of its association with a Malaysian government organization, Malaysian Institute of Microelectronic Systems (MIMOS). MIMOS operates the country's first Internet Service Provider, JARING, and also administers government funds for the Demonstrator Application Grants Scheme. MIMOS officials asked if Cisco Systems could support some of the DAGS projects, and the rural telecenter project in Bario was selected. Initially, a sum of 20,000 Malaysian Ringits (approx. US$5,250) was provided in the form of wireless networking devices. In return, the university will test and report on their performance.

The University

The role of the university has been to create the conditions necessary to make it attractive for the partners to participate in the research and to contribute their resources towards achieving desirable outcomes for the communities within which the research is being conducted. In the case of the IDRC, the research results contribute to their wider programs for using ICTs for development. The IDRC actively supports such programs in Africa and Latin America, as well as in Asia. Researchers from the Sarawak project have been able to contribute to various IDRC activities. For the Malaysian Government, policy makers are able to explore the various options available to them in closing the digital divide in Malaysia. The Sarawak experience has sensitized government officials to the rural telecenter concept. The commercial partners, Comserv Multech and Cisco Systems, have been able to demonstrate their social awareness as well as gain experience in the application of their products and services in the particular circumstances of the Sarawak research. By synergizing the resources of the various partners, the university has been able to construct and implement a research program in an emerging area of academic interest and to provide direct benefits to marginalized sections of Malaysia's population.

The potential now exists for the university to achieve a position of international influence in the field of ICT-induced rural development in the developing world.

In order to differentiate their skills and knowledge, developing country institutions should lean on their strengths and exploit the advantages they have over institutions in the developed nations, rather than trying to emulate them. The geographical and social conditions of Sarawak are unlike those found in most developed countries, yet they resemble those of many developing nations. The state's underdeveloped infrastructure and the low living standards of its rural population, combined with Malaysia's burgeoning economy with its emphasis on ICTs, presents a unique opportunity for the university to address problems that affect huge sections of the world's population. In such a position, the university is able to reduce reliance on developed country sources of knowledge and adopt a leadership role in what is known as South-South collaborations, whereby developing countries provide assistance to each other.

Future activities in the research partnership include further installations in communities of differing ethnic, cultural and economic backgrounds. These will test the extent to which early successful outcomes can be replicated under changed circumstances. Further partnerships will be sought. For example, the United Nations Development Program country office in Kuala Lumpur has expressed an interest to fund further activities. Other modes of computer and Internet access are also being considered by the research team. For example, there is a proposal to equip a riverboat with computers as a mobile telecenter to serve the many communities in Sarawak that depend on rivers for communications and transport. A possible outcome of this proposal is for the university to partner with a boat builder and operator who will construct the necessary boat and then lease it to the university for the duration of the research.

CONCLUSIONS

In this chapter we outlined the argument for rural development in developing countries through the deployment of ICTs. We have highlighted the emergence of Community Informatics and promoted it as a field of study that provides a framework for the development of methodologies that can inform practitioners of rural development. It has been shown how the use of existing participatory techniques can assist in this process through the example of research in rural Sarawak, Malaysia. Arising from these experiences, a formal university-community research partnership has been proposed that will exploit the geographic and demographic characteristics of Sarawak for the purpose of creating the new knowledge that is needed for successfully furthering the diffusion of ICTs into rural communities in developing countries.

The proposed university-community partnership offers a timely opportunity for implementing a research agenda in an area of pressing need for which new knowledge is urgently required. The location in Sarawak provides a highly suitable setting for such an endeavour, given the Malaysian Government's emphasis on ICTs for equitable development and the dispersed nature of the state's population. The needs for integrating rural populations into mainstream national life will drive the solutions that are currently being sought towards diffusing ICT into areas where rural and remote communities live. Blending the development paradigms that already exist in the shape of participatory practices and those which are emerging from the Community Informatics field offer an exiting opportunity for enriching the methodological armory of a wide range of academic pursuits and practitioner communities. Focusing research onto the problems of rural ICTs in developing countries carries the promise of accelerating the alleviation of the plight of even the world's poorest people, dispelling the myth that computers are artifacts only of urban life. The ideals of rural development stand at the forefront not only of the digital divide but also of crushing inequality that characterizes the differences between the high-income countries and their low-income neighbors. Developing countries must take the lead in embracing the information revolution before they are crushed by it, but by doing so in a way that contextualizes technologies within their own circumstances instead of blindly imitating inappropriate foreign models. Third-world institutions should leverage their advantages and strengths in building solutions for their own unique problems. Only in this way can they find a voice in international forums and compete effectively against dominant western institutions.

While it appears inevitable that ICTs will continue to heap advantage on the already advantaged, this need not be the case, provided it is understood that it is not the technology that causes disparities of access and benefit but it is the actions of ourselves and of the institutions within which we shape our lives that cause them. Partnerships for knowledge are capable of providing solutions that deploy existing technologies in locally specific settings and in a fashion particular to the circumstances. Rural communities are extremely knowledgeable with regard to their own circumstances and that knowledge can be successfully blended with approaches to technology and system design that will help them incorporate ICTs into their own development agendas. The proposed university-community partnership will accelerate the learning that is now essential in order to bring that about.

REFERENCES

Barui, Fraser (1998). Research Officers Urged to Work Closely with Farmers, *Sarawak* Tribune, November 26.

Chambers, R. (1997). *Whose Reality Counts?* London: Intermediate Technology Publications.

CIA World Factbook. http://www.cia.gov/cia/publications/factbook/indexgeo.html.

Davies, S. (1994). Information, knowledge and power, introduction to knowledge is power? The use and abuse of information in development. *Institute of Development Studies Bulletin*, 25(2), 1-13.

Dienes, B. (1999). The role of low-cost technology for improved access to health care programs throughout Africa: A Community Informatics approach to health care for rural Africa. *The African Telemedicine Project Conference '99*, Nairobi, Kenya, February 19-21.

Gardner, K. and Lewis, D. (1996). *Anthropology, Development and the Post-Modern Challenge*. London: Pluto Press.

Gomez, R., Hunt, P. and Lamoureux, E. (1999). *Telecentre Evaluation and Research: A Global Perspective*. Ottawa, Canada: International Development Research Centre.

Gurstein, M. (2000). *Community Informatics: Enabling Community Uses of Information and Communications Technologies*. Hershey, PA: Idea Group Publishing.

Harris, R. W. (1999). Rural information technology for Sarawak's development, Sarawak. *Development Journal*, 2(1), 72-84.

Harris, R. W. (2001). Malaysia's multimedia super corridor: An experiment in employing information and communication technologies for national development. In Palvia, P., Palvia, S. and Roche, E. (Eds.), *Global Information Technology and Electronic Commerce: Issues for the New Millennium*. Hershey, PA: Idea Group Publishing.

Harris, R. W., Bala, P., Songan, P. and Khoo E. (2001). Challenges and opportunities in introducing information and communication technologies to the Kelabit Community of north central Borneo. *New Media and Society*, 3(3).

Lynch, M. (Ed.). (1998). *An Introduction to the Community Information Systems Centre at University of the West of England, Bristol*.

Preece, J. (2000). *Online Communities: Designing Usability, Supporting Sociability*. Chichester, England: John Wiley and Sons.

Songan, P., Harris, R., Bala, P. and Khoo E. (2000). Awareness and usage of information technology in a rural community of Bario, Sarawak. *Sixth*

Biennial Borneo Research Conference 2000, July 10-14, Kuching Sarawak.

UNDP. (1999). *UNDP and the Communications Revolution, Communications and Knowledge-Based Technologies for Sustainable Human Development*. United Nations Development Program.

Webb Collins, R. (2000). Academic-community partnerships for advanced information processing in low technology-support settings. In Gurstein, M. (Ed.), *Community Informatics: Enabling Community Uses of Information and Communications Technologies*. Hershey, PA: Idea Group Publishing.

World Bank. (1998/99). *World Bank Development Report, Knowledge for Development*.

Chapter XIII

Service-Research Partnerships: Research Projects that Help Bridge the Digital Divide

Jonathan Lazar
Towson University, USA

Anthony F. Norcio
University of Maryland Baltimore County, USA

The concept of service-research is described in this chapter. Service-research is the integration of community service with faculty research. It can benefit the researcher as well as community agencies. For organizations, such as non-profit agencies and schools, service-research can help provide free training, documentation, and help with systems development or management. For the researcher, service-research can provide inexpensive access to research subjects or data. This chapter discusses the data collection techniques that can be used with service-research, and how service-research can help bridge the digital divide, as well as the usability divide. Possible applications of service-research are presented, including user training, documentation, information systems management, systems design methodologies, and policy awareness. Two case studies of service-research are also discussed.

INTRODUCTION

Teaching, research, and service – it is the trilogy of academic life. The service part of the trilogy usually refers to service to the academic community. One type of service in which faculty engage is service to the university, through curriculum committees, promotion and tenure committees, academic advising, faculty advisor of clubs, and similar responsibilities. Another type of service is to the respective research communities, through serving on conference planning committees, professional association leadership positions, reviewing papers, and journal editorships. One type of service that is less frequent is service to the local community. Faculty are often overwhelmed with their other responsibilities, and service to the local community may not be given a high priority by the university. Although faculty may have the desire to serve the community, it may be difficult to find the time.

If community service can be successfully integrated with faculty research, this combination can offer numerous advantages. This chapter discusses the concept of service-research, where community service and academic research are successfully integrated. In service-research, the process of academic research is structured in a way that it can make an immediate impact on the community. Although all research should eventually have a positive impact on the community through its findings, in service-research, the process of performing academic research provides an immediate, useful service to the local community. In this chapter, the theoretical foundations of service-research are presented. The problem of the digital divide is discussed as it relates to service-research, and appropriate areas for applying service-research are conceptualized. In addition, two case studies of service-research are presented. The goal is that this chapter will provide the background needed, to enable researchers to apply the concept of service-research to their own research initiatives, to help their communities.

GENERAL RESEARCH ISSUES

The goal of research, in general, is to increase knowledge. It is hoped that the research can also improve the human condition. The goal of research in information systems or human-computer interaction is to improve the human experience by increasing the understanding, use, management, functionality, and usability of information technology. In this modern and rapidly changing technological society, the effective use of technology directly impacts on the community's ability to function well. Consequently, service-research partnerships provide enormous symbiotic opportunities for both the researchers and the particular community. The data that are collected and analyzed during these studies become much more than just a set of numbers. These data become information that can be transformed into knowledge. At the same time, there is a secondary, more immediate benefit to the community. Community-based agencies can receive immediate services related to technology, as a part of the research process. The process and procedures for this relationship will be discussed later in the chapter. Through service-research partnerships, both the researcher and the community benefit.

Data Collection and Research Methods

The foundation of academic research is data collection. There are several data collection techniques that are commonly used for research on information systems and human-computer interaction (Preece et. al, 1994). While a detailed discussion of the different research methods is beyond the scope of this chapter, a short overview of each method might be useful. These different research traditions can all be applied when forming service-research partnerships.

- **Controlled Experiments**. With this technique, formal and rigorous experiments are designed and conducted, by developing specific research hypotheses. Subjects are appropriately selected and placed into groups where they may receive different treatments. Quantitative and qualitative data are collected, which may relate to the subjects' performance, satisfaction and perception under these different controlled conditions.

- **Questionnaires**. Questionnaires (also called surveys) are a set of prepared, detailed questions that relate to the overall research questions. Subjects in the study are asked simply to complete the questionnaire form. There are many different types of questions, including open-ended questions, closed-ended questions, and Likert scales (Oppenheim, 1992). Furthermore, surveys can be distributed via paper, e-mail, or web pages.

- **Data Logging**. In data logging (also called interaction logging), the computer is programmed to record the different tasks and actions performed by the user, as well as the computer system responses. The data collected over time (and over different users) is then analyzed to look for patterns.

- **Focus Groups and Interviews**. In focus groups and interviews, a researcher (or researchers) asks questions of the participants. Interviews usually involve only one participant, whereas focus groups generally include more participants (Krueger, 1994). Focus groups and interviews tend to be less structured than questionnaires, allowing for more flexibility in data collection. For instance, when the subject makes an interesting comment, the researcher can follow up on it.

- **Case Studies**. A case study is a detailed documentation of a specific organization, systems development project, partnership, or other situation or process. Case studies are valuable because they can present theoretical concepts through a real-world setting, allowing readers to see how theories can be implemented, as well as what challenges exist.

- **Observational Studies**. With this technique, unobtrusive observations are made in the natural settings of the subjects (Marshall and Rossman, 1995). This approach allows for a more realistic examination of the environment in which subjects use technology. However, with this approach, great care must be taken so that the observations do not change the environment, or the behavior or actions of the subjects.

Subjects

Whichever data collection technique is employed in the research, subjects are needed to participate in the study. Although theoretical frameworks are useful, much of the knowledge required to advance the fields of information systems and human-computer interaction must be based on data collection. In order to ensure that the results are statistically valid, large numbers of subjects should take part in research. No generalizations can be made about interface design with, for example, two subjects. However, if a strong pattern is observed in over 100 subjects, this is stronger evidence. The size of the subject population is a very important consideration in the validity of the research, especially if there are many different research treatments.

Acquiring access to subjects can be a challenge. And great care must be taken in choosing subjects so that that the subjects accurately represent the user population of interest. For instance, it would be inappropriate to use high school students to represent the decision-making behaviors of business managers. It would also be inappropriate to use stockbrokers to represent users of hospital or airline information technology. If a representative population of subjects is not used, then results cannot be generalized to the user population. Furthermore, in many cases, subjects expect to be paid for their time, so the financial costs of performing research can increase. So, at the same time that there is a need for large numbers of subjects, there might be financial considerations that limit the number of subjects that can take part in the research. Service-research partnerships can help ameliorate the cost, because the subjects themselves are receiving a useful service, therefore, it is likely that it is not necessary to provide financial compensation, as the subjects are already receiving a non-financial compensation (the useful services). Both the researchers and the subjects benefit from the experience.

As in any type of research, with service-research partnerships, the rights of human subjects must be carefully protected. For most data collection efforts, subjects have a number of rights. The subjects have the right to know the purpose of the research, the right to know what will be asked of the subjects, the right to have all of their questions answered, and the right to leave the experiment at any time without any penalty. In addition, the data collected should not be identified by the name of the subject. Usually, before any data collection begins, the subjects must fill out a "Human Subjects Form" or a similar instrument, informing them of their rights, notifying them that the research has been approved by some oversight body (usually an institutional review board), and offering the subjects the option to leave at any time. While this might not be necessary for all information systems research, and in fact, information systems research tends not to be harmful in any way, shape, or form to humans, these are important considerations, which are just as relevant in service-research partnerships.

THE DIGITAL DIVIDE

There has been much talk recently about the "digital divide." The digital divide is a growing gap between those who have access to information technology and communication networks, and those who do not have access (U.S. Department of Commerce, 1999). In an information economy, there are many ramifications to not having access to computer networks such as the Internet. Not only do many jobs require familiarity and comfort with using computer technology, but job and resume postings are now largely Internet-based. Educational materials and news are also provided via computer networks, causing a disadvantage for someone who does not have access to those resources.

A number of different approaches have been developed for bridging the digital divide. For instance, community technology access centers provide access to technology in economically disadvantaged areas. Some schools provide access to their computer labs during the evening hours for local residents. Public libraries provide access to the Internet as part of their mission to provide knowledge to the entire community. Some community-based groups collect, refurbish, and donate computers to non-profit organizations. Other groups create volunteer efforts to assist in wiring schools and other community buildings. Many non-profit organizations in the community are connecting to the Internet but are barely able to afford the hardware, software, and Internet service provider costs. But having access to information technology is not equivalent to being able to use the technology effectively. There are a number of additional factors that help determine successful use of technology. To ensure effective use of technology, there should be adequate user training. Understandable documentation is also necessary. Proper maintenance and management of the technology is necessary. Appropriate use policies and guidelines must be set up. Although university professors could help community groups in writing grants to purchase technology, academic research usually cannot help with the costs of acquiring computer hardware, software, networking equipment, and Internet service. However, academic research can be structured to assist with other technology expenses, such as user training, documentation, and management.

THE USABILITY DIVIDE

Along with the problems of access to information technology, there is a corresponding problem in ease of use for information technology. This could be called the "usability divide." Many information systems and software applications are not easy to use. Software applications continue to become more complex, offering many more features than the users could ever need, and using terminology that the users cannot understand. User interfaces, while improving, are still a major headache for many users. Two important trends are the related areas of universal design and universal usability. Universal design is the process of designing products and infrastructures that can be used by the largest number of people. Universal usability is the process of designing information systems that are easy to use for a large number of people (Shneiderman, 2000). Universal usability means designing informational systems that are easy to use for diverse user populations (different levels of computer experience, different educational levels, different age levels, different disabilities, etc.) and under diverse technological settings (different platforms, different monitor sizes, different connection speeds, different physical locations, etc.) (Shneiderman, 2000). The concept of universal usability relates closely to the problem of the digital divide. If access to technology is provided for larger numbers of users, and if more and more people are to going to be encouraged and required to use information technology, this information technology must be easy to use. How will a new user feel when they receive an error message such as: *"A fatal exception OE has occurred at 017F: BFFAADOB. The current application will be terminated."*

As more users with little computer experience begin to use information technology, the usability of the information technology becomes even more important to ensure successful use of the technology. If the digital divide can be bridged, that means that more users from diverse populations will have access to technology, but will they want to and be able to effectively use the technology once they have access? More research needs to be performed related to the usability of software applications, web sites, and information appliances. Service-research is a golden opportunity to help bridge the usability divide. As research is performed, the research has an immediate impact on the community, and helps to bridge the digital divide. The research may involve novice users (or other user populations), and will then help to bridge the usability divide by creating informational systems that are easier to use in the future. The research then has a double impact on the community.

THE BENEFITS OF SERVICE-RESEARCH

Universities are incredible collections of resources. The vast knowledge and experience of faculty, staff, students, and alumni are valuable resources. Universities also have capital resources such as buildings, classrooms, and computer equipment. When possible, these resources can be used, and should be used, to help the community. In the last decade, there has been an increasing focus on getting students and faculty involved with community service. For instance, during winter and spring break periods, some students and faculty work on building homes for those who are economically disadvantaged, through programs such as *Habitat for Humanity*. Students take part in weekly tutoring programs for children in the local neighborhood. Students are increasingly taking part in structured community service as a part of their course work (see Chapters 1-4 in this book). Faculty may run programs to assist local schools in network wiring, or in acquiring computer software and hardware. Service-research is an extension of this service trend, to meet the current needs of the community, relating to technology.

There are real needs in the community. Acquiring information technology is expensive, and managing that technology can also be expensive. If universities can help meet some of the community's needs through research projects, this is an excellent benefit to the community. The community not only benefits from the expertise and/or services provided by the university, but the community ultimately benefits from the research, which is used to improve the experience of using information technology. And when a local community is stronger and more productive, that can only strengthen the university that resides in the community. A service-research partnership creates a synergy, which is mutually beneficial and may even provide some unexpected benefits. Faculty and staff of the university, when involved in the local community, can help offset some of the traditional "town and gown" tensions. Those living in the local community may have a more positive view of the university. The possibilities are endless.

POSSIBLE AREAS OF SERVICE-RESEARCH PARTNERSHIPS

There are many ways in which local communities can be involved with, and benefit from, academic research. The next section lists some possible application areas of service-research. These are by no means the only areas in which service-research is applicable. Researchers are encouraged to apply the concepts of service-research in creative and innovative ways.

- **User Training**. Although user training is an important aspect for the effective use of information systems, training is frequently omitted due to the lack of budgetary funds. Service-research can help fill the training gap. There are a myriad set of options to consider when planning and organizing technology training sessions. For instance, training sessions can have different physical settings (e.g., room layouts, air temperature, lighting, furniture), different presentational methods (e.g., procedural training versus exploratory training), or different combinations of instructors. Research should help to determine which approaches to training are most effective for specific training needs (different types of users, different types of software applications, etc.). The research area of training is a good match for service-research. Community members can agree to take part in a research experiment as subjects, and data is collected on the effectiveness (or some other aspect) of the training. At the same time, those community members receive training in software applications, usually free of charge (Lazar and Norcio, 2000). The training helps users to more effectively use specific software applications, or information systems as a whole. Both researchers and trainees benefit from the partnership.

- **Usability**. An important concern in the design of informational systems is the usability, or ease of use. Usability research with large numbers of people differs from usability testing on products. Usability research usually focuses on some inherent aspect of interfaces, and which presentation methods or input/output methods are most effective. Usability testing usually focuses on a smaller number of users, with the goal of finding and uncovering usability problems in a specific system. Many experiments are performed in the area of usability research. In return for taking part in an experiment on usability, there could be many possible benefits or services provided to the community. For instance, if the research is on how novice users interact with an interface, then it might be appropriate to provide introductory training beforehand on using a system (which would be useful for novice users). This would be similar to the training through service-research described above. The difference is that with usability research, the multiple experimental conditions would not be focused on different training methods, but rather, all subjects would receive similar training, but receive different experimental interface treatments, and then data collection could relate to those different interfaces.

- **User Behavior**. Closely related to the area of usability is user behavior. What tasks do users perform most often? Which specific approaches do users take when performing a task? How do users perceive the technology, and do users feel satisfied? Which tasks are most frustrating? These are important research questions, and it is therefore necessary to study users and collect data. Data can be collected through session logging, and users can also fill out surveys. In return for allowing their computer actions to be logged, subjects can receive some sort of benefit. For instance, after researchers determine which tasks are most frustrating, the user might then receive suggestions or extra training on how better to respond to those tasks. Also, many organizations have "help desks" set up to respond to user questions and complaints. Help desks are perfect places to study user behavior as well as user perceptions of technology. In return, researchers could provide suggestions on how to improve the system, training, or documentation, so as to lessen the number of calls to the help desk. The researcher learns more about user behavior, while the user and/or community organization receives help in improving the experience with technology.

- **User Documentation**. Research in human-computer interaction may focus on different ways of presenting user documentation. For instance, user documentation can be a complete how-to guide for performing all tasks, or the documentation could present minimalist approaches, where only the simple, easy-to-understand steps are presented (Carroll, 1990). Researchers can learn more about the effectiveness of different approaches to user documentation by helping non-profit organizations develop appropriate user documentation. Data can then be collected on the effectiveness of these different approaches to user documentation. And if user training does not take place, the importance of good documentation increases.

- **The Effects of Computer Usage on Education**. A number of communities, schools, as well as the homes of teachers and students, have been provided with computers and Internet access, through the financial generosity of corporations or funding agencies. Researchers can study the impacts of the technology on learning, and on the educational process and school management. The goal of the research is to learn more about the effects of technology, but the community immediately benefits, as they receive free computer equipment, software, and Internet service. This type of service-research occurs less frequently, because of the large amount of funding needed to begin such research.

- **Information Systems Management**. Whole books have been written about the topic of managing information technology, dealing with topics as diverse as project management, systems migration, acceptable use policies, and outsourcing (Martin et al., 1994). Community organizations often are in need of assistance with managing their information technology, and it would be helpful if researchers could assist community organizations with suggestions for managing their technology. At the same time, researchers can gain access to the community organizations to learn more about the problems and challenges of managing information technology in non-profit organizations. Case studies and examples of best practices can then be developed, which will possibly be able to help other organizations with effectively managing their information technology resources.

- **Policy Awareness**. For decision-makers, it is frequently important to determine current levels of compliance with certain national or international policies. For instance, the U.S. Government now requires that technology purchased by the federal government, as well as Federal web sites, be accessible for users with disabilities (Lazar, Kumin, and Wolsey, 2001). Similar requirements exist for web sites in Australia (Astbrink, 2001). Research could be undertaken to determine the current levels of accessibility, for technology both inside and outside of the government. At the same time, when organizations are asked to take part in the study, the researchers could use this opportunity to inform and educate respondents about the need for accessibility of information technology. Accessibility is not limited to government web sites; other research studies have looked at accessibility levels of popular e-commerce web sites (Sullivan and Matson, 2000). This would provide a public service, as it would help educate the community and community organizations to the needs of users with disabilities.

- **Design Processes**. Over time, the design processes for information systems have changed. New development lifecycles have been created that focus more on user involvement. For instance, participatory design, where users become a part of the design team, has been successfully used with educators (see the chapter by Carroll et al. in this book), senior citizens (Ellis and Kurniawan, 2000), and children (Druin, 1999). Many information systems development projects never get fully implemented, because users were not sufficiently involved in the development (Hoffer, George, and Valacich, 1999). Researchers can assist community groups with their information systems development, by helping to determine what functionality and usability needs exist, offering suggestions on appropriate ways to integrate users into the development, and pointing out possible problems. At the same time, the researchers can learn more about the effectiveness of or problems in currently existing development models, or entirely new development models can be created and tested. Just as new systems development models have been created for web sites (Lazar, 2001) and other distributed populations (Lazar, Hanst, Buckwalter, and Preece, 2000), appropriate development models will need to be created for handheld and wireless devices. This is a promising area for service-research.

CASE STUDIES

The following are examples of experimental research using the service-research paradigm. The next section describes a service-research project that was successfully completed, and a service-research project that is currently in progress.

Archdiocese of Baltimore

In 1998, the Archdiocese of Baltimore connected all of their parishes, schools, and offices to the Internet. With this large technology expense, the Archdiocese was not able to afford Internet training for their staff members. As part of a research experiment on different training methods for web browsing, free training was offered to employees of the Archdiocese of Baltimore (Lazar and Norcio, 2000). The information technology office at the Archdiocese advertised the experiment to employees, and the researchers coordinated registration. At the end of the research experiment, more than 250 people had taken part in the experiment, and therefore, had received Internet training at no cost. The researchers gained access to a large subject pool of novice users, and were able to learn more about how different training methods for web browsing affected performance and satisfaction (Lazar and Norcio, 2000).

Howard County Office on Aging

We have currently formed a service-research partnership with the Howard County Office on Aging. This is an office that serves the needs of senior citizens in Howard County, Maryland, which is located between Baltimore and

Washington, DC. Staff members in the office are interested in receiving training on the effective use of Web browsers, however, training funds are not available in the office budget. The current plan is to provide training, and in return, the staff members will take part in a research experiment. The purpose of the research experiment is to learn about novice user perceptions of error on the web. The planned methodology for the experiment is available in Lazar and Norcio (2001).

SUMMARY

Scholarly research in information systems has a positive impact on the community; however, the impact might sometimes be realized long after the completion of the research. There are many technology needs in the community that go unfulfilled due to lack of funds. Through a concept called service-research, some research experiments can be structured so that they provide an immediate benefit to the community. By forming a service-research partnership, researchers can get access to large numbers of subjects, while at the same time helping the local community to meet their technology needs. Service-research can be applied in many different research areas, such as training, documentation, usability, management, and policy.

REFERENCES

Astbrink, G. (2001). The legislative impact in Australia on universal access in telecommunications. *Proceedings of the Universal Access in Human-Computer Interaction 2001 Conference*, 1042-1046.

Carroll, J. (1990). *The Nurnberg Funnel: Designing Minimalist Instruction for Practical Computer Skill*. Cambridge, MA: MIT Press.

Druin, A. (Ed.). (1998). *The Design of Children's Technology*. San Francisco, CA: Morgan Kaufmann Publishers.

Ellis, R. D. and Kurniawan, S. (2000). Increasing the usability of online information for older users: A case study in participatory design. *International Journal of Human-Computer Interaction*, 12(2), 263-276.

Hoffer, J., George, J., and Valacich, J. (1999). *Modern Systems Analysis and Design*. Reading, MA: Addison-Wesley.

Krueger, R. (1994). *Focus Groups: A Practical Guide For Applied Research*. Thousand Oaks, CA: Sage Publications.

Lazar, J. (2001). *User-Centered Web Development*. Sudbury, MA: Jones and Bartlett Publishers.

Lazar, J., Hanst, E., Buchwalter, J., and Preece, J. (2000). Collecting user requirements in a virtual population: A case study. *WebNet Journal*, 2(4), 20-27.

Lazar, J., Kumin, L., and Wolsey, S. (2001). Universal usability for Web sites: Current trends in the U.S. law. *Proceedings of the Universal Access in Human-Computer Interaction 2001 Conference*, 1083-1087.

Lazar, J. and Norcio, A. (2000). Service-research: Community partnerships for research and training. *Journal of Informatics Education and Research*, 2(3), 21-25.

Lazar, J. and Norcio, A. (2001). An exploratory study of situational error on the Web. *Proceedings of the Human-Computer Interaction International (HCII) Conference*, 111-114.

Marshall, C. and Rossman, G. (1995). *Designing Qualitative Research*. Thousand Oaks, CA: Sage Publications.

Martin, E., DeHayes, D., Hoffer, J., and Perkins, W. (1994). *Managing Information Technology: What Managers Need to Know*. New York: Macmillan Publishing Company.

Oppenheim, A. (1992). *Questionnaire Design, Interviewing, and Attitude Measurement*. London: Pinter Publishers.

Preece, J., Rogers, Y., Sharp, H., Benyon, D., Holland, S., and Carey, T. (1994). *Human-Computer Interaction*. Wokingham, England: Addison Wesley Publishing.

Shneiderman, B. (2000). Universal usability: Pushing human-computer interaction research to empower every citizen. *Communications of the ACM*, 43(5), 84-91.

Sullivan, T. and Matson, R. (2000). Barriers to use: Usability and content accessibility on the Web's most popular sites. *Proceedings of the ACM Conference on Universal Usability*, 139-144.

U.S. Department of Commerce. (1999). *Falling Through the Net: Defining the Digital Divide*. Retrieved from the World Wide Web: http://www.ntia.doc.gov/ntiahome/fttn99/contents.html.

About the Authors

Jonathan K. Lazar is an Assistant Professor in the Department of Computer and Information Sciences, in the College of Science and Mathematics at Towson University. He has a number of research publications focusing on human-computer interaction issues in the Internet environment. Specifically, Dr. Lazar is interested in user error, user training, user satisfaction, user-centered design methods, web usability, and online communities. He is the author of the book, *User-Centered Web Development*, published by Jones and Bartlett Publishers. Dr. Lazar has integrated service-learning in a number of different information systems courses, and was named the Towson University *Faculty Advisor of the Year* in May 2000.

***

John Borton is currently Chair of the USC Department of Computer Information Systems. He has been with the university since 1983. Prior to coming to USC, Dr. Borton worked in industry as a programmer, systems analyst, and database administrator. He received his BA in Social Studies and Math Education from Purdue University, his MS in Statistics from the University of Northern Colorado, and his PhD in Information Systems from the University of Colorado at Boulder. He recently completed a one-year sabbatical with Oracle Corporation and became an Oracle Certified DBA.

Roger Boyle won a mathematics doctorate from the University of York in 1978, and has worked in Computing at the University of Leeds for over 20 years. He has devoted much of the last 10 years to student recruitment and has put special effort into recruiting from non-traditional and under-represented groups. He has published widely in the teaching of computing in higher education. His primary research interests are in AI and computer vision.

John M. Carroll is Professor of Computer Science, Education, and Psychology, and Director of the Center for Human-Computer Interaction, all at Virginia Tech. His research interests include methods and theory in human-computer interaction, particularly as applied to networking tools for collaborative learning and problem-solving. His most recent books are *Minimalism Beyond "The Nurnberg Funnel"* (MIT Press, 1998) and *Making Use: Scenario-Based Design of Human-Computer Interactions* (MIT Press, 2000).

George Chin Jr. is a Senior Research Scientist at Battelle Pacific Northwest Laboratory. Prior to joining Battelle, he was a PhD candidate in the Center for Human-Computer Interaction at Virginia Tech. His research has been in the areas of participatory design, ethnographic methods, computer-supported collaborative work, computer-supported collaborative learning, problem-solving environments, and human-computer interaction.

James R. Coakley is an Associate Professor in the College of Business at Oregon State University. He received his PhD in Accounting Information Systems from the University of Utah in 1982. His research interests include strategic alignment of IT infrastructure, applications of artificial neural networks, and the use of information technology to teach information technology. Dr. Coakley has published in journals such as *Expert Systems with Applications, International Journal of Intelligent Systems in Accounting, Finance and Management, Journal of Management Education, Journal of Systems Management, Journal of Informatics Education and Research,* and *Management Accounting.*

Daniel R. Dunlap is a Research Associate for the Center for Human-Computer Interaction at Virginia Tech, where he is conducting social science research related to computer use. He is currently pursuing a doctoral degree in Science and Technology Studies and is a former public school science and math teacher. His research interests include ethnomethodology, philosophy, and sociology of science and technology, especially as these areas relate to education, collaboration, and computing.

Roger W. Harris received a PhD in Information Systems from the City University of Hong Kong in 1997. By 2001, he was Associate Professor at a university in Sarawak, Malaysia, leading a team of researchers concerned with the use of the Internet for development in rural and remote communities. He now coordinates the learning and evaluation activities of a group of Asian telecentre projects, know as the PanAsia Telecentre Learning and Evaluation Group (PANTLEG), an off-shoot of the Canadian Government's International Development Research Center (IDRC). In September 2001, he took up a visiting position at Central Queensland University, Australia.

Steven Hawley is a Visiting Assistant Professor at Wright State University. He currently serves as Principal of the Cincinnati Virtual High School and co-founder of the Cyberstars program. In addition to serving as Director of the Hamilton/Clermont Cooperative Association of Boards of Education, he has taught youth at all levels and served as director of a teacher training program that provided a collaborative for five regional universities. His current focus is on urban youth empowerment through technology.

Philip L. Isenhour is a Research Associate with the Center for Human-Computer Interaction at Virginia Tech. His research is currently focused on adaptable software infrastructure to support networked and collaborative applications.

Kathy S. Lassila is Associate Professor of Computer Information Systems (CIS) at the University of Southern Colorado (USC). She has over 11 years of IT industry experience as a systems analyst, software developer, technical services manager, and IT consultant. Her current research interests include the societal impacts of IT, the effectiveness of web-based IT education, and the organizational impact of information systems. Dr. Lassila received her BA in Economics from the University of Wisconsin–Eau Claire, her MBA with an emphasis in Organization Development from the University of Wisconsin-Milwaukee, and her PhD in Information Systems from the University of Colorado at Boulder. She is responsible for the Senior Professional Project course in the CIS curriculum.

Cindy LeRouge, CPA, is a PhD student in Information Systems and Decision Sciences at the University of South Florida. She received her MS in accounting from the University of New Orleans. Her research focuses on information technology education and training, organizational learning, and telemedicine. Ms. LeRouge has served consulting, training, and analyst roles for two enterprise system software companies; provided audit, tax, and consulting services for two "Big 6" public accounting firms; and worked as a controller in the medical supply, intellectual property, and petrochemical industries.

Doris K. Lidtke is a Professor of Computer and Information Sciences at Towson University. She has been an active member of ACM serving as SIG Board Chair, on Council, and on the Education Board. She was a member of the committee which developed Curriculum '91 and Information Systems-Centric Curriculum (ISCC '99). She is a member of the IEEE-Computer Society Golden Core. She has been deeply involved in computing accreditation, served as one of the first Team Chairs, as President of CSAB, and as Principal Investigator for the NSF-funded grant which developed the "Draft Criteria for Accreditation of

Information Systems Programs." She is currently Adjunct Director of Accreditation for Computing for ABET.

Carlos J. Navarrete is Associate Professor in the Computer Information Systems Department at the College of Business Administration of the California State Polytechnic University, Pomona. He holds a BSc from Instituto Politecnico Nacional, Mexico, and a PhD in Management Information Systems from Claremont Graduate University. Before joining California State Polytechnic, Professor Navarrete worked for Universidad Iberoamerican, Mexico, where he was the Chair of the Information Systems Department. His research interest is the use of information technology to support individuals, groups, and organizations' productivity. Dr. Navarrete has received several awards through his academic carrier. He was Fulbright Scholar from 1991 to 1994.

Dennis C. Neale is a Human Factors Engineer who recently worked as an Evaluation Specialist for the Center for Human-Computer Interaction at Virginia Tech. He is currently pursuing a doctorate degree in Industrial and Systems Engineering at Virginia Tech. His current research interests include usability engineering, collaborative systems, and video-mediated communication.

Anthony F. Norcio is a Professor of Information Systems at the University of Maryland-Baltimore County (UMBC). Dr. Norcio is also the Co-Director (with Dr. Marion J. Ball) of the World Health Organization (WHO)/Pan American Health Organization (PAHO) Collaborating Center for Health Informatics. He serves as an External Advisor to the PAHO and to the Inter-American Development Bank (IDB) on computing and health informatics. He is an invited member of the PAHO/IDB Health Task Force of the Informatics 2000 Initiative for Latin America and the Caribbean. He also currently serves as a Computer Scientist at the Artificial Intelligence Center of the Naval Research Laboratory, and has served as the Scientific Advisor to the Mathematical, Computer, and Information Sciences Division of the Office of Naval Research. He regularly participates on planning and program committees for national and international conferences. Dr. Norcio has published dozens of scientific papers in various journals, as well as the proceedings of numerous national and international conferences.

James Pick is Professor in the School of Business at University of Redlands. He holds a BA from Northwestern University and a PhD from the University of California, Irvine. He has authored seven books and more than 90 scientific papers and book chapters in geographic information systems, management information systems, demographic studies of Mexico and the U.S., environmental systems, and simulation. His most recent book is *Mexico City in the World Economy* (Westview Press, 2001). He received the outstanding faculty teaching and research awards from the University of Redlands, and recently a Ford Foundation grant and senior Fulbright senior lecturer/researcher award.

Randal D. Pinkett is a member of the Epistemology and Learning Group at the MIT Media Laboratory, and the President and CEO of MBS Enterprises, an educational services and community technology consulting company headquartered in Plainfield, New Jersey. Dr. Pinkett received a BS degree in Electrical Engineering from Rutgers University, MS degree in Computer Science from the University of Oxford as a Rhodes Scholar, and MS in Electrical Engineering, MBA, and PhD degrees from MIT. He has been featured in *Black Enterprise* and *Ebony* magazines, in their "30 Leaders for the Future" issues, and is also listed in *Who's Who Among American Entrepreneurs* and *Who's Who Among African-Americans*.

Ann Roberts graduated from the University of St. Andrews and the University of London. She has worked in Computing at the University of Leeds for over 15 years. Her main responsibility is school and industrial liaison. Her chief interest is in providing summer schools and introductions to the university for pupils from schools in the inner-city areas of Leeds.

Mary Beth Rosson is Associate Professor of Computer Science and Fellow of the Center for Human-Computer Interaction at Virginia Tech, where she is working in the areas of human-computer interaction, computer-supported cooperative work, and usability engineering. She has recently co-authored a book with John Carroll, *Usability Engineering: Scenario-Based Development of Human-Computer Interaction* (Morgan Kaufmann).

Cynthia Ruppel is an Associate Professor at Crummer Graduate School. Her research interests include the introduction and use of telecommunications technology to conduct business, including telecommuting, e-business, and virtual organizations. She has published in *IEEE Transactions on Professional Communications, IEEE Potentials, Journal of Business Ethics, Information Resource Management Journal,* and *Journal of End User Computing.*

David Ruppel is a PhD student in the EECS Department of the College of Engineering at the University of Toledo. He has an MS in Mathematics and a Computer Science Certificate from the University of Akron, and a BS in Secondary Education from Concordia College in Seward, Nebraska, with additional work in

Computer Science from Kent State University. He has been a Visiting Instructor in Mathematics and Computer Science at the University of Akron and in Computer Science at Cleveland State University. His research interests are in networking, with particular interests in the areas of ATM networks and active networking.

Ruth V. Small, PhD, is a Professor at the School of Information Studies, Syracuse University. Dr. Small is widely published in the instructional design, development, and evaluation areas. She has authored or co-authored a number of research articles and books, and consults actively in these areas.

Craig K. Tyran is an Associate Professor in the College of Business and Economics at Western Washington University. He received his PhD in Management Information Systems from the University of Arizona. His research interests include the organizational applications of collaborative technology, systems development and implementation, and the educational applications of information technology. Dr. Tyran's research has been published in a number of publications, including *MIS Quarterly* and the *Journal of Management Information Systems*. He has also presented his research at numerous national and international conferences.

Murali Venkatesh, PhD, is an Associate Professor at the School of Information Studies, Syracuse University, where he teaches courses in systems and telecommunications. He founded CAL and CITI, and currently directs CITI. His research interests include telecommunications systems planning and design, and broadband community network development. Dr. Venkatesh's research has been presented at leading academic research conferences and other scholarly forums.

Harold W. Webb is an Assistant Professor in the College of Business at the University of South Florida. He received his MBA and PhD in Management Information Systems from Texas Tech University. His work experience includes the development of advanced systems requirements for the United States Army. His research interests include the effects of information technology on learning at the individual and organizational level. He is also interested in research into the behavioral aspects of software testing, as well as decision support systems and electronic commerce.

Index